Festivals of the *World*

NETHERLANDS

Gareth Stevens Publishing
MILWAUKEE

D0102441

Written by
JOYCE VAN FENEMA

Edited by
GERALDINE MESENAS

Designed by
LOO CHUAN MING

Picture research by
SUSAN JANE MANUEL

First published in North America in 1998 by
Gareth Stevens Publishing
1555 North RiverCenter Drive, Suite 201
Milwaukee, Wisconsin 53212 USA

For a free color catalog describing Gareth
Stevens' list of high-quality books and multimedia
programs, call
1-800-542-2595 (USA)
or 1-800-461-9120 (Canada).
Gareth Stevens Publishing's Fax: (414) 225-0377.
See our catalog, too, on the World Wide Web:
http://gsinc.com

All rights reserved. No part of this book may be
reproduced or utilized in any form or by any
means electronic or mechanical, including
photocopying, recording, or by an information
storage and retrieval system, without permission
from the copyright owner.

© TIMES EDITIONS PTE LTD 1998
Originated and designed by
Times Books International
an imprint of Times Editions Pte Ltd
Times Centre, 1 New Industrial Road
Singapore 536196
Printed in Singapore

Library of Congress Cataloging-in-Publication Data:
van Fenema, Joyce.
Netherlands / by Joyce van Fenema.
p. cm.—(Festivals of the world)
Includes bibliographical references and index.
Summary: Describes how the culture of the
Netherlands is reflected in its many festivals,
including Sinterklaas, Carnaval, and Queensday.
ISBN 0-8368-2016-9 (lib. bdg.)
1. Festivals—Netherlands—Juvenile literature. 2.
Netherlands—Social life and customs—Juvenile
literature. [1. Festivals—Netherlands. 2.
Holidays—Netherlands. 3. Netherlands—Social
life and customs.] I. Title. II. Series.
GT4854.A2F46 1998
394.269492—dc21   98-11038

1 2 3 4 5 6 7 8 9 02 01 00 99 98

CONTENTS

It's Festival Time . . .

The Dutch are a very warm and hospitable people. A festival in the Netherlands is simply called a *feest* [faist] and is a favorite time for the Dutch, who love to have a good time. Whether it's in celebration of their religion, their beloved queen, or their beautiful country, the Dutch always do it with perfect style. When it comes to partying, the Dutch have only one rule: have lots of fun!

WHERE'S THE NETHERLANDS?

The Netherlands is a small and densely populated **monarchy** in northwestern Europe, and its neighbors are Belgium and Germany. The country got its name from the fact that most of the country lies below sea level, and it consists of 13 provinces. It is often called "Holland" as well, although this name actually applies only to the two provinces of North and South Holland.

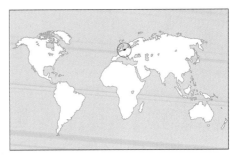

Two Dutch boys having fun by the beach in winter.

Who are the Dutch?

The first people in the Netherlands were the Frisians from Germany and Batavians from the Celtic tribe. Since those early days, the Dutch people have fought the Germans, the French, and the Spanish. It was only in 1579 that the Netherlands became an independent country.

The sea has always been important to the Dutch, who are mostly fishermen and traders. At the same time, much land has been reclaimed for farms, which the Dutch prevent from being flooded by building **dikes** and windmills.

NETHERLANDS

NORTH SEA

GRONINGEN

FRIESLAND

DRENTHE

NORTH HOLLAND

Alkmaar

FLEVOLAND

Haarlem

AMSTERDAM

Aalsmeer

OVERIJSSEL

Leiden

The Hague

UTRECHT

GELDERLAND

SOUTH HOLLAND

GERMANY

N

ZEELAND

NORTH BRABANT

LIMBURG

BELGIUM

Maastricht

Typical country houses in the Netherlands.

When's the Feest?

AUTUMN

- ✪ **PRINCE DAY**—On the third Tuesday in September, the royal family rides through The Hague in gold coaches, and the Queen opens the parliamentary year.
- ✪ **ANIMAL DAY**—On this day, school activities center around animal welfare. Children take their pets to school.
- ✪ **SINT MAARTEN**—The Roman soldier who cut his cloak in half and gave it to a shivering beggar is the inspiration for the door-to-door begging of alms.
- ✪ **ELEVEN/ELEVEN NIGHT**—Eleven is a fool's number. Therefore, the 11th day of the 11th month of the year is the day of the fool's carnival.
- ✪ **SINTERKLAAS**

Would you care for some cheese? Come to page 25.

WINTER

- ✪ **CHRISTMAS**—The birth of Jesus is widely celebrated in churches and schools.
- ✪ **HOLY INNOCENTS DAY**—The 28th of December centers around the youngest in the family, who chooses the day's menu.
- ✪ **NEW YEAR'S EVE**—On this festive occasion, noise and fireworks abound, and of course, snowball fights (if there's snow).
- ✪ **THREE KINGS DAY**—Children carry lanterns and dress up as the three kings, wearing paper crowns they make themselves.
- ✪ **CARNAVAL**

A colorful and "flowery" experience awaits you on page 20.

SPRING

- ✪ **TREE-PLANTING DAY**—Care for the environment has made this a day where the whole nation celebrates nature together.
- ✪ **PALM SUNDAY**—The entry of Christ into Jerusalem is celebrated by making your own palm tree and carrying it in a procession.

Have a crazy time with us at the Queensday carnival on page 16.

- ✪ **EASTER**—Children wake up in the early morning to go on an Easter egg hunt in their own gardens or in public parks.
- ✪ **QUEENSDAY**
- ✪ **LIBERATION DAY**—The day after Memorial Day, the Dutch celebrate the end of the Second World War.
- ✪ **LUILAK**—The idea on this day is to make fun of the person who wakes up last on the Saturday before Pentecost. Children go out into the streets making noise and ringing doorbells.
- ✪ **NATIONAL WINDMILL AND BICYCLE DAY**

SUMMER

- ✪ **FLOWER FESTIVAL**
- ✪ **RING RIDING**—A version of the tournaments of the medieval knights, it is held in August, on the third day of Pentecost.
- ✪ **CATTLE MARKET**
- ✪ **CHEESE MARKET**

7

SINTERKLAAS

Around November, the days grow shorter in the Netherlands and the weather turns nasty and bitterly cold. However, this is the favorite time for most children, as it's the time of Sinterklaas [sin-ter-KLASS]! At this time, Sinterklaas and his servants, the Black Peters, arrive at the port of Amsterdam by boat. This signals the start of St. Nicholas season, which will end on December 6th, when the Dutch celebrate the Feast of Sinterklaas.

Sinterklaas and his Black Peters arriving by boat at the port of Amsterdam.

Who is Sinterklaas?

Sinterklaas, or St. Nicholas, was a **bishop** in the fourth century who became famous for his good deeds and his selfless ways in helping the poor and the unfortunate. When he died, he became a legend who calmed the stormy seas and rescued children from boiling tar. In the Netherlands today, he has become the **patron saint** for sailors and merchants—and especially children.

Clowning at the Sinterklaas festivities.

Opposite: After arriving, Sinterklaas climbs on his milk-white horse and starts his tour through all the Dutch cities.

Have you been naughty or nice?

On Sinterklaas, the Black Peters carry large sacks full of candy and sweets for all the good children. But all children who have been naughty in the past year, be warned. The Black Peters also have birch rods for spanking all the naughty children, who will be carried away in the empty sacks. This doesn't really happen, of course; it's just part of the storytelling tradition.

On Sinterklaas, children put big carrots or hay in their shoes and place them under the chimney for Sinterklaas' horse. It is the Black Peters' duty to make sure the children's carrots and hay are exchanged for small gifts or sweets.

Sinterklaas is not only celebrated by children. Today, Sinterklaas has become a nationwide event, with elaborate parades and general merry-making. Here, we see Sinterklaas's golden carriage moving through the streets of Amsterdam.

Where did Sinterklaas come from?

Having a bit of fun in the Sinterklaas parade.

Ask the Dutch children, and they will tell you that Sinterklaas lives in Spain, although most adults know that this merry old man lived in Asia Minor a very long time ago. It is not clear how this happened, but many old songs and nursery rhymes tell children that Sinterklaas comes from "sunny Spain."

Sinterklaas is always accompanied by Moorish servants called Black Peters or *Zwarte Piet* [zwar-ta PEET]. Many Moors, people from Africa, lived in Spain a long time ago. On Sinterklaas, the Black Peters will throw gingernuts to the crowds of singing children.

Think about this

Sinterklaas is a jolly old man who loves children and gives presents and sweets to all the good children. Do you know of another festival where good children are rewarded with presents? Are these presents also given by a merry old man?

CARNAVAL

C arnaval [CAR-na-val] used to be a feast for grown-ups, but, today, children start taking part as soon as they can walk. There are many exciting events for children, such as fancy dress contests, singing contests, and colorful parades. Teenagers have plenty to occupy them, too, as they group together in the streets, singing and jumping around, bringing the traffic to a complete standstill.

In the Netherlands, Carnaval is celebrated differently in every region and village. However, the "true Carnaval" is definitely the Maastricht Carnaval held in the south of the country.

Little clowns drumming up loads of fun in the Maastricht Carnaval.

How did Carnaval start?

Like many historic feasts, the Dutch Carnaval is based on a religious event. In the old days, a six-week fasting period (Lent) was held before Easter, starting on Ash Wednesday. During the fast, people **atoned** for past sins by **abstaining** from meat and alcohol—children were not allowed to eat sweets. In those days, this seemed a terrible sacrifice. Therefore, on Pancake Tuesday, the day before Ash Wednesday, people got themselves stuffed with good food.

Above: In the three weeks leading up to Carnaval, shop owners decorate their shop fronts with carnival characters in preparation for the big event.

Below: Masked musicians in elaborate costumes are a common sight in the Maastricht Carnaval.

Let's play the fool

Over the years, the desire for revelry grew into a street carnival which lasted all of the five days before Ash Wednesday. People took to the streets to live it up as much as they could. They went around doing **outrageous** things, such as making fun of everyone and hiding behind masks so they wouldn't be recognized.

Parades, mascots, and more

Every town and village has one or more Carnaval clubs, with a
house band and a **mascot**. The mascots are made from paper
and other materials way beforehand, and can be anything from
a frog to a sausage or a witch—the madder, the better. These
clubs organize events such as singing contests, pageants, and
parades. They also perform musical serenades in hospitals and
retirement homes. The parades in the big towns are fantastic,
with giant floats that have but one goal—to make people laugh.

  When evening comes, the fun is taken to the pubs and
dance halls, which fill to the brim with partygoers. In the
Carnaval, everything (well, almost everything) is allowed, as
long as it's funny.

No carnival is
without lots of loud,
stomping music—by
a strange bunch of
musicians in fancy
dress and make-up.

Think about this
Carnaval starts the period of fasting in Lent. There are several other religions that also observe a fasting month. Do you know these other religions? Do you know anyone who fasts? Why do they do so?

The one rule in the Carnaval is, "the madder, the better." True to this rule is this man who has strapped a bird to his head as a **bizarre** headdress!

Let's party!

A big festival should end with a bang. So on Tuesday at midnight, the crowds gather at the marketplace to burn or bury their paper mascots. Those who still have a voice left sing a last farewell song. Then the crowds hurry home or back to the pub.

Clowns, clowns, and more clowns.

QUEENSDAY

April 30th is the official birthday of Queen Beatrix. This is celebrated in the Netherlands as Queensday, when Queen Beatrix visits a different town each year. In this lucky town, people line the streets wearing national costumes, singing and dancing to music bands. They also decorate their houses with the national red-white-and-blue flags and orange ribbons.

The birth of a queen and three princes

Queen Beatrix was actually born in February, the coldest month of the year. When she ascended the throne, she chose to celebrate her birthday on April 30th, the birthday of her mother Juliana. Spring in April is still pretty chilly, but at least there is a chance that the sun will warm up the people and the outdoor festivities!

Queen Beatrix and her husband, Prince Claus, have three sons: Willem-Alexander, Constantijn and Johan Friso.

A talented boy entertains on the saxophone in the Queensday carnival.

A day for celebration

Over the last 20 years, Queensday has been celebrated with an exciting, country-wide free market (or flea market). It is the one day when people are allowed to sell anything and everything, wherever they like. From as early as six in the morning, you will see lots of things for sale—from household items and old pieces of furniture to foodstuff like shish kebabs and spicy hot dogs. Even schoolchildren try to make extra pocket money by selling books and toys they have outgrown.

To add to the already noisy and festive mood, musicians take out their instruments, and acrobats perform stunts for the excited crowds.

The Dutch royal family in the garden of Huis ten Bosch Palace. Queen Beatrix and Prince Claus are in front. The three princes are in the back, from left to right: Prince Constantijn, Prince Willem-Alexander (the Crown Prince) and Prince Johan Friso.

A prettily painted "kitten" at the flea market.

Think about this
Queensday is a big birthday bash for all Dutch people. Even the Dutch who live abroad are invited to join in the festivities at the homes of the Dutch ambassadors all over the world!

Colorfully costumed musicians and revelers live it up at the Queensday carnival. Everybody wears a dash of orange on Queensday—even dogs wear an orange ribbon!

Why is orange the national color?

That's because it is the Queen's last name. Queen Beatrix is the greater-than-great-granddaughter of Prince Willem of Orange, who freed the Netherlands from the Spaniards and became the country's first ruler. The Dutch people only use the color on special occasions, such as the 1995 World Cup which the Dutch soccer team won. On that day, the whole country was decked out in orange. People even painted their cars and the front of their houses orange!

The statue of Prince Willem of Orange at The Hague. The Dutch have placed beautiful orange flowers at the foot of the monument of the Dutch national hero.

Opposite: A painted "kitten" plays a recorder at her mother's bag stall, at one of the many flea markets on Queensday.

WINDMILLS AND FLOWERS

The west of the Netherlands is flowers and windmill country. Throughout spring and summer, the Dutch people celebrate their windmill **heritage** and the beauty of the bulb fields with parades and splendid celebrations—Dutch style!

Opposite: The second Saturday of May, when the Dutch national flower, the tulip, achieves its full bloom, has been declared the National Windmill Day—in celebration of two of the Netherlands' most popular symbols.

National Windmill Day

The second Saturday in May is National Windmill Day, when windmills all over the Netherlands are opened to the public, and their sails are **unfurled**. On this day, everybody gets a chance to admire the beauty of the windmills and also discover the workings of a windmill from the inside.

Today, windmills are not used as much as before. Of the thousands of windmills that were once used by the Dutch, only about 1,000 survive.

For over 600 years, the Dutch used windmills to drain the land for farms, grind corn, and crush seeds to make oil. In fact, the Dutch even communicated and sent messages through their windmills—for example, the windmill sails are decorated with flowers and other special items during special occasions.

Blossoms and bulbs

The Dutch love flowers, which can be seen all over the Netherlands. In fact, flowers are found in every garden and on the tiniest balcony. Throughout spring and summer, the Bloembollenstreek, the bulb-growing area between Haarlem and Leiden, boasts a wondrous display of flowers of every color under the sun.

Right: The most famous flower in the Netherlands is, of course, the tulip, which was first grown on Dutch soil by Carolus Clusius in 1593. Other flowers **cultivated** in the Netherlands include daffodils, hyacinths, irises, lilies, and dahlias.

Above: One of the most spectacular flower gardens in the world is Keukenhof in Holland. It is planted with over seven million bulbs and is at its most brilliant from late March to late May.

Flower parades

The highlight of the flower season occurs in the summer, when flower parades are held in various parts of the Netherlands. In these parades, huge floats made of fresh flowers drive in procession through the town, complete with flower girls and a flower queen. These are huge local celebrations where the streets come alive with brilliant colors from the giant floats, as well as bands, cheerleaders, and hundreds of merry-makers.

The most famous flower parade is held in Aalsmeer—the center of the flower industry.

Think about this

In the 17th century, tulips were considered such precious flowers that they were as expensive as gold. This became known as "tulipomania," which means a craze for tulips.

SUMMER FESTIVALS

I n the summer, the Netherlands comes alive with numerous activities all over the country. With so much to do— from traditional sports and art fairs, to street theater festivals and fascinating markets—it's no wonder the Dutch look forward to summer every year!

Early summer is the time of the cattle markets, where cows, pigs, sheep, horses, and other domestic animals are displayed and traded.

Ringrijden is a tournament where riders on horseback and couples in traditional horse-drawn carriages gallop past and try to unhook a ring with their **lance**.

Fascinating markets

Cattle markets have, over the years, grown into enormous fairs with numerous stalls selling everything from dresses and toys to handicrafts and pancakes. Often, there are sheep shearing shows and pony rides as well. All summer long, you will also discover the many exciting food markets that spring up all over the Netherlands. Each and every town and village in the country has its own "folklore" and special trade.

Alkmaar's traditional cheese market features porters in colorful historic uniforms.

Traditional sports

Perhaps the biggest crowd-pullers are the traditional sporting events held in different regions in the Netherlands, such as ring-riding, pole-jumping, and pony-racing for boys.

Ring-riding or the *Ringrijden* [RING-ray-den] is held in the provinces of Zeeland and Friesland in August. Pole-jumping (across a ditch of course) and pony-racing are popular in North Holland.

THINGS FOR YOU TO DO

If there is one thing that Dutch children love, it's the outdoors. All over the Netherlands, you will see children playing or cycling in the streets and in the country, enjoying the warm sun in summer and the cool wind in winter. There is only one rule in the games that Dutch children play—have fun!

Windmill fun!

This colorful little wonder is fun to make and gives you hours of fun in the outdoors. At the same time, it shows you how wind can be turned into energy—the secret behind the success of the windmill.

Make a windmill

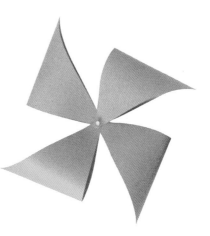

To make a windmill, you will need two squares of colored paper—get the sturdy kind (about 4 inches x 4 inches, or 10 centimeters x 10 centimeters). Fold each piece of paper diagonally in half and cut along the folds with a scissors. Now, you have four triangles. Glue the two identical corners of each triangle together. Don't fold! These are the four sails of the windmill. Then, take all the glued ends and place them on top of one another, and spread them out to four different corners (like the sails of a real windmill). Pin the sails onto a wooden stick (about 12 inches or 30 centimeters long) with a small pin, and you have your windmill!

Make as many windmills as you like and run around your garden as you hold them in your hands. The faster you run, the faster they turn!

Games that never get old

Do you ever play hopscotch or rope-skipping in the schoolyard or on the pavement outside your home? In the Netherlands, these games are still very popular and are played in spring and autumn, when the sun is shining and the air is cool.

Things to look for in your library

Amsterdam (Cities of the World). Deborah Kent (Children's Press, 1997).
Anne Frank: the Diary of a Young Girl. B. M. Mooyaart [translator] (Doubleday, 1967).
Art for Young People: Vincent Van Gogh. Peter Harrison (Sterling Publications, 1996).
Flower Parades. (video).
Inside the Netherlands. Ian James (Franklin Watts Incorporated, 1990).
Kinderdike. Leonard Everett Fisher (Atheneum, 1994).
The Little Riders. Margaretha Shemin (Beech Tree Books, 1993).
Netherlands (Where We Live series). Donna Bailey (Steck-Vaughn Library Division, 1992).
Netherlands Bureau of Tourism. (http://www.nbt.nl/holland, 1997).
The Royals. (video).
Saint Nicholas. (video).

MAKE A PALMPAAS

When Easter is just around the corner, and you've painted all the eggs in your kitchen, try your hand at making a *palmpaas* [palm-PAS]. When you're done, you can stick it into a pot of soil, and you've got a great decoration for your living room or your garden. You could also attach it to a Christmas tree stand, and you've created your very own "Easter tree!"

You will need:
1. A paint tray
2. Tempera paints
3. A few packets of chocolate eggs
4. Two bamboo sticks—4 feet (1.2 m) long and 2 feet (60 cm) long
5. Paintbrushes
6. Pencil
7. A ball of strong thread (yarn or twine) or tape
8. Scissors
9. Paper clay
10. Colored tinsel
11. Gauze (to hold the eggs)
12. Four oranges
13. Colored ribbons (and any other decorations you like)

1

2

3

4

5

6

7

8

9

10

11

12

13

1 Shape a rooster out of paper clay and poke a hole at the bottom of the rooster. Let it harden. When it is hard, paint in the rooster's eyes, crown, beak, etc.

2 Tie the two sticks together into a cross (as shown above)—you can use tape if it's easier.

3 Wrap the colored tinsel around the sticks. Then carefully pierce two oranges over the top until they sit at the crossing. Stick two more oranges on the outside of the cross-beams. Ask an adult to help you make cuts on the oranges so that it is easier to pierce the stick through them.

4 Hang the eggs and other decorations on both crossbeams, and tie as many bows in between as you like. Then, gently place the rooster on top—and you've got your very own palmpaas! (If you like, you can even make a palmpaas with two crossbars for more colorful decorations!)

MAKE SUGAR HEARTS

Sinterklaas, good children, and sugar hearts go together. But since Sinterklaas is not celebrated in the United States, you don't have to wait until December 5th to make these sweet treats. Can you think of other special days when you can give a special person a heart? If there are, here's a recipe to make your very own sugar heart!

You will need:
1. Wax paper
2. ½ cup (120 ml) milk
3. A wooden spoon
4. 2 teaspoons cocoa powder
5. A teaspoon of butter
6. Measuring spoons
7. A saucepan
8. 1 or more heart-shaped baking dishes
9. 1 cup (200 g) sugar
10. Measuring cup

1

2 and 10

3

4

5

6

7

8

9

30

1 Mix the sugar and cocoa in a saucepan. Add milk, stir well, and bring to a boil.

2 Let the mixture simmer till it thickens into syrup. Once the syrup is slow to fall back from the spoon, remove the syrup from the fire and stir till cloudy.

3 Line the baking dishes with wax paper. Pour the syrup into the dishes before it hardens. Then scrape the hard sugar off the inside of the saucepan.

4 Let the hearts cool off and harden, then carefully lift the sugar heart out of the baking dish. Remove the wax paper and you've got your sugar heart!

GLOSSARY

abstaining, 13 Holding yourself back from something you enjoy.
atoned, 13 Made amends for a wrongdoing.
bishop, 8 A high priest in the Catholic church.
bizarre, 15 Very odd in manner or appearance.
cultivated, 22 Plants or crops grown from seeds, bulbs, shoots, etc.
dikes, 4 Walls constructed to keep the sea from flooding inland.
heritage, 20 Traditions or bloodlines handed down from past generations.
lance, 24 A weapon with a long wooden pole and a pointed steel head, used by horsemen when charging.
mascot, 14 Person, animal, or object that is supposed to bring luck.
outrageous, 13 Shocking.
patron saint, 8 A saint looked upon as the special guardian of a person or place.
unfurled, 20 To have opened or spread out something that has been rolled up tightly.

INDEX

Picture credits
Haga Library Japan: 8 (both), 9, 10, 11 (both), 23, 24 (top); Dave G. Houser: 1, 3 (bottom); International Photobank: 2, 5, 20, 21, 22 (top), 25; Life File: 3 (top), 18 (top); Keith Mundy: 7 (bottom), 16, 17 (bottom), 18 (bottom), 19; Netherlands Ministry of Home Affairs: 17 (top); Photobank Singapore: 6, 7 (top), 22 (bottom); David Simson: 12, 13 (both), 14, 15 (both), 24 (bottom); Liba Taylor: 4

Lincoln Christian College

P9-DDY-904

MORE POWER FOR YOUR CHURCH
•
BUILDING UP YOUR CONGREGATION

MORE POWER FOR YOUR CHURCH

•

BUILDING UP YOUR CONGREGATION

By WILLARD AUGUSTUS PLEUTHNER

*With the Assistance of
Several Hundred Clergy and Church Workers
of Different Denominations and Faiths*

FARRAR, STRAUS AND CUDAHY   NEW YORK

COPYRIGHT © 1950, 1951, 1952, 1959
by WILLARD A. PLEUTHNER

Library of Congress catalog card number 59-6589

All rights reserved, including the right
to reproduce this book or portions thereof
in any form.

All the author's royalties from the sale of this combined edition will be sent by Farrar, Straus and
Cudahy directly to the following organizations:

AMERICAN BIBLE SOCIETY
NATIONAL CONFERENCE OF CHRISTIANS AND JEWS
RELIGION IN AMERICAN LIFE

MANUFACTURED IN THE UNITED STATES OF AMERICA

250
P72m
c.1.

This condensed version is dedicated to those hard-working saints who serve so many . . . so long . . . in so many ways, yet often receive so little appreciation or recognition. To the clergymen we all love so well and without whom our lives would lose purpose, inspiration and depth.

In particular, the author dedicates this book to those men of God who have had a profound influence on his life:

ALBERT G. BUTZER

WILBURN C. CAMPBELL

HORACE B. DONNEGAN

WALTER LORD

WALTER MC NEELEY

AUSTIN PARDUE

21670

INTRODUCTION

WHILE READING THIS WONDERFUL BOOK by Willard Pleuthner, the thought came to me how excited and disturbed we would be if the Communists should issue such a suggestion manual for their workers. We would be aware that they were employing the highest efficiency in their activities, and as a result would make tremendous gains.

Mr. Pleuthner's book will render such service to the Christian cause. It is the most amazing compilation of practical and workable suggestions that I have ever seen. The author has drawn ideas from churches everywhere. Seemingly every project, idea, or plan that has ever worked anywhere is described in these pages. I firmly believe that, if ministers and laymen study and apply the ideas herein contained, any church (and I mean any church anywhere) can increase attendance, improve its financial position, make a greater impact on the community, and attain the supreme objective of winning people to Jesus Christ.

I am going to give a copy to each of my official associates in the Marble Collegiate Church. I shall ask each man to study the methods of church activities outlined and bring his suggestions for our consideration. We shall use the volume as a source of fresh, new ideas.

I am enthusiastic about the practical value of the book. May I underscore the author's emphasis that this is not merely a "reading" book. Rather, it is a working manual. It is not only to read and meditate on, but it is a direct action, new idea source book.

Efficiency methods work in business and in every other phase of human activity. Why not in the church, as well? The Bible says, "The Kingdom of God is within you," meaning among other things that within us are enough creative capacities to meet all our problems and enter into the richness of God's blessings. This book will stimulate our own creative powers and give a great impetus to the whole Christian movement.

I, for one, want to give thanks that the Church can produce such consecrated, enthusiastic, and efficient laymen as Willard A. Pleuthner. We owe him a great debt of gratitude for his book, *More Power for Your Church*.

Norman Vincent Peale

CONTENTS

Chapter 1

GETTING MORE PEOPLE
INTO CHURCH

THIS IS A FAVORITE chapter of the author for two reasons. First, its caption was almost selected as the title for the first book, instead of *Building Up Your Congregation*. Second, this chapter was voted one of the seven most helpful, most needed chapters, in the advance survey made among 2600 clergymen and lay workers.

While no sincere church worker is interested in *just* getting people into church, this is usually one of the necessary *first steps* in exposing more people to religion. Most of us must get into church first *before* religion can become a bigger influence in our lives.

There are so many proven ways to get more people into church or into synagogue that we hardly know where to begin. This desirable and needed form of evangelism is being accomplished week after week by inspired individuals, organized groups, committees, councils of churches, and individual hard-working clergymen. The religious press carries a continuous flow of proven plans for building up a congregation. Any lay worker who is charged with the responsibility or accepts God's challenge to bring in more worshipers should subscribe to his own denominational publication, plus a general interdenominational magazine like *Christian Herald, Christian Century, National Council Outlook* or *Protestant World*. The religious publications offer a rich storehouse of ideas and plans which can be adapted to your church . . . your neighborhood . . . and your city.

In this chapter we will describe some of the plans which have brought more people into houses of worship. You'll find other proven ideas in other chapters of this book. The problem is not to find them, but to *start* using them in your house of worship.

.1. George E. Sweazey, secretary of the *New Life Advance*, points out that "in Spain Protestant churches are not allowed to advertise—not even by a notice on the door saying, 'Preaching at 11 a.m.' No cross or symbol is allowed to mark their meeting place. They are utterly dependent upon person-to-person advertising. Because there is no other way, the church members are extraordinarily zealous in giving invitations to the church, and Spanish Protestant Church membership is said to have doubled or tripled in the past twelve years."

2. When Dr. Joseph Sizoo went to the famous New York Avenue Church in Washington the congregation had become very small. They stayed small until some of the men of the church had an informal meeting to discuss the problem. Each man promised to tell several others during the week about the splendid services at the church. By this method alone, within a year the congregation had more than doubled.

3. A prominent leader said: "The great discovery about evangelism in our generation is that it is best done by training and assigning lay church members to go out and make calls. This method, often called 'Visitation Evangelism,' is bringing more adults into Protestant Anglican and Orthodox churches today than are all other methods combined—bringing more than mass evangelism ever did in its heyday. Experience during two decades has worked out highly practical and spiritually sound methods for this. There are several excellent books on the subject. I would recommend 'How to Increase Church Membership and Attendance' by

Crossland, Abingdon-Cokesbury, $1.75, and 'A Handbook of Evangelism for Laymen' by Bryan, Abingdon-Cokesbury, 50¢."

Tidings of 1908 Grand Avenue, Nashville 4, Tennessee, offer four briefer leaflets on this same subject.

4. "The good people of Jacksonville, Florida, rode to church—*any* church—free of charge last summer, thanks to a generous good-will gesture by Wiley Moore, president of the Jacksonville Coach Company.

"On Sunday morning, all a churchgoer had to do was get on a bus and tell the driver, 'I'm going to church.' After services, 'I've been to church' won him a free ride home.

"The possibility of persons using that as an excuse for a free ride on Sunday didn't bother Mr. Moore much. 'I figured if anybody cheated, it would be on his conscience,' he explained, 'and that would drive him to church anyway.' "

"To fill our churches we must advertise more," the Reverend Guy Perdue, minister of the White Rock Methodist Church of Dallas, Texas, advised. "God was the original advertiser. He hung out the stars to let 'the Heavens declare the glory of God.' "

The bus company in Buffalo took people to church free on the Sundays in Lent. Perhaps there is an equally public-spirited transportation company in your city. It's worth finding out.

5. St. Matthew's Lutheran Church in White Plains, N. Y., secured a 25 percent increase in attendance by training the entire congregation for evangelism. Prior to the beginning of their official program, each member was sent a copy of a special booklet, entitled, "Let's Put First Things First." Prepared under the direction of John H. Wagner, this booklet gives the details of a complete program of evangelism. As this plan worked, it's worth sending for this material.

6. The Reverend E. Hoyt Kerr, Jr., pastor of the First Presbyterian Church in Clarksville, Arkansas, se-

cured a 20 percent increase in church attendance
through the following program:

"Our plan involves the signing of an enrollment card
or a registration of each person present each Sunday.
The results of this signing are tabulated in a notebook
each week. The notebook contains, in alphabetical
order, the names of each member—or close friend—of
the church. Then before the service the following Sunday each absentee—not each family that is absent but
each person—is sent a postal card reminder which also
contains the coming sermon topic and any important
announcements."

This plan is used once a year for a two- or three-
month period. It is used at different times each year . . .
spring . . . fall . . . or summer.

7. Several synagogues in the East have a special service which helps one fulfill that religious axiom, "The
family that prays together, stays together." It is known
as *"Family Night Service"* and is held the first Friday
in each month. All children with a birthday that month
attend this service *with* their families. Here is an ideal
way to add religious significance to a child's birthday
and to make it an occasion for worshiping *together*.

8. The Reverend Gerald V. A. Barry of Christ
Church, Riverdale, N. Y., sends each member a birthday card every year. But it is not the usual type of
greeting. This card arrives the week of the birthday and
announces that on the next Sunday "we will remember
you in our prayers . . . we hope you will worship with
us on that day." Few churchgoers can resist going to
church on their "Birthday-Sunday."

9. During the past 10 years more than 5,000 attended
Sunday church services in Philadelphia, yet an hour before services not one had planned to go.

They went because 75-year-old Fred Werner, layman
at Holy Trinity Church, asked them to go.

Leaving home about an hour before church Mr.
Werner patrols principal streets and parks of downtown
Philadelphia on the lookout for servicemen.

With a friendly smile he says to them: "Come on boys and go to church with me. It won't hurt and it won't cost you a cent." Mr. Werner says of his direct technique: "I don't talk religion to the boys . . . I'm not a sheep-stealer. I just figure if a boy is lonely and in a strange town and hasn't anything else to do, he might as well be in church."

Usually, he says, from half a dozen to 40 servicemen respond and accompany him to church. A decrease in the number of servicemen after World War II didn't lessen his activities. He brought in foreign sailors.

This is a method which can be adopted in hundreds of cities. As the Information Service Bulletin of the National Council of Churches says,

"Though people come into the Church in groups, it is very frequently under the influence of one strong, deeply converted man or woman within the group. One such layman is worth his weight in gold."

10. The Reverend H. P. Alexander is a retired Presbyterian minister who has an enviable record of getting more people into the six small churches he has built up in Oklahoma and Kansas. The secret of his success was to call in the families . . . call on families . . . and keep calling on families. All families! He called on farmers who hadn't been visited by a clergyman in almost 20 years.

11. Getting more people into church on a mass scale was dramatically illustrated by the successful state-wide crusade of the Iowa Methodists. In a single week these inspired workers rang enough door bells to convert more than 11,000 to active membership. The drive was directed by Dr. Eugene Golay of Nashville, Tennessee, as an associate of the Methodist United Evangelistic Mission. Despite severe weather 32,518 people were interviewed.

More than 6,000 professed the Christian faith for the first time and 5,022 others transferred standing membership—mostly inactive—to local churches. This was all accomplished by two-member teams who visited non-churchgoers and persuaded them that "the Church is never more needed than now."

This state-wide crusade is additional proof that countless thousands are ready to go to church, if only someone will talk to them about it. God bless Bishop Charles W. Brashares of Des Moines and the Iowa Methodists for their leadership in setting an example which should be followed in other states by other denominations.

12. The Church of the Ascension, Fifth Avenue and 10th Street, New York, has kept its doors open around the clock since 1929. Is it worth it?

The church released figures for the last eight months in 1951. Total attendance during the night hours from 9 p.m. to 6:45 a.m. was 10,441, about equal numbers of men and women and preponderantly adults. About one-fourth were members or constituents of the church. There were only 23 requests for relief.

Is yours a church which can duplicate this "Around the Clock" service?

13. The DeWitt Memorial Church uses a "block captain" technique for stimulating church interest among tenants of the apartment buildings on New York's lower East Side. "Under the plan, a member of the congregation living in each of the 16 buildings of the new Lillian Wald Houses that cover a 16-square-block tract near the church is the church's representative for his building.

"His job is to call on each family, acquaint it with the church's work and services and extend an invitation to join the congregation.

"Each block captain also organizes children in his building for Sunday school attendance. He meets them in the lobby at a set time on Sunday morning and shepherds them to and from Sunday school."

The Rev. Donald J. Walton has found that this block captain plan has resulted in greatly increased church attendance and Sunday School enrollment.

Chapter 2

GREATER INSPIRATION
THROUGH MORE
CONGREGATION
PARTICIPATION

SPORTS, MUSIC AND RELIGION have one basic factor in common. Those who personally participate get far more out of it than those who are merely spectators. People in the pews who are listening are more like spectators than when they actively put themselves into the service by praying, singing or reading responses. There's nothing like participation to build morale and give a sense of belonging.

Many of the churches which are showing the greatest growth are those in which more and more of the service is being given back to the people in the pews. Here are some of the many ways in which your church can increase its congregation participation. Yes, they will result in more inspiration.

1. During "Laymen's Sunday," held every third Sunday in October, laymen read the Bible lessons, among their several activities in this service. This does something to deepen the reader's religious life. From that Sunday on, his religion, his attendance at church services mean more to him. So why not let this experience of pulpit reading of the Bible be enjoyed and shared by more members of the congregation? Why not have the Bible read by laymen at least once a month? The congregation likes this change of pace and it permits the clergyman to save more of his energy and thoughts for the sermon.

9

The Reverend Robert Anthony of the North Presbyterian Church in Flushing, Long Island, carries out
this congregation participation regularly. So does Dr.
Samuel Harkness of the Winnetka, Illinois, Congregational Church. To vary the practice, have the good
ladies read the Bible lesson every now and then. In
addition to the good it does them and others, they
deserve the recognition for the overwhelming amount
of church work done by the distaff side.

2. In Grace Church, Utica, New York, a group of
laymen read the litany each weekday noon. In addition
they pray for peace and pray for parishioners having
anniversaries.

3. Has your church ever used a prayer hymn? St.
Joseph of Arimathea in Elmsford, New York, uses the
first verse of the hymn, "Lead Us, O Father, in the
Path of Peace," in the latter part of the Reverend Walter McNeely's closing prayer. The First Presbyterian
Church in Sebring, Florida, has a Prayer Hymn right
after the first lesson. Listening to "God Be in My
Heart" is just the right sort of musical background for
one's personal silent prayer. Why not try letting a
prayer hymn lift the praying souls to greater heights?
How about starting this next Sunday?

The First Presbyterian Church of Sebring, Florida,
opens its 11 a.m. Sunday service in a most unusual and
tuneful way. The organist plays the Westminster
"grandfather's clock" chimes at 11 o'clock. If you have
a chimes stop on your organ, try this opening on special
Sundays. If your congregation likes this chiming introduction, use it once a month as a change of pace.

4. Better congregational singing is one of the surest
and easiest ways to increase congregation participation.
This can be done simply by singing favorite, well-
known hymns. One key to which hymns are most popular and best-loved is a list of those which are sung on
Sunday radio programs. For example, the Fred Waring
program, sponsored by the General Electric Company,

closes with hymns that people love to sing. Another source is the hymns played on the bells at the famous Bok Singing Tower at Lake Wales, Florida. Mr. Anton Brees, the world's master carillonneur, tells us that the following hymns are favorites with the millions who come from all over the United States to listen at this mountain lake sanctuary:

> Hymn of Thanks
> Faith of Our Fathers
> The Old Rugged Cross
> In the Garden
> The Bells of St. Mary's

"The Word of Life" TV program asked listeners to send in their favorite hymns. Out of thousands of letters, these were the best-loved:

> The Old Rugged Cross
> What a Friend We Have in Jesus
> In the Garden
> It Is No Secret
> The Love of God

Of course you will always get better congregational singing when the service includes such standard favorites as:

> Dear Lord and Father of Mankind
> Onward Christian Soldiers
> America the Beautiful
> Lead Kindly Light
> Jesus Lover of My Soul
> Come Ye Thankful People Come

One of the best ways to find out the individual favorites of your own congregation is to make a "Favorite Hymn Survey." This is described in detail in the book, *Building Up Your Congregation.*

For the best congregation participation in your church singing, make sure that the opening and closing hymns are favorite hymns. Let the people in the pews sing what they know best, even if you schedule the same favorite every month or six weeks.

5. There are some churches which cannot afford the time or money to have an adult choir. Or they do not have enough musical talent among their members for an adult choir. This is not a serious problem. A junior choir of girls from 12 to 17 singing favorite hymns is an acceptable alternate to an adult choir.

St. Joseph's of Arimathéa, at Elmsford, New York, does this, even without choir practice, for their junior choir. The Rector frequently uses hymns in place of such canticles as the "Te Deum," etc. to promote greater congregation participation. A decimeter (sound measuring device) would show that the singing at St. Joseph's is the height of congregation participation.

St. Mark's Methodist Church in Brooklyn, New York, goes so far toward youth singing that it has a choir of "cherubs." These tots (2-5 years old) look like cherubs in their white surplices, scrubbed faces, shining hair and little mouths open in song. They appear at the Christmas and Easter services and other special features. Think of little children singing and you hear silver bells on a soft summer's night; the twinkle of a brook running deep in green woods; the laughter of angels.

6. Some of the best-loved hymns are the glorious resurrection ones for Easter. Notice how much better the congregation sings such inspirational music as: "Jesus Christ Has Risen Today."

There is no reason why those lovely popular hymns should be sung only at Easter. The truth and inspiration of Christ's resurrection is with Christians all through the year. So why should we sing about this joy just during the all too brief Easter season. Why not plan to sing Easter hymns at a "Resurrection Sunday Service," the first Sunday after Labor Day? That's when the fall season of church services starts. There's no better way to begin another church year of worship than with Easter hymns and a sermon on Christ's resurrection . . . what it means to all of us.

R. W. Dale, the great English Congregationalist preacher of over half a century ago, had his congregation sing an Easter hymn almost every Sunday morning. A visitor to his church commented, "When I first attended the service there, I was surprised to hear on a November morning the hymn, 'Christ Is Risen, Allelujah!' I mentioned it to Dr. Dale afterwards and he said: 'I want my people to get hold of the glorious fact that Christ is alive, and to rejoice over it.' "

7. For many years leading clergymen and laymen have longed for some way to add more congregation participation to the wedding service. It is true that in some wedding ceremonies the Lord's Prayer is repeated, or some responses given. But even the Lord's Prayer doesn't answer the longing of those who would like to see a wedding service participation which enables the married people of the congregation (usually in the majority) to renew their own wedding vows.

At last this need has been filled by a special wedding hymn with words by Catherine Haydon Jacobs and music by Lee Hastings Bristol, Jr. (Mr. Bristol, interestingly enough, is a descendant of another hymn-tune writer, Thomas Hastings, who wrote—among 1,000 others—the tune TOPLADY to which "Rock of Ages" is usually sung). This inspirational wedding hymn by Mrs. Jacobs and Mr. Bristol is reproduced in this book with their permission.

Copies can be secured from Lee Bristol, Jr., Room 1155, 630 Fifth Avenue, New York, New York. To enable the congregation to join in the singing of this wedding hymn, it is suggested that enough copies be ordered for everyone. These attractive little leaflets make an interesting personal memento to carry away from the wedding. Some people order them far enough

WEDDING HYMN

1. Dear Lord, a man and woman bring
      Their consecrated love.
   Hear Thou our voices as we sing;
      Receive their vows above.
   Remember them as children who
      Are Thine through hope instilled.
   O, God, our Father, bless these two,
      Thy sacrament fulfilled.

2. Through paths untraveled and unknown
      Dear Lord, speed Thou their ways
   And bid the radiance of Thy throne
      Illuminate their days.
   Grant them a lasting faith renewed,
      Courageous hearts that dare
   To blend with selfless gratitude
      The holiness of prayer.

3. Before Thine altar, Lord, they kneel
      In humble reverence,
   Entrusting earthly woe or weal
      To Heavenly consequence.
   Receive their union through Thy rite
      Ordained within this hour,
   Fidelity in Thy clear sight,
      Thine everlasting Dower.

4. Before Thine altar, Lord, may all
      Who took the marriage vow
   Kneel once again! Let them recall
      Their spoken pledges now,
   Their love to each as theirs to Thee
      Beyond our silent claim.
   O, Father, bless this marriage, we
      Ask now in Jesus' name.   Amen.

Catherine Haydon Jacobs

WEDDING HYMN
(C. M. D.)

"JOEL"

LEE H. BRISTOL, Jr.

Music copyright 1952 by the composer.

ahead of time so that a local printer can imprint them with a personalized identification at the top of the page. This might read as follows:

Wedding Hymn

sung at the wedding

of

_____   and   _____

on (date) at (name of church and town)

By now, my dear reader, you may think that the author has spent too much of your time and your book discussing hymn singing. For that normal reaction, I don't blame you. Yet, I was encouraged by many people to go all-out in discussing this important part of church services. One big encouragement was the following item in the *Episcopal Churchnews.*

BISHOP SAYS INSPIRING HYMN
WORTH A THOUSAND SERMONS

"In California a hymn is worth a thousand sermons. At least this was the opinion implied by the Right Reverend Karl M. Block, Bishop of California, when he addressed the first Diocesan Church Music Conference recently in San Francisco. Said the Bishop: 'The spiritual upthrust gained from the lilting songs of the church, the very antiquity of some of the chants, and the beauty of the familiar, will catch and change a person more often than a dozen sermons.' Calling for close association between rectors and organists, Bishop Block said, 'Get to know your rector and you'll know what's in his heart.' "

8. Speaking of the relationship between clergy and organist leads us logically to the relationship of clergy, congregation, and choir. To cover this vital subject the author was able to secure the help of an experienced specialist in that field . . . a Mr. Paul Swarm. He is Director of the Church Music Foundation (P. O. Box 7, Decatur, Illinois), a non-profit corporation dedicated to serving church musicians of all faiths and creeds and to improving church music in America. By conducting local "workshops" and other programs and by publishing helpful reference material, the Foundation has done much in its short existence to further its objectives. Here is his sound advice on contacts with the clergy.

Chapter 3

TURNING MAN-POWER
INTO CHURCH-POWER

"NEVER UNDERESTIMATE the power of a woman" is the slogan of a well-known woman's publication. Few people do. Men aren't so highly regarded, it seems. Churches, clergymen, even laymen themselves, are underestimating the power of men.

We men, at least most of us, sit back and watch while the little ladies carry on the main part of church work. The women make and serve the chicken dinners; they sew, knit and mend for the needy. They take care of choir and altar. They are the missionary conscience of the church. They run the bazaars, the socials, and most money-making affairs. True, we men usually foot the bills, pay for the tickets, or allow ourselves to be dragged out for the occasions. Yes, we're nice when some hard-working gal talks up a wonderful value in a handmade apron.

But how many major or helpful activities are started, and carried out, completely by men? Outside of the every-member canvass, board meetings, the men's club dinners, or Boy Scout sponsorship, do we males make much of a contribution toward keeping our church going and growing?

When we remember that the original twelve who spread Christ's word were *men*, we realize how far we've slipped from our duty, opportunity and privilege. We once had the alibi of being busy everlastingly working to make a living. No more. With the eight-hour working day and five-day week in so many communities, the old excuse doesn't hold water.

One specific situation which should be ours to solve is the problem of getting more men to attend the Sunday services. As it is now in most churches, women outnumber men in the pews by a most discouraging percentage. This can be corrected in two ways.

First, by our making it an established practice—a regular habit—to attend worship services ourselves, with our wives and families. Out of our 168 hours of time per week, let's give God's hour back to him by being in church on Sundays. It does something for us. It is amazing how much better the service makes us feel the rest of the week. It does something for others, too. Each one of us sets the example for at least twenty other people who follow what we do, who consciously or unconsciously imitate many of our actions and activities. Some of these think they can lead a "good life" without going to church, and they point to us as an example.

Second, we should all assume the duties of Sales Manager of Church Attendance. Or, we can call ourselves Vice-President in Charge of Building Congregations, if we like a more impressive title. In either case, our steady job is to invite men, with their families, to worship with us in our church. We should ask these non-churchgoers on Thursday or Friday, so they will have plenty of time to arrange their Sunday schedule. When we are turned down, we'll keep on at regular (but not annoying) intervals asking them to come. As Sales Manager, we should set for ourselves a yearly quota of new men and families to get into the church. It may be two or six or ten. But set the quota and then work regularly at achieving or exceeding it. That is the greatest con-

tribution which most of us men can give our churches
—more valuable, ministers say, than money.

There are many activities which the men of the
church can take over, and put over. Why not a definite
Christian objective for your men's club each year? This
could be increased contribution to foreign missions,
local missionary work in your community, a clothing
campaign for Korean children, a teen-age club or other
recreation for the young people in the church. Why
shouldn't we men organize a stag Saturday painting
party and paint the church rooms that look unworthy
of God's house? Our church is a sanctuary which should
invite reverence.

An annual Father-and-Son Sunday helps to increase
male attendance. Wives, mothers, and daughters are
welcome, too. But for just this Sunday, fathers and sons
sit down in front.

Instead of having Laymen's Sunday only once a year
in October, why not another Men's Sunday in May? At
that service we men could read the Bible lessons, give
the prayers and perhaps even the sermon. That's a
tested way to step up male attendance. Some churches
have different men read the Scriptures every Sunday.
Why not start this practice in your church?

Have you ever asked your minister to pray for business men? Today business men need such prayers more
than ever. Business workers and executives can't help
gravitating to those churches where their pressing work-
day problems are recognized and an effort made to help
in their solution on a Christian basis.

Many men like a garden. A churchmen's garden club
will appeal to those who do. It's a privilege to create
and maintain a church garden that is a joy and inspiration for members, visitors and passersby. A good place
is the front yard of the church facing the street, the
garden shape a well-proportioned cross.

These are just a few of the obvious ways we men can
be real builders, not merely well-behaved pew-warmers.
You will think of other helpful, Christian things to do.

Mr., Mrs., Miss _____

Address _____

_____ Phone _____

Business Address _____ Phone _____

has indicated an interest in participating in the following areas:

☐ Attendance at Worship Services

☐ Affiliation with _____
                              (Organizations)

☐ Daily Personal Devotions   ☐ Family Worship

	Has	Will		Has	Will
Teaching			**Youth Groups**		
Children	☐	☐	Counselor	☐	☐
Youth	☐	☐	Member	☐	☐
Adults	☐	☐	**Men's Work**	☐	☐
Music			**Women's Work**	☐	☐
Choir	☐	☐	**Visiting**		
Instrument:			Sick	☐	☐
	☐	☐	Visitors	☐	☐
_____			New Members	☐	☐
Ushering			Absentees	☐	☐
Morning	☐	☐	**Church Dinners**		
Evening	☐	☐	Assist in Kitchen	☐	☐
Office Work			Serve Tables	☐	☐
Typing	☐	☐	**Church Maintenance**		
Bookkeeping	☐	☐	Carpentering	☐	☐
Mimeographing	☐	☐	Painting	☐	☐
Floral Arrangements	☐	☐	_____	☐	☐

Other:

_____ ☐ ☐

_____ ☐ ☐

_____ ☐ ☐

_____ ☐ ☐

Interviewed by _____

Date _____

The Judson Press   Form W. No. 3—Price, $1.25 a hundred

But don't stop with thinking about them. Write down your ideas, discuss them over the phone with a fellow member, talk about them with your preacher or a church official at next Sunday's service.

Dr. Charles O. Wright of the First Baptist Church in White Plains, New York, makes sure that their man-power is geared into church-power . . . in writing on cards. Reproduced on this page is the handy card on which each new man (and woman, too) puts down how he would like to personally participate in the various activities of the church. This gives the Reverend Mr. Wright and the church organizations a visible inventory of the available man-power.

You can get a supply of these cards from The Judson Press, 703 Chestnut Street, Philadelphia, Pennsylvania, for only $1.25 per hundred. Ask for form W No. 3. This card is one of a series of cards and folders developed by the Council of American Baptist Men. Headquarters at 152 Madison Avenue, New York City. The Director of this active laymen's group is Edward Parsons.

Very few churches have an up-to-date and adequate library of religious books. Although this needed project is listed under the chapter on women's organizations, it is a religious building plan that is worthy of the personal interest and support of any red-blooded male Christian.

Here's a congregation building plan which some man in your church can duplicate. Maybe *you* will volunteer to be its starter and sponsor.

A chain of ribbons promises to fill Emanuel Evangelical United Brethren Church, Cleveland, Ohio, to its very rafters.

In a unique "Church Loyalty Crusade" each man, woman and child attending the church this month is given a colored ribbon every Sunday to give to a friend with the friend's promise to be at church next Sunday.

The first Sunday of the campaign ribbons were distributed to 105 attending the service. The next Sunday, Mother's Day, a crowd of 197 nearly filled the auditorium, anteroom and balcony to capacity. All received ribbons to give to their friends for next Sunday.

As a feature of Mother's Day, Mrs. Emilie Hartwig, 85, was given a bouquet as the oldest mother present, and Mrs. Richard Spears, 21, received flowers as the youngest mother. Some 75 mothers were given potted plants, "To watch grow, signifying your growing with your children."

You business executives may have the opportunity of getting a religious basic theme or church-going slogan included in the advertising for your own company or for your trade association. Look how effectively the Washington Automobile Trade Association did this in the following well-read newspaper advertisement.

You will be interested to know more about the basic theme "Bring Your Problems to Church this Sunday . . . Millions Leave Them there." It was developed as one of the many sound and effective appeals by and for the "Religion In American Life Campaign." From reading about it on pages 278 to 289 you'll see they have many things your executives can use.

We like the little folder put out by Paul Swarm, President of the Church Music Foundation of Decatur, Illinois. It is entitled "How to Hold a Church Position Without Working." Inside you get the answer in these three short sentences:

> Don't fool yourself
> It can't be done
> Study your profession and go to work

That is sound advice for us business men. But Paul means it for choirmasters. He has developed a manual work book which some man in your church should get and give to the choirmaster or organist. It is entitled "Guideposts for the Church Musician." One section tells "Fourteen Ways of Maintaining Choir Interest." Are *you* the man who will be a hero and helper by giving this great guide to your choir? It is written for all three faiths!

By now you may be saying the author is certainly lining up a lot of jobs for *one* man to do. Of course, you cannot do them all, even if you want to disprove that dire Old Testament prediction, called to my attention by Charles Brower . . . a good friend of mine at B.B.D.&O. It is from Ecclesiastes, Chapter 26, Verse 29, and reads as follows:

> A Merchant shall hardly keep himself from doing wrong:
> and a huckster shall not be freed from sin"

We are sure you'll keep from doing wrong by doing right by those jobs in this list which you can do *best*. Jobs which are *not now* being done in or for your congregation and church.

At All Saints Church, Syracuse, New York, two laymen read morning prayer and two others read evening prayer, *every day of the week* except Sunday. At the beginning of their effort to have DAILY services at their church these men found they were all alone each day. But now after several years of this daily worship lead by 24 laymen, they find that other laymen and women stop by the church during weekends for prayer and meditation.

Most laymen serving are business men. The work started under the leadership of W. Dexter Wilson, an insurance executive, who for 20 years has been a leader in central New York's laymen's work.

Did you ever see your minister cutting a stencil or mimeographing a church bulletin? If you did you should have a guilty feeling about it. It is not his job. He has far more important things to do. A qualified layman should do this or be responsible for getting it done.

Yes, men, this *is* your business. It is the biggest and most important business in the world.

Chapter 4

PROJECTS FOR
TEEN-AGE GROUPS

Baked bean suppers . . . hymn sings . . . and even religious movies are not enough to keep a young people's group growing in interest and in numbers. (However, all are real helps in the over-all plan.) Young people look for, and live on, action. They want to be doing things . . . different things . . . as much as possible.

Group leaders and adult advisers have the constant problem of directing youthful enthusiasm and energies into paths which develop character and religious principles. Their activities should also benefit the church . . . the congregation . . . and the community. To help in this planning we give you herewith a list of some projects which can help you in the fine work needed for these future leaders of the church.

1. The Bells. This is a great project for the God-fearing young people of our nation: To go to their places of worship and ring the bells or chimes or carillon from 7 p.m. to 7:15 p.m. every Saturday evening, to remind hearers to worship God, to tell the world that we are a God-fearing people, and to wordlessly ask people week after week to work for true brotherhood through all the world.

The inspiration for this project: Upon hearing of the century-old custom in Europe of ringing Roman Catholic, Anglican and Protestant church bells from 7 p.m. to 7:15 p.m. every Saturday evening, the 1950 Brotherhood Week committee for Washington, D. C., adopted as one of the Brotherhood Week features the ringing of the church bells of the nation's capitol every Saturday evening of 1950. The bells were first rung on February 18th, the eve of Brotherhood Week.

A project is born: A church youth group in northern Virginia, hearing of this feature of the Brotherhood Week plans in Washington, decided to ring the bells of their own church at the same time that the Washington church bells were being rung, and to ask young people of other churches near Washington to do the same thing.

Ringing the bells on Saturday night is not the only time your church should use this truly religious music. They should be rung daily at 12 noon. This reminds listeners of all that church and Christ offer them.

The Hitchcock Presbyterian Church uses its bells to play hymns when the men are coming home from the Scarsdale, New York, station at night. What a fine welcome back to one's neighborhood!

St. Bartholomew's in New York City uses its bells for a special purpose on Good Friday. At the close of the service the chimes toll thirty-three times to denote the years of our Lord's life on earth.

St. Paul's Cathedral in Buffalo, a typical downtown church, plays favorite hymns on its carillon every weekday noon. When repairs were needed for its bell tower, the neighboring business men were big contributors. This is the best testimonial that the bells are appreciated and loved by those who hear this traditional ministry of religious music.

2. Youth Counseling. Compton Hill (Congregational Christian) Church in St. Louis is in a blighted tenement area with a city mission job. The minister, Kenneth Murphy, writes in *Advance*: "We have instituted a youth counseling program that has become an integral

part of our program. We give basic vocational and personality analyses to as many of our young people as possible—750 tests thus far. With these as a basis, we do our counseling. Dr. Nathan Kohn, of Washington University and our associate minister for counseling, who is nationally known in the vocational field, is in charge of this program. Adult members are also interested in this program and come in for their own testing."

3. *Presbyterian Life* magazine carried this stimulating story of how Kentucky youth sponsored religion in high school:

"Teen-agers of a Kentucky town united recently to stage a week-long religious emphasis program in their high school.

"The young people were members of Protestant churches in Elizabethtown, Kentucky. Early last fall they went to the Ministerial Association and requested an extended program of religious talks and meetings for all the youth of the town. With the help of the churches and the school, they planned and carried out the *town's first Religious Emphasis Week.*

"In the high school each day a radio worship program was prepared by the young people. They wrote a devotional guide which was used for home-room devotionals. Out-of-town speakers addressed the school in daily convocation programs and individual conferences and consultations were held.

"A mass meeting led by the young people was held each evening in a central church. The boys and girls led prayers, sang in a forty-voice chorus, played the organ, and ushered. One of the high-school cheer leaders led singing.

"Evening meetings were overcrowded and every young person in the high school attended the meetings."

4. Historic Christ's Church in historic Tarrytown, N. Y., makes teen-age boys an integral part of its church

life by forming a Junior Vestry. This body of willing helpers meets once a month. If a member fails to attend three meetings in a row, he is notified by letter that if he has no excuse for the three absences he is no longer a Junior Vestryman.

This Vestry appoints a committee to help on these important activities: ushering, music, finance, and property. Naturally, the Junior Vestrymen are regular in their church attendance. Here is the service of Installation used by the Rev. C. Kenneth Ackerman of Christ's Church:

WARDEN "Reverend Sir, I present unto you these persons to be inducted as Junior Vestrymen and Associate Junior Vestrymen in the service of God and in this Parish of Christ Episcopal Church, Tarrytown, New York."

MINISTER "Shortly after the Day of Pentecost, when the Apostles received power from Almighty God to carry on the task of building His Church, the numbers of new converts increased so rapidly that assistance was needed to minister to them. And we read, 'Then the Twelve called the multitude of the disciples unto them and said, It is not reason that we should leave the Word of God and serve tables. Wherefore, Brethren, look ye out among you seven men of honest report, full of the Holy Ghost and wisdom whom we may appoint over this business.' You young men of the Junior Vestry have been selected to follow in that tradition. Therefore, that this present congregation of Christ may know your fitness and resolution for this task, you shall answer plainly to these things which we, in the name of God and His Church, demand of you concerning the same."

MINISTER "Are you ready and willing to accept the office to which you have been appointed?"

VESTRYMAN "I am."

MINISTER "Will you earnestly give yourself to this office by your faithful attendance at the services of the Church; by your ready and willing acceptance of the duties of your office; by your loyal support of and cooperation with the Rector of the Parish in the discharge of his canonical duties; by doing all in your power to promote the welfare of this Parish and of the whole Church of which this Parish is a part?"

VESTRYMAN "I will earnestly endeavor to do so, the Lord being my Helper."

MINISTER "By reason of the promise you have just made and by virtue of my office as Rector of this Parish, I heartily welcome you into this official relationship and hereby install you into the respective offices to which you have been appointed; and on behalf of this Parish, I declare that you are now charged with the responsibilities and privileges of said offices."

MINISTER "Let us pray. (All kneel and recite the Lord's Prayer)

"O Lord, we beseech Thee to pour Thy Heavenly Blessing upon all who are engaged in serving Thee through Thy Holy Church, especially these Thy servants called to be Junior Vestrymen in this Parish. Prosper Thou their understanding, grant them strength and wisdom for their task, and perseverance therein. Grant that by their efforts and example they may win others to zealous and faithful service in the work of Thy Church, through the same Jesus Christ our Lord. Amen.

"O God, the Creator and Preserver of all mankind, grant that these Thy servants to whom we have entrusted a portion of the affairs of this Parish may ever act with courage, prudence, justice and love. May they be of one mind and of one heart in the upbuilding of Thy Church and in the spread of Thy Kingdom. We ask it in the Name and for the Sake of Jesus Christ our Lord. Amen."

5. Many loyal churchgoers in their teens are disturbed at the way their older brothers, sisters, and friends let their church attendance slide when they go away to school. It is too easy for the student to get out of the habit of Sunday worship. Therefore, college days become dangerous days for the away-from-homers. Before they know it, they become away-from-churchers, too.

Thinking teen-agers do not want this to happen any more than their parents and clergymen. One way to help solve this problem is to have it discussed by teen-age groups *before* they go away to school. Have some popular college graduates in the church tell how they met and solved this problem in their own personal lives. The clergyman can explain how he will write a fellow-minister in the school town to ask him to look up the home town student . . . and gear him or her into the life of the school town church. In the Episcopal faith the Reverend Roger W. Blanchard has developed some helpful materials in this work. As Executive Secretary of the Division of the College Work he prepared a "Letter of Commendation" which the student presents to the rector of a school town church; a duplicate of this is sent by the Rector to the College chaplain or school town clergyman. This "Letter of Commendation" is such a constructive factor in maintaining the church-going habits of students that we reproduce it here in full.

On the back of the right half, used by the clergyman, is a space for "Comments on Student." This includes printed subject headings for: Parish acitvities, Interests, and Miscellaneous Comments.

This same Division of College Work at Church Missions House, 281 Fourth Avenue, New York 10, N. Y., also produced two other folders of great help to teen-agers going away to school. One is entitled "So You're Going Away to College." The other is "The Local Parish and the College Student." The ideas and suggestions

Letter of Commendation

Student will present this to Episcopal chaplain or clergyman in college community

_____ a _____
NAME OF STUDENT   BAPTIZED, CONFIRMED

member of _____,
              PARISH

_____, is commended
CITY   STATE

to your spiritual care while attending_____

_____. He will be
NAME OF SCHOOL OR COLLEGE

_____
YEAR IN SCHOOL

[SIGNED]_____
           RECTOR OF

Student's Home Address_____

_____

Student's College Address_____

_____

Parents' Names _____

_____

_____

Letter of Commendation

Rector will send to Episcopal chaplain or clergyman in college community*

_____ a _____
NAME OF STUDENT   BAPTIZED, CONFIRMED

member of _____
              PARISH

_____, is commended
CITY   STATE

to your spiritual care while attending_____

_____. He will be
NAME OF SCHOOL OR COLLEGE

_____
YEAR IN SCHOOL

[SIGNED]_____
           RECTOR OF

Student's Home Address_____

Student's College Address_____

*Living Church Annual, pp. 68-83

----------------------------------- TEAR HERE -----------------

Letter of Commendation Received

to be sent by college clergyman to the student's home parish

Letter of Commendation given to_____
                                     NAME OF STUDENT

_____has been received by mail_____and

from the student_____.

[SIGNED]_____
           COLLEGE CLERGYMAN

---

in these folders are so general and so constructive that they can be used by any church of any denomination.

6. Teen-agers like a real reason to meet and talk to the older members of the church. Also they want to help on vital church projects. They can do both when they cooperate in making the congregational surveys described in Chapter 6, "Improving the Services Through Every-Member Surveys." The teen-agers can distribute questionnaires . . . interview members . . . collect the filled-out forms . . . and then help tabulate the results.

7. Here is a project which a teen-age group can ar-

range and finance all by themselves. It is to get the local radio stations to broadcast that wonderful song "Let's Go to Church on Sunday Morning" every Saturday, at least once during that day. First, calls should be made on the station manager and on the program director. Explain how the majority of listeners will like to hear this lovely and inspiring song on Saturdays. That's because the majority of listeners are churchgoers; are religious-minded. Then find out if the station has a recording of "Let's Go to Church on Sunday Morning." If not, the teen-age group has the opportunity of buying one for the station. This builds good will and encourages the station to use it frequently. This song was recorded on a Capitol record.

8. When young people go away to college, it is widely recognized that this is the time when many drop out of church forever. At Colby College, Waterville, Maine, a religious census showed that over 10 percent of the students were Anglicans. Yet only five attended the downtown church. Several college students decided that they knew the reason. The downtown church was poor and dirty. It couldn't keep a clergyman over a year. Its parishioners fought among themselves. So the students got permission to paint and clean up the church, they never fought among themselves and showed a united front before the townspeople. The result was that although the college still didn't have a chaplain for them, they became a working lay team.

After a year, a young Army Chaplain, John Knight, came to serve at both the church and the college. In two years he had built the small downtown mission, for 75 years dependent on outside funds, into a self-supporting church. With his student aides, he opened up a mission in a cellar at a nearby town, and after two years, they have built their own church. This and many other examples at St. Mark's, Waterville, show that when laymen assume responsibility they can help their church help them. Thus college students without a chaplain helped a downtown church and got a chaplain.

9. Several Boy Scouts in a Syracuse Sunday School opened the eyes of a public relations director when he found out how they had got out of the habit of going to church. These youngsters had been faithful in their attendance during the year, until they went to summer camp. When they came back in the fall, they didn't show up in church any more. The lay leader went out to Constantia, New York, the next summer, and talked with another group of boys. They told him, "We're doing all right here, we seem to get along without church services such as we attend at home. So why bother?" The public relations man tried to talk to his bishops to point out the importance of picking up the ministry at the camp, which was formerly under the jurisdiction of one of their clergymen. But they didn't show much interest.

So several laymen got together and with the help of the Christian Boy Scouts Board Members and other clergy who were interested, arranged to have a morning prayer service read at the camp, even though it was inconvenient for the lay readers—but not for the Boy Scouts. The record next year showed that not one Boy Scout dropped out of the church after his being able to share in the ministry of the young lay leader at Trinity Church, Constantia.

10. The youth at the First Presbyterian Church in Ponca City, Oklahoma, don't just sit around discussing things. They have raised $3,000 for Sunday School supplies. They sent $750 for youth work in other countries. Last year they paid the expenses of 40 boys and girls at summer camps. In addition they raised funds to bring a twenty-year-old Ukrainian D. P. to Ponca City to join her parents and small sister whom the First Presbyterian adults had already brought to town.

11. Teen-agers are given a practical and personal training in the parable of talents by the Reverend W. Hamilton Aulenbach of Christ Church and St. Michael's in Germantown, Pa. Each year certain older

Sunday School students are given ten talents, or one dollar, and told to multiply them. The report of their Christian stewardship is given on a rally day. There one boy tells how he multiplied his talents five-fold by selling dish cloths and brings back five extra dollars. Another explains how he doubled his talents through sales of dish cloths. What a sound way to show why and how teen-agers should develop their talents.

12. The Rev. James E. Ewalt, pastor of the First Presbyterian Church in Pittsburgh, Pennsylvania, writes us this good news about their "Boys and Girls Club":

"We have been running it for three years now and grow more enthusiastic for it all the time. The morale of the faculty and parents is equal to that of the boys and girls. Here is a description of it. Immediately after school on Wednesday afternoons a swarm of eighty-five boys and girls from grades three through eight come buzzing into our Church School building. On the first day of each semester you find them bringing two cans of fruit or vegetables as their registration fee for their club. Having registered, the boys go to the gymnasium for basketball, volley ball, or group games under the leadership of a certain gym teacher and her high school age son. This drains off all that energy which has been pent up from the day's confinement in school. The girls go to handcraft classes where they are taught ceramics, weaving, leather crafts, and embroidery.

"Next comes the Bible hour, a forty-minute period where the Club is divided into four classes for definite Bible study. Emphasis is laid on the application of Bible teachings to everyday life. In the spring semester the pastor conducts his Communicant's Class at this hour. Then comes the supper hour when the club members for forty cents are served a nutritious dinner. A permanent committee of four women staff the kitchen and a rotating committee of four women (parents) each week handles the dining room duties. After the dinner, the boys and girls go to the assembly room where they are led in devotions by the pastor. Twice during the semester he gives a consecration talk. At other times he gives a junior sermon or shows a missionary film.

"After that, the girls go to gym class and the boys to handcraft where they made model trains and airplanes, pocketbooks, belts, lanyards, book-ends, and hammered aluminum bracelets. Cost for the handcraft materials is defrayed by a banking system in which the club members make weekly deposits to their own accounts. A price is set for the raw material for each article they make and is charged to the member's account. Returning to the assembly room the boys and girls sing hymns for fifteen minutes which are projected on a screen and then they are dismissed with a benediction.

" 'I have never seen my boy so anxious to go to Church,' was the remark of one father about this Club.

" 'You don't know how much we parents appreciate your having this Club. My child would not think of missing it,' was the comment of a mother.

" 'The kids that don't come here, just don't know what they are missing,' one member announced."

PRAYER FOR THE YOUTH OF TODAY

"Hear the cry of our souls, O God, for the youth of today. Shower upon them Thy special providence, that they who will lead tomorrow may follow Thee now, and be girded against the issues of life or death. Take their courage and refine it until it becomes like that of Him who set His face toward Jerusalem and dared alone the cross for Thee. Take their enthusiasm and turn it to moral passion. Temper their zeal with patience, their fervor with discipline. Let their hearts' devotion be no longer misguided, or claimed by those who trifle with the lives of men and barter the righteous for silver.

"Allow no easy road or pleasant prospect to lure them into a betrayal of Thee. Meet them at every crossroads of decision, that they may discover Thy presence when tempted to forget it. In the hour when the youths shall faint and be weary and the young men shall utterly fall, bring them to wait on Thee and renew their strength. In the day when they rush to save the world and take the kingdom of heaven by force, give them pause by Thy question thrice repeated: 'Lovest thou Me?'

"We pray for the young people who are perplexed and bewildered today, for all who are separated from their loved ones and from the work of their choice. Above their hindered plans, their thwarted dreams, may they see Thee who will never fail them, nor swerve from that which is right. Keep them from bitterness, despair, and the sense of futility. Guard them against weak resignation to the low estate of the world and blind acceptance of its follies.

"Help them to choose those of strong character and lofty aims as their friends. Enable them to keep their minds and bodies clean, as befits Thy dwelling-place. Assist them in every new opportunity to witness to Thee by word and kindness to others. Preserve their bodies from danger and their souls from the sin of war. Keep alive their reverence for all human beings, their uneasy conscience, their good will for friend and enemy. So may they glorify each shameful cross they have been made to bear, and through each sacrifice bring us all to repentance and sanity. We ask it for Thy goodness' sake. Amen."

by Marion C. Allen

In conclusion, we would like to recommend to those who plan and direct teen-age projects, an excellent book for stimulating discussion. Entitled, "Whatever You Do," it contains 96 well-written pages on stewardship and Christian vocation. The author, Clarence C. Stoughton, worked out these talks and discussions with a summer school class of boys and girls.

Chapter 5

GOOD WORKS
FOR YOUNG MARRIEDS
OR YOUNG ADULTS

ALL THE "PROJECT-CHAPTERS" in this book are grouped under the table . . . "Faith Without Works is Dead." Today the faith of our young adults is far from dead. It's filled with good works!

Religion should and does mean more to our young adults than to almost any other group in this country! Why? Simply because young marrieds want their children to be raised in the same kind of God-living land which our fathers founded. A land where we can have "In God We Trust" on our coins . . . and really mean "In God We Trust." They realize that only through religion can their children grow up with those individual opportunities for development found only in a religious country.

So today you see groups of young adults adding their drive, enthusiasm and hundreds of worth-while "good works" to the life of churches, synagogues, shrines, and cathedrals. Instead of having a "return to religion" of older people, our younger groups are carrying right on with those Godly principles they learned in Sunday School. Yes, they are carrying on with *action*, not just holy thoughts. They do not stop with prayers and hymns. Their religion goes on good works to further God's way in this world.

Here are some typical, inspiring examples, and some projects which are worth the God-living energies of our young adults:

1. Nineteen young adults from the local Protestant churches in New Brunswick, New Jersey, spent a weekend renovating the building of the Piscatawayton Baptist Chapel. They painted the Sunday School room, hung curtains, put hymn book racks on the pews. On Sunday the group helped the Reverend Lloyd A. Williams conduct the church service. This is a perfect example of how we can love our neighbors with good works. The Piscatawayton Chapel was a "pilot" weekend camp project of the United Christian Youth Movement which sponsors similar activities annually throughout the country during the fourth week in January.

2. The "Couples Club" of the Westminster Presbyterian Church in Buffalo, New York, raised funds to buy pictures for the Sunday School rooms, to send the Junior Choir on field trips and to provide "sitter service" for babies during the regular Sunday service. This same group took over the responsibility of calling on newcomers to Buffalo . . . inviting them to the meetings . . . and introducing them to young adults of their own age. This friendly religious welcome prevents new people from being "strangers within our gates."

3. In a large midwest synagogue the young adults organize the "Family Worship Service" for the first Friday night in each month. At this 8 p.m. service they honor all children who will have birthdays that month. (Note: Would that more religious groups organized special services in which families would worship together as families.)

4. The Emmanuel Baptist Church is probably one of the few churches in the country to sponsor an orchestra. Its Clinton Hill Symphony is composed of interfaith members who rehearse Tuesday nights. This new and unusual activity has enabled Clinton Hill to meet a

basic need in a neighborhood which has no other social center.

5. The young adults of the First United Presbyterian Church in Cincinnati, Ohio, add an extra convenience to their baby-sitting service. A file of available sitters is always available to parishioners in the church office.

6. The First Methodist Church in Bridgeport, Connecticut, has one of the most successful and progressive young couples' clubs in this country. It believes in sharing the responsibilities so completely that a man and his wife are elected to each of the clubs' offices. The evening meetings of the young adult club feature a wide range of speakers. A local rabbi talks and brings with him some of the young people from his synagogue. A librarian discusses "Interesting Discoveries of Early Connecticut." A Y.M.C.A. staff member analyzes "Experience and Trends in Race Relations." A popular radio commentator talks on "What America Is Reading." An outstanding psychologist leads a discussion on "Being An Adult." Each year one outstanding leader in the cooperative program of the church is brought from New York City.

7. The Interracial Fellowship of Greater New York has a most practical good works program. Their young adults spend weekends working to clean up run-down tenements in New York's East Harlem. They paint, plaster and clean up. This is a useful way for young people to express their religious and social concern for their less fortunate fellow-men.

8. The Youth Fellowship Council of Virginia sponsors the training and sending out of Youth Caravans. The purpose of these caravans is to deepen religious experience of the young people in the churches visited, to strengthen the existing youth program, and to show others how to organize and plan a vital program. Each caravan team serves for a three-weeks' period, spending a week at each church.

9. In the spring of 1951 young adults of Grace Episcopal Church in Jersey City, New Jersey, met at the Rectory to discuss what Christians might do about the dreadful housing conditions in the church neighborhood. They formed the "Grace Church Social Action Committee." Then they studied housing laws, tenement codes, and, most important of all, the seats of responsibility for enforcement at City Hall. This church group found that an active informed committee *can* get results!

Approving this project, members of other churches joined the Social Action Committee. Now there are over 100 members in the four groups with a Central Action Committee. Besides improving housing, the committee is providing playground equipment for placement in vacant lots and defending civil rights. Jersey City can well be proud of her young adults and young marrieds.

Here are some of the worth-while projects which are ideal activities for young adult groups:

EARN money to buy the minister a tape recorder machine. Then he can take church services right into the homes of the shut-ins, elderly people who cannot get to church. The tape recorder brings them hymns, prayers, and the sermon. This extra service is now being carried by many ministers like the Reverend Gibson T. Daniels of Saugatuck Congregational Church in Westport, Connecticut, and the Reverend G. Earle Daniels of St. James' Episcopal Church in Cambridge, Massachusetts.

VISIT hospitals and prisons on Sundays . . . taking the inmates magazines . . . reading the Bible to those who want that spiritual uplift . . . writing letters or postcards. Inmates of hospitals and prisons would deeply appreciate getting a birthday card from the church on their natal days. This would be tangible evidence that the church cares about its children no matter what their age is, no matter where they are . . . lending them radios owned by the young adults' group.

COLLECT inspirational quotations for the church bulletin, so that each issue contains thoughts which give the readers an extra spiritual lift. These quotations will be found in our leading magazines, in speeches by great leaders, in newspaper editorials, or in the ads prepared by the Religion in American Life Campaign.

Many promising young men are unable to study for the ministry because of the lack of financial backing. This should become the concern of the parish, and particularly the men of the parish. To assure such a young man of an education is one of the greatest services you can render. So why not—

GIVE "scholarship plate banquets" to help support students who are preparing for full-time Christian service? This is an annual event of the First Christian Church of Portland, Oregon. The scholarship charge can run from $10 to $25 per plate depending upon the average income of the parishioners.

RAISE funds to buy a church flag to fly over the doorway on Sunday. This flag gives the front of the church a "Lord's-Day-Look" on Sunday. It reminds all who pass the church of God's love for His children, of all that churches and synagogues offer to worshiping families. The flag also reminds us to worship more frequently.

PROVIDE the church or temple with a rack for the back of the church. This rack is to hold booklets, religious books, and church magazines. This is one of the surest ways to increase the religious readings of the congregation.

MAKE SURE that all your church's or synagogue's printed material includes a basic theme or slogan. This could be: "Worshiping Families Are Happier Families," or "Families Who Pray Together Stay Together," or some basic theme developed by your group and approved by the adult board. Make sure it's used on all bulletins . . . Letterheads . . . printed folders and appeals . . . and in your newspaper advertisements.

FORM a "Bell Ringing Committee" to use your church's bell more frequently and more effectively. This committee will arrange to have some members ring the bell every Saturday night from 7 to 7:15 p.m. This is a century-old custom in Europe among Roman Catholic, Anglican and Protestant churches. The pealing of the bells at the close of the Jewish Sabbath and on the eve of the Christian Sabbath proclaims from our Nation's Capitol—

That we are a God-fearing people,

That each week we re-affirm our trust and faith in God,

And that each week we are dedicating ourselves anew to work for true brotherhood under God through all the world.

PROJECTS FOR YOUNGER MARRIEDS

Some of the more advanced young adult programs in America's houses of worship are modeled on the pioneering efforts of the First Community Church in Columbus, Ohio. Tucked away in a middle-class suburb, this far-famed nondenominational church has a congregation of over 5,000 drawn from all levels of the city's social strata. Under the inspired leadership of a tireless fifty-year-old pastor named Roy Burkhart, it has imbued in its members a spirit of Christian fellowship which many visiting clergy say is unmatched anywhere in the U. S.

To an outsider the Young Couples' Circles are the clearest demonstration of the way the Church has wrought extraordinarily beneficial changes in the lives of these young folk. A Circle is an informal gathering of ten married couples who meet once a month at one another's homes, with Dr. Burkhart or one of his associate ministers present. What goes on? There is seldom any definite agenda, but conversation always gravitates unaffectedly toward issues of real Christian living. It may center around an exchange of ideas on the significance of some Bible passage—which in turn, may bring up a moral principle and its pertinence in twentieth-century life.

Having discovered that Christianity works in some-body else's parlor, they begin to test it out in their own. This starts them on the adventure of re-examining their prejudices and hostilities in the light of their changing natures. They become more tolerant, less prone to self-pity and over-dramatization of their personal troubles. Perhaps for the first time, they look for the good in their neighbors rather than for the bad. The inevitable result is happier, better-adjusted young people. And perhaps the proof lies in the fact that of the more than 1,100 marriages performed by Dr. Burkhart only nine have ended in divorce.

No wonder Dr. Karl Menninger, director of the Menninger Psychiatric Institute, says of the First Community Church program, "It is the finest example of organized mental hygiene I have ever encountered."

Like freshly converted young adults everywhere, those at the First Community Church are forever exploring the relationship between a person's faith and his job. With a missionary zeal they have in several instances changed the whole atmosphere in their places of work. For example, a group of bank workers report: "It has meant more smiles and less impatience, fewer clock-watchers, less time out for smokes, less swearing, less grousing about higher-ups and lower-downs, and even fewer suspicions about anyone's lifting stamps from the stamp drawer!"

When young people adopt a religious faith, it isn't long, as Dr. Burkhart puts it, before they are anxious to "make a contribution to the spiritual and economic welfare of all men." Thus a few years back young adults at the First Community Church responded to the challenge of a Columbus judge who pointed to a neighborhood that spawned ninety percent of the city's juvenile delinquents. First, the young men of the church accompanied marauding boy gangs on their escapades, seeking their confidence and discovering the influences that forced them away from wholesome living. Then they sponsored a settlement house, organized picnics in the country, staged indoor pageants at Easter and Christmas, and gradually introduced devotional prayers. The project's success is reflected in the latest statistics on juvenile crime in Columbus. Today only eighteen percent of the city's delinquents live in this neighborhood.

The same deep-felt will to help others was shown when a district of three hundred Negroes in Columbus bemoaned the lack of a place for worship. Some of them had been attending the First Community Church but complained that it was too far from their homes. So young peoples of both races joined to build a church in the Negro neighborhood. They dug the foundation, hauled the bricks and lumber, and gave up every leisure hour until the building was finished. Not even the subtlest racial bigot could unshackle the bonds of fellowship and cooperation that exist between the two churches today.

Evening programs in the First Methodist Church in Bridgeport, Connecticut, contain such variety as an address by the rabbi who attends with some of the young people from the nearby synagogue; a librarian's discussion on "Interesting Discoveries of Early Connecticut"; a Y.M.C.A. staff member's analysis of "Experience and Trends in Race Relations"; the pastor's presentation of "What Actually Happened on Easter"; a popular radio commentator on "What America Is Reading"; the council secretary's presentation of "Cooperative Work of the Community"; a trip to New Haven to hear Dr. Frank C. Laubach speak on "Literacy"; the pastor's presentation of the organizations of the Church; "Being an Adult," led by an outstanding psychologist; and two of the older members of the church presenting its history and episodes in the building of the present edifice. Each year one outstanding leader in the cooperative program of the Church is brought from New York. Home friends who have traveled abroad usually find this young adult group one of the most interested audiences upon their return. Some Sunday evenings are supper nights; others just "snack" nights.

Social meetings, such as a progressive dinner party, moonlight boat ride, picnic, Halloween party, New Year's Eve party, and Christmas party, have been part of the program.

In addition to the bi-monthly programs, the suppers and the social gatherings, the young adult group finds expression in four other areas. One, the Labor Day Week-End Camp has become a yearly event. Program planning, fun, inspiration, and fellowship make up the program.

First United Presbyterian Church in Cincinnati, Ohio, (the Reverend G. Barrett Rich III, pastor) offers a helpful service to its parishioners. There's a file of available baby-sitters in the church office.

The first Toledo (Ohio) marriage preparation course for young people from Protestant homes ended with a notable accomplishment.

It succeeded in holding the attention for ten weeks, of more than two hundred youths seventeen to twenty-three and broke even optimistic attendance estimates.

When 193 youths jammed the classrooms of the Whitney Vocational High School on opening night, the course's sponsors—Toledo's Family Life Education Program—moved to more spacious quarters in the parish house of Glenwood Lutheran Church. Course subjects ran the gamut from "Dating and Courtship" and "Love and Sex" to "Mixed Marriages" and "The Creation of New Life."

"Laymen and ministers alike have not been alert as they might have been to discern symptoms and learn how to deal with them effectively before they reach an advanced stage," says Reverend Herman L. Barbery, Associate Pastor of the Marble Collegiate Church, New York City. "Mr.-and-Mrs. clubs, which make some discussion of marital counseling part of their yearly program, are helpful in encouraging parishioners to seek help."

Plenty of expert counseling is available through ministers, but people must be encouraged to seek it. Churches had better be showing individuals, *before* their marriage gets to the breaking point, where and when to ask for help.

Here is where your group comes in. Whether you are the Young Folks, the Young Adults, the Couples Club, or the Women's Group, you can spark the organization of a program of education for family living, a marriage institute, or whatever you wish to call it. Tell your church, "We want to plan it and take the responsibility for getting people there."

In the First Community Church of Columbus, Ohio, when a young couple begins to look forward to a family event they will meet with one of the ministers of the church in the Family Workshop. Their interest in the Family Workshop will be in the pre-natal group which meets regularly the fifth Tuesday of the month (where there are five Tuesdays). This is a fellowship of young parents anticipating their first child. In the three or four evenings together the church will try to unravel with them the concept of the family, preparing them for the psychological, physiological, and spiritual aspects of the forthcoming event.

With the family now three, with a pre-school child, it will center its interest in the Family Workshop for pre-school children. This group meets on the first Tuesday of each month. So it goes. There is a Workshop to follow the parent through the various stages of his child's growth: elementary school, the second Tuesday; intermediate grades, the third Tuesday; parents of adolescents, the fourth Tuesday.

Young adults not yet married will find their fellowship in the Cambridge Club. This is a regular Sunday evening fellowship of young people beyond the college age, either as graduate students or employed. The Cambridge Club group, which meets on Tuesday evenings for a prayer cell experience, is primarily a fellowship group. The prayer cell experience is a deeper spiritual search. The whole group also finds fellowship on occasional weekends at the church's camp.

Married couples with or without children are also grouped in fellowship groups known as Couples Circles composed of ten couples to a Circle.

FELLOWSHIP AND SCHOLARSHIP

How is the attendance at young adult meetings in your church? This vital area of church activity is always worthy of careful thought and planning. The young people of today face a troubled future; besides fun and games they seek practical guidance in Christian living.

Varied programs that provide an opportunity for learning and intelligent discussion of life's daily problems can also stress religion in daily living. Lectures by doctors, psychologists, teachers, businessmen, and other clergy that are followed by a discussion period will stimulate both interest and attendance.

Proven many times, this thesis was proven again by the young adult group of the First Methodist Church in Bridgeport, Connecticut. After the general business meeting and worship service, and preceding the social hour and refreshments, a varied program was offered.

One Sunday they were addressed by the rabbi of a nearby synagogue, who brought some of his young people, and another time a Y.M.C.A. staff member spoke on "Experiences and Trends in Race Relations," a pressing problem today. A leading psychologist provided a thought-provoking group discussion on "Being an Adult." Sometimes members themselves accepted responsibility for programs on the history of their church, its edifice and denomination. The pastor frequently leads the group on subjects like church organization, how its money is spent, and its purpose.

This is in addition to a full and varied schedule of social events that include group junkets outside the church. The attendance has grown and interest runs high. A democratic system gives everyone a job to do in preparing for these meetings. They earn what they learn while meeting in fellowship through Christ.

The youth at Arch Street Methodist Church represent Philadelphia's most active young-adult program. Every Sunday afternoon they conduct a supper forum meeting. They provide a Sunday night choir of fifty voices. And after evening service they join in a church "Friendly Hour" that brings to lonely hearts a wholesome touch of Christian companionship.

AUDIO-VISUAL AIDS TO RELIGIOUS RELATIONS

There are now available many movies on religious themes that can be used to add spice to the meetings of the various groups and circles in your church. In addition there are film strips, records, and tape recorders. All can be used by you to advantage. The cost need not be prohibitive; some are available on a rental basis and those you buy could be lent out to other churches in return for what they may have in their film libraries.

Your young marrieds would be interested in films discussing the problems of raising children, the home, religion, and many other such topics. Films, sound or silent, black and white or color, will add variety to the programs of the Young People's Groups and in the Sunday schools. Adults like them, too, and some churches include them in the services to illustrate some point. If followed by well-led discussion periods it will add another dimension to group activities. For information on films and film strips write to the Religious Film Association, 35 West 45th Street, New York 19, New York, or your denominational board.

An enthusiastic young adult at Westminster Presbyterian Church in Buffalo, N. Y. writes as follows:

"As you probably know, the young married groups at Westminster are very active. They bring a great many new people to the church who eventually join. I can't tell you how many newcomers to Buffalo have told us that they wouldn't have known what to do with themselves if it had not been for Junior Parish or Couples Club or Children's Activities. All the friends Ted and I have made together as a couple we have met through some activity at church. One of the pleasures of going to church for me is the exchange of greetings with the many people we know while waiting for our children. And you don't meet those people and get to know them on Sunday mornings. One of my pet subjects is the purpose of a church group. Beyond the purpose of making money for a favorite charity I feel that a church organization serves the individual member by helping him or her to make new friends, to gain new outlooks and activities, and to make a place for himself in the church. Then he can say 'This is my church.'

"The Couples Club at Westminster was formed about seven years ago. Four couples who had discussed the need for such a group asked eight other couples (ourselves included) to meet with the ministers to make plans. We decided then that the most important thing was to meet together as couples and to become better acquainted. Everyone still feels the same way. They have no money-making project, but of their small dues they have managed to give the church a few gifts— *pictures for the Sunday school and a trip to Rochester for the Junior Choir. They also run a 'sitter service' for babies during church on Sundays.* Their membership numbers about 250 with an average attendance of from 90 to 120 for their monthly dinners held at the Church. This year they have tried to vary the usual after-dinner speakers by showing a movie once and by going to a pop concert at Klinehaus Music Hall after dinner another time. For the last meeting in May they have usually had a dinner dance, but this year they plan to make it a smörgasbord dance. When the program as planned is finished, they always bring out cakes for everyone which helps people to sit around and talk a little longer.

The bowling alleys are opened and I think there are ping-pong tables, too. We usually play a short game of bridge in the library.

"I am going to tell you about Junior Parish and Children's Activities groups because they really feed the Couples Club. And I feel they are quite separate from the Women's groups.

"Junior Parish you know about, but I'll bring you up to date. The girls are all 'young marrieds' and can't be over thirty-five years old. Their only charity is Westminster Camp, which they support in full, as far as I know. And you know what a beautiful spot that is. Last year they made over $3,000. They now have an annual fashion show at the Statler on which they make around $2,000. (Most of that on their programs.) Then at the linen sale in November they sponsor the luncheon, the baked goods booth, flower booth, and doll and toy booth. Their membership numbers about seventy, with an average attendance of fifty at weekly luncheons. They now have two sitters in the children's building during the meetings—one for babies and one for toddlers. At their meetings they have the usual unpaid speakers. Their only strictly religious activity—and this applies to the other groups, too—is a series of Lenten talks usually by Dr. Butzer. During the summer they still follow my suggestion of seven years ago. They meet once a month at the home of one of the members. It is purely social and keeps the group together over the summer months. And it is fun to go to the various homes.

"The Children's Activities Group was formed about seven years ago when a few of the Junior Parish girls became thirty-five and hated to go into the Women's Parish and sew all day. It grew very fast because there were so many girls with children who couldn't keep up the fast pace of J.P. but wanted something different from Women's Parish. The average age is between thirty-two and forty-five. There are one hundred members with an average attendance of fifty to sixty at monthly luncheons. Because they had to be part of Women's Parish, 60 percent of the money they make goes there. The other 40 percent they keep for their own projects, all concerned with the Church School. They try to do whatever is needed for the school. We have an altar guild which has flowers for the school altars every Sunday. *We supply the uniforms for the thirty children* in the junior choir and decorated their dressing room. We have bought tables and special chairs and books and toys every year. Last year we built a partition in the upstairs parish hall to make two separate Sunday school rooms and avoid some confusion. Our projects to raise money are a spring bridge luncheon and a white elephant and clothing sale in the spring. Then, of course, our linen sale activities, which include the knitting booth, sewing booth, favors booth (those felt angels I sent you last year) and the tea. The luncheon meetings are similar to those of the Junior Parish.

"Perhaps the greatest service of the Children's Activities Group is furnishing 'Parent Assistants,' as well as some teachers, in the Church School. Almost each grade has a Parent Assistant for the teacher. You can understand the need for this when you realize we have almost 1,500 enrolled in our Sunday school. Dr. Butzer feels these social church organizations to be very important. For example, at Easter we took in eighty new members, a good many of those being people introduced to the church through attending these outside clubs or organizations.

Chapter 6

PLANS FOR MEN'S CLUBS

Here is an outline of "good works" which are worthy of the "church-power in your man-power." Most of them can be adapted to any size church in any size town or neighborhood. Plan to discuss them with the other officers of your men's club.

1. Why not have a committee go to the local newspaper editor or editors to ask that once a week, the paper publish a religious statement or editorial by a local churchgoer. This can be rotated among the various denominations and faiths. This weekly "witness" is done well in the Miami *Herald* newspaper. The column is entitled "What My Religion Means to Me." The Nashville *Tennessean* also features a similar testimony written by local business men.

2. At the Grace Church in Detroit they have vocational groups who get together and discuss how they apply their Christian standards in their work. For example, a group of industrial managers met and talked on how they can use their religion in their weekday work. Then the union members talk with themselves as to how they can run their unions and their factory lives on Christian principles. The groups meet monthly. There is no permanent leader. There is a different chairman each season. The notes are mailed to each member after each meeting. Here is a practical and challenging project for your church. For more complete

details, write Ralph Hiteman of the Detroit, Michigan, Y.M.C.A., at 2020 Witherell St., Detroit, Michigan.

3. From upstate New York comes this example of what a Men's Club can do when an industry moves into or out of a town:

Often when industry moves a new plant into a town, there is a golden opportunity for your church to win some new members. A recent good example of this was when Pneumatic Tube moved from Detroit to Utica, New York. The minister and vestry of Grace Church in Utica did the following:

a. Wrote to clergymen of their faith in Detroit asking for the names of their members who would soon be leaving Detroit to come to Utica. These would be naturals to join up at Grace.

b. Wrote to the company and obtained their help to get the names and addresses of the men being moved into Utica.

c. Having obtained the names, they wrote a letter to those families saying that they were most welcome in Utica. Could the church and its members do anything to help the move? Only at the end, did it say that if they were members of another faith, it was hoped that they would join the local church in Utica, but if they had no church, they would be welcomeed at Grace Church. This Christian act of fellowship and welcome not only resulted in good new families, but it prevented many from dropping out of church altogether during the move, and won national recognition.

4. Men's Clubs can perform a real religious function by getting more firms to subscribe to *Guideposts* . . . the inspirational magazine . . . for all their employees. This monthly magazine builds the morale and spirit of of all who read it. Interesting articles tell how individuals have overcome trouble . . . achieved success . . . or started life anew, through their faith. Approved by all three faiths, *Guideposts* has one of the few calendars in the world which gives the holidays and Holy

Days for Protestant, Anglican, Roman Catholic and Jew. Leading firms like R. J. Reynolds and Hotpoint Electric send *Guideposts* to all their thousands of employees. A year's subscription costs only $1.33 so any firm can afford this proven morale builder. The address is *Guideposts*, Pawling, New York.

Here is how James J. Nance, now President of Packard Motors, announced *Guideposts* subscription to his top executives:

TO THE KEY MEN:

For some time past, I have been reading a small magazine called *Guideposts* which was originated in 1945 by a small group of practical thinkers, including Lowell Thomas, Eddie Rickenbacker, Branch Rickey and Dr. Norman Vincent Peale. This little magazine endeavors to translate religion into the practical terms of everyday living and business relationships.

I have long felt that the Key Men might benefit from reading the down-to-earth writings that it carries, but I have been hesitant about taking any action because I have always believed that a man's religion is an intensely personal and private thing, which he must work out for himself. I am, however, convinced that the magazine is nonsectarian, completely unbiased, and not at all preachy, and further, that it has only one purpose: to be helpful to those who care to read its messages.

With this in mind, I have entered a subscription in the name of each Key Man for *Guideposts* to be mailed to your homes. I hope that you and your family will receive it in the spirit with which it is sent, and that you will find it thought-provoking and beneficial in your daily lives, both in and out of business. I would be glad to receive your reactions to the magazine after you have received a few copies. With all good wishes.

James J. Nance

5. The church men of White Plains, New York, have developed an activity which bears duplication in other

cities. In 1945 they established the Laymen's Inter-church Council. Its objective is:

"To unite the Christian Churches of the City of White Plains in common programs for their mutual welfare and the benefit of the City, with special emphasis on increasing the influence of the individual churches and of the churches as a unit in the lives and work of the residents of this City."

Some of the Council activities include:

a. Observance of Laymen's Sunday (third Sunday in October).

b. Getting outstanding preachers for city-wide Lenten services.

c. Religious census of White Plains.

d. Cooperation in Christian Education for weekday public schools.

e. Youth program for high schools.

f. Reformation Day Service, on the anniversary of Martin Luther's historical event on October 31, 1517, in Wittenburg, Germany.

g. City-wide Visitation Evangelism, which brought many new people into the churches.

h. Cooperation with the American Bible Society in getting daily Bible readings broadcast over station WFAS.

Three to six men represent each of the churches in this Council. This group action accomplishes projects which would otherwise be impossible or impractical for individual churches. The Council puts extra steam behind a drive which goes beyond the power of one church.

6. Portland, Oregon and Cleveland are among an increasing number of cities which open city council meetings with prayer. Representatives of various faiths are usually invited to invoke seriously the Lord's guidance. Suggestions from councils of churches to city officials are sometimes instrumental in introducing this practice.

A resolution by your Men's Clubs and the Men's Clubs of nearby churches can be the means of getting your city to open its council meetings with prayer.

7. Many of the men in your club work for firms which publish company magazines. Here is an opportunity for them to spread God's word among fellow workers. These members should contact the editor of their house magazine and get him to include some religious editorial material in *each* issue. This can be an editorial . . . a prayer . . . or a sermonette.

The writing and selection of this material should be rotated among the three faiths.

Charles R. Riegler, Editor of "Johnson and Johnson's Bulletin," is one of many who have found and proved the value of using religious editorial material. He has used the back cover for inspirational ads and, in a recent issue, carried a short but inspiring sermonette by a local clergyman entitled: "Thought for the Month." Think what an inspired group of laymen could do to spread this religious editorial policy. In their talks with house magazine editors your fellow club members should point out today, more and more *general* publications are running more and more religious editorials. That's because their readers want this material and respond to it. Readership studies show that religious articles, stories and news get above the average reading. When you read a good religious piece in a general magazine, don't sit on your hands. Send a post card or letter to the publisher or editor. Tell him how much you liked it . . . urge him to run more religious material. When all we church-goers keep sending in our notes of appreciation to publication people, the quantity of religious material will be at least double what it is today. So don't sit on your hands!

8. Your Men's Club can be a powerful factor in getting your city to celebrate Christmas in a religious way. They can greatly increase the religious observance of this festival. For example, your Men's Club can organ-

ize a plan to follow Little Rock, Arkansas, in giving witness to the religious meaning of the Christmas season. On December 15, local churches of eight denominations, plus the Y.M.C.A., stage their annual Christmas parade. This portrays the Life of Christ. The procession of more than 40 floats go down the main streets to the steps of the State Capitol. Here a Christmas lighting ceremony takes place. The parade is so newsworthy it is televised by a Memphis station.

9. Here is an answer to a popular alibi for not attending church, which should be read at the next meeting of your Men's Club.

"If I were a layman, I'd go after my non-churchgoing male friends, who say, 'My parents made me go to church so often when I was a kid that I swore when I was grown and had my independence I would never go again.'

"The woods are full of that brand of opposition. The field is white unto the harvest. Such a man needs to be made to think. He needs to have his conscience aroused. Generally, he is a likeable sort, but the average parson hasn't a chance with him. He is allergic to parsons.

"But a smart layman he often respects. A business associate has a good chance of winning him, particularly if as much time is put on the 'Christian sales talk' as the average business salesman devotes to the task of learning how to sell his particular product. Generally he can be reminded that he has a good reputation in town. He is a success. He has the respect and confidence of his fellow men. Ask him why.

"The basic reason is that his father and mother saw to it that he was brought up in the Christian faith, that he went regularly to church, that he learned to believe in and respect Christian principles of human conduct. The truth is, he is blaming his parents for the very things that put him where he is today. Besides hurting the cause of Christ at a time when the world desperately needs his abilities and witness, he is ungrateful for the heritage his parents gave him."

This is quoted from that helpful and inspiring folder "If I Were a Layman" by James W. F. Carman. These folders are available at 3¢ each or $2.25 per hundred, from the Presiding Bishop's Committee on Laymen's Work, at 281 Fourth Avenue, New York 10, N. Y. If all the men in your club had a copy of this folder they could do a better sales job on and for the church.

10. Speaking of educating laymen, the Lutheran Laymen's Movement for Stewardship has taken a forward step by establishing a lay school of theology at Wittenberg College. It is designed to prepare laymen for increased responsibility in congregational administration, stewardship and evangelism. Classes include Bible studies, basic Christian beliefs, psychological problems, for laymen, practical church work, church history and sociology. Conducted by Hamma Divinity School, Wittenberg's theological department, the classes will be held on eight consecutive Saturdays. They will be repeated twice each semester in the future if demand warrants.

11. Students at Wittenberg College made front page news when they organized their own Chapel Council. The newly formed Chapel Council at this Springfield, Ohio, college is a full-fledged, self-governing church. Your Men's Club can help the students at your local college to organize their church and chapel services. In too many schools chapel services are being curtailed or dropped.

Our Men's Clubs can strengthen the determination of the college president to continue these religious services and help him make them more inspiring.

12. How long since your Men's Club offered to help the Sunday School? Providing some badly needed new equipment . . . visiting and providing speakers for opening services . . . getting religious pictures for the walls? By doing this and other helpful things one of your members may become so interested that he helps give new life and growth to the Sunday School. For example, Luis Weil, a top executive at Young and Rubicam ad-

vertising agency became so interested in the Sunday
School at Noroton, Conn., that he plunged into its work.
As a result of Mr. Weil's activities, the size of the Sunday School quadrupled in four years. This contribution
was made despite the fact that Mr. Weil is one of the
busiest advertising men in New York City. He proved
we men all have time to help our Sunday Schools if we
are inspired to find it.

The Hotel Biltmore in New York City has a prayer
room. Conrad Hilton is establishing a prayer room in
the famous Waldorf-Astoria Hotel in New York. Your
Men's Club can help spread this religious development
in hotel and community life. Suggest to your local hotel
manager that he follow the example of these two hotels
who serve their guests and fellow townsmen by providing the facilities for prayer and meditation. Then
help the hotel publicize the room and encourage its use.
It would be most constructive if your club could get
groups of people to use such local prayer room in
group praying for specific causes like world peace, industrial peace, religion in government.

13. At the risk of being accused of having a one-track
mind, we are going to close with the same idea which
ends the chapter on "Activities for Active Old Timers."
This idea or activity is just as right and logical for
Men's Clubs as it is for Active Old Timers. It is the
project of getting local plants to hold religious services
regularly. The men in your club *can* persuade local industries to follow the example of the Gerber Plumbing
Fixture Co., of Plymouth, Indiana.

Here is how their program led to greater church
membership according to the special news story in the
Protestant World.

An increase in church membership and a lessening
in industrial tensions among the workers of the crate
factory of the Gerber Plumbing Fixtures Company here
can both be traced to the ten-month old program of religious services in the factory on company time. The

interdenominational services started early this year at a request from a number of workers in the plant, are held every Wednesday morning as the working day starts, at 7 a.m., and last for 30 minutes.

Seven Plymouth clergymen take turns in leading the services. They are: the Reverend Ernest R. Armstrong of the Presbyterian Church, the Reverend William Van Winkle of the Assembly of God, the Reverend Ivan R. Woods of the Church of the Nazarene, the Reverend Milton Petsold of the Evangelical Reformed Church, the Reverend Merlin Cassell of the Church of the Brethren, and the Reverend R. Richmond Blake of the Methodist Church.

Max Gerber, president of the company, is convinced that the investment of half an hour of company time once a week has paid big dividends in improved management-employee relations, better interfaith understanding and increased church membership.

The common bond established by prayer and song has served to reduce the number of grievances that normally arise among people working together.

On the basis of their experience, those who have shared in this successful experiment in factory religious services believe that their success can be readily duplicated elsewhere as long as a few simple rules are followed. The services must not be imposed upon the factory workers, but must come in response to their demand; services must be interdenominational; attendance must be voluntary; ministers in the area must support the plan; and the whole plan must be under the eye of a committee representative of all company departments.

One of the clearest indications that such a plan can work elsewhere is the fact that the employees of three smaller plants near the Gerber crate plant have recently been permitted to punch the time clock on Wednesday mornings and then take time off to attend the Gerber services.

Chapter 7

PROJECTS FOR WOMEN'S CLUBS

G OD MUST LOVE WOMEN dearly. He made them so attractive in so many different ways. He gave them patience and understanding to get along with their husbands and children. He keeps them from being bored with housework. On top of all this, God blessed women with a sixth sense—the sense of intuition.

Ever since the Church was founded, women have been showing their appreciation for God's many blessings by being God's greatest helpers. No church could get along without the *daily* support of the women. Women do so much more church work than men, that the men in many families should be ashamed for letting the "little lady" do so much more than they do. For too long church men have depended upon the clergy and the women to do most of the church work. Too many men have been visible examples of a description given by someone who reworded a familiar hymn to read:

> "Take my wife and let her be
> Consecrated, Lord, to Thee;
> Help her now Thy will to see
> But please, dear Lord, don't count on me."

The authors and sponsors of this book do not agree with the above last line. That's why there are two chapters on how men can do their share of God's work. Yet there are three words in that last line which are true of women . . . "count on me."

Ever since the time of Mary and Martha, God has always been able to count on women. Women's organizations are always looking for new ways to serve God . . . to spread his religion . . . and to help others. Here are some projects which are worthy of being extended to and adopted by other women's church groups.

1. Wouldn't your group like to provide your church and clergyman with a valuable device that extends the ministry of service and of music? Of course it would! Especially as the cost is within the means of most women's organizations.

The device is a tape recording machine. With it your minister can bring your own church services to shut-ins, to the hospitalized and parishioners. They can actually participate in services which they are unable to attend. A tape recording machine brings your choir these unusual advantages. It can rehearse entire numbers without interruption. Then the choir leader can play back the rehearsal with individual group choir members to suggest improvement. Also the recording permits rehearsals when an accompanist cannot be present.

Many ministers use the tape recording machine for practicing sermons and developing a still better delivery. The Minnesota Mining and Manufacturing Company of St. Paul, Minnesota, can tell you all about the useful machines because they make the recording tape for them.

2. Here is a worth-while project which costs only the time and postage of individual letters. It is to encourage motion picture companies to produce more religious films to combat our godless common enemy . . . Communism. The production and showing of more religious films will also remind more movie-goers to attend their houses of worship more frequently. They show the unchurched some of the values of life which come only through a religious life.

How do you organize this project? Simply by forming a "Motion Picture Committee." The members report regularly on religious films that deserve the support and commendation of churchgoers. The committee urges the members to take four steps concerning religious films.

First: Have the family see it.

Second: Recommend the film to friends, neighbors, and relatives.

Third: Write the motion picture company, thanking them for getting out the picture and urging them to produce more religious films of similar high calibre.

Fourth: Write or phone the manager of the local movie theater where you saw the film. Tell him how much you liked the picture and encourage him to show more religious films.

The Johnston Office of the Motion Picture Producers recently began to consider having films reviewed by critics from the religious press. This project is worthy of support, and adoption by your religious journal.

Here is what Spyros P. Skouras, president of Twentieth Century Fox Film Company, says on religion and the movies:

"The screen will never cease to be conscious of its tremendous responsibilities to the cause of religion. Church and screen are joined together in the defense of the spiritual heritage of Western civilization against the threats of a pagan philosophy. Among civilized people no medium of communication is more sensitive to the spiritual aspirations of humanity than the screen.

"Combining all the classical arts, the screen has long been able to present religion as a living experience, identifying the individual in the audience with the characters he sees on the screen. The screen's unlimited scope, in terms of time and geography, can make people relive again the story of Calvary, or report events of the present moment showing the influence of Christ upon the minds and hearts of men. The camera can penetrate into the greatest cathedral or the smallest country chapel."

By organizing a Motion Picture Committee, your group can help increase the number and quality of religious films shown to the 70,000,000 movie-goers in this country.

3. Instead of giving just a certain percentage of money from your group's treasury for foreign missions, plan to earn or give money for a definite project. Here are some examples. Provide a horse and saddle for a missionary in the Philippines. Send automobile snow tires for a traveling missionary in South Dakota. Get a printing press or a cow for the Kiyosato Educational Experiment in Kiyosato, Japan. Dr. Paul Rusch can let you know more of the needs of this pioneering rural project to bring Christianity to Japan if you write him at 2720 North Greenview Street, Chicago 14, Illinois.

The Foreign Mission Board of your denomination can give you specific needs which can fit the earning or giving capacity of any size women's group. You'll get more support from more members and more non-members through this method of filling definite needs.

4. Does your church have a lending library of religious books? If not, here is a real opportunity for your organization. Nearly all of us churchgoers do not read enough religious books. We would read more of them if the books were made more available . . . easier to get . . . could be picked up in connection with services of worship. Yes, a church library will stimulate the religious reading of the congregation.

Most churches have plenty of space for a church library. Some handy man or home workshop hobbyist in the church can build the bookcases. A book collecting committee plus pulpit appeals will bring in the volumes. Families with means can be urged to buy one new religious book per month, read it, and then turn it over to the church's library.

Each month the church bulletin can list the new

books and two or three favorites, like *In His Steps, The Big Fisherman, A Certain Woman, The Robe, A Man Called Peter,* The Religious Book Publishers Association of 2 West 46th Street, New York City, can supply your local book stores, or you, with a list of 350 religious books which can make a church library complete. Get this list and then use it as a guide for your new additions.

5. Have your group put on a skit before the congregation, visualizing your activities. It's a lot of fun. And oh, so worth while! The Women's Auxiliary of the Diocese of Chicago produced such a skit, entitled "Visions of a Parish President." The skit *sold* the value of women's work so thoroughly that new support, new members, new cooperation came from many sources.

The skit is well-written. It combines serious thought and lighthearted humor. You can easily adapt it to the work of your organization. So why not write for a copy of this script? The source is Women's Auxiliary, Diocese of Chicago, 65 East Huron Street, Chicago 11, Illinois.

6. All of us like to receive greeting cards on our birthdays. We would enjoy having our church remember us on that day. Why not form a "Greeting Card Committee" among your organizations? It's the responsibility of the group to send out birthday cards to each member . . . get-well cards to the sick and temporarily hospitalized . . . congratulation cards to the parents of newborn babies. The good will and friendship generated by this activity is far more than the low cost.

Mary and H. C. Mattern are the world's greatest example of the good will and friendship developed by birthday cards. This remarkable couple have developed a birthday card list of names which exceeds 12,000 lucky recipients. And the Matterns keep this flow of friendship going out every day, despite the fact that they have no permanent home and are "on the road" constantly. Their motto, "God Bless You," "Keep Smiling Always," is known throughout the U.S.A. and the world.

7. In an inspiring article in *The City Church,* Mabel G. Wagner tells how Methodist women teach neighborliness in community centers. Under the title, "Chaotic Cities or Christian Communities?" she writes as follows:

"Home missions have a significant responsibility for creating a Christian America by reaching the neglected areas of cities and developing in them a sense of neighborhood or community. Feeling this challenge, the Woman's Division of Christian Service of the Methodist Board of Missions and Church Extension has neighborhood houses and community centers in cities all over the United States.

"How are we carrying the Christian gospel through these centers? By seeking those whom society has spurned and sometimes our established churches have neglected. Our workers take people where they are, trying first to meet their most pressing needs, be they spiritual, health, social, or whatever else.?

"Respect for every personality, regardless of race, nationality, or religion, is basic, stemming from Christ's teaching of the worth and dignity of each individual. Sometimes this means we are serving people of other faiths in our program. The missionary spirit—'Go ye into all the world'—impels us to serve all, even those of another faith if there is human need. We are not carrying the Gospel only to our own little group.

"Always there is hope that our workers and programs will be able to give inspiration and guidance in the religious fundamentals of life. Such a response may not come in a week or a month or even longer. Years later we may discover that an individual was lifted up."

St. Mark's Community Center in New Orleans is an example of this home mission work so badly needed in so many cities. It is located in the famous French Quarter. Here young and old are welcomed. Under Christian leadership a program of wholesome recreation is provided to help young people to develop a sense of neighborliness and responsibility for helping themselves and the community. This includes clubs, Boy Scouts, Girl Scouts, Explorers, crafts, game room activities, family night programs, truck rides for teen-agers, parties and outings. Home calls and personal conferences minister to special individual needs.

Wesley House in Atlanta, Georgia, and George and Marcy Center in Chicago, are similar projects where church women sponsor a Christian social center to meet the community needs.

8. Re-establish the fine old religious habit of saying grace at your meals. We in America have so much for which to thank God, that we should take these family gathering opportunities to count our blessings *out loud*. And also start the practice of ending your grace with ... "And keep us ever mindful of the needs of others." That's one of the surest ways to keep your children conscious of Christian charity and Christian stewardship.

9. How about having a bush-planting party in the spring or fall on the church grounds? In this way your church property can have the background of one of the most beautiful and inspiring grounds in the city. Flowering shrubs are especially effective. A chairman of the Garden or Grounds Committee can tell the congregation a week ahead of time what plants and bushes are wanted. For a complete plan of a church garden project, read Chapter 18, starting on page 255.

10. Women are the ideal ones to increase religious reading in the home. They are the ones to subscribe to the magazine published by your denomination, and to an inter-denominational publication like *Christian Herald, Christian Century, National Council Outlook,* or *Protestant World*. Yes, the fair sex are the best ones to start carrying out the suggestions in Chapter 26 on religious reading, starting on page 334.

Your women's clubs can start by organizing a rebirth of Bible reading in the home. The need for this is found in the Bible survey made for Thomas Nelson & Sons by

Batten, Barton, Durstine and Osborn. One question in
this survey was: "How often do you read your Bible?"
(Survey included all faiths and the majority of denominations.) The answers were as follows:

When I feel the need of it	33%
Once a week or so	24%
Every day	22%
Once a month	3%
Less frequently	9%
Never	3%

No religious group can feel very proud of this record.
Let's hope that your church members read the Bible far
more often. An inspired questionnaire, asking the same
question, would be an interesting piece of research for
your club members. Simply distribute slips of paper
asking the same question, then ask the members to answer it, not signing their names. After the answers are
tabulated, see how their Bible-reading habits compare
with the above percentages.

Then start an all-out campaign to increase Bible reading in your members' homes. Point out that every family *has time* to read the Good Book. For example, no
one is busier than the star, Red Skelton, with his TV
and radio shows, personal appearances, etc. Yet Red
Skelton finds time to read his Bible every day. Urge
your members to put a Bible on the night table next to
the bed. Then it is more convenient for husband and
wife to pick it up and read it just before they go to
sleep at night. If you wonder where to begin, start with
the "Sermon on the Mount," Matthew, chapters 5
through 7. That is the talk which 8 out of 10 college
students wished they had heard given at first hand. It
contained more familiar quotations than almost any
other part of the Bible. Some people read the "Sermon
on the Mount" once a month. Yet regardless of what you
read in the Bible, you will feel better for the reading.
Some families stimulate the Bible reading of their chil-

dren by giving them a brand new Bible in a different translation, for example, the "New Revised Standard Version."

Other ways of increasing Bible reading in the home are as follows:

a. Let each member of the family have his own copy and share in the reading, using the version best suited and liked.

b. Sometimes read the life of Jesus right straight through.

c. The Sunday School lessons may be followed.

d. Also readily accessible are booklets of daily devotional readings, selections from religious magazines, or leaflets which the American Bible Society makes available such as "Stories of the Bible," "Men and Women of the Bible," "Poetry of the Bible," "Wisdom from the Bible," "Forty Favorite Chapters," "A Month of Devotional Readings," "Bible Alphabet," or "Daily Bible Readings for the Year," which takes note of special days and religious events. The address of the American Bible Society is 450 Park Avenue, New York 22, N. Y.

If your church is getting a new minister *and wife,* we sincerely recommend your sending for a reprint of an article which appeared in the July 19, 1952, issue of Presbyterian Life Magazine. It was entitled "Directions for the Care and Use of Your Pastor's Wife." The author, Margaret Johnson Hess, points out the unsoundness and unfairness of taking it for granted that the new minister's wife can, and will, take over *all* the activities of the previous parson's bride. She will be better at some things and may not be as good at others. That's natural! She may even do things which were impossible for her predecessor.

Chapter 8

ACTIVITIES FOR
ACTIVE OLD-TIMERS

Lᴇᴛ ᴜs ᴛʜᴀɴᴋ Gᴏᴅ for the development of "geriatrics"—for all medicine and health habits created for older people. It has given our churches a larger number of longer-lived members and communicants than ever recorded in the religious history of the world. These fine men and women are a priceless asset to any congregation. Properly directed, the energies, talents and experiences of these "active old-timers" can give your parish extra ways to serve your community, your congregation and Our Lord.

The size of this group is described in an article written by Jean Begeman. Entitled "Work Longer, Live Longer," it states:

"Primarily because of modern medicine's emphasis on longevity, there are now three million more old folks in the United States than there were 10 years ago. There are today in the United States 13 million persons 65 years of age or over. Those retiring at 65 now have an average of 13 years of life remaining and half of them will live longer."

These fine people are growing more important in the religious life of this country. Here are just some of the ways their abilities and experiences can build your church.

1. The Reverend P. T. Graetz of the United Congregational Church in Avon Park tells us about the un-

usual activities of a woman who at seventy-two suddenly found herself confined to a wheel chair. Some people could have become either bitter or *resigned* to this confinement. But not this grand soul. She started a new Christian life for herself by devoting her wheel-chair time to writing comforting letters to people in trouble. Even though she doesn't know the recipients personally, her notes of cheer and encouragement are an inspiration which often comes at the most opportune time. If a person cannot compose individual letters, he or she can now find attractive and inexpensive greeting cards which express many of the desired sentiments.

2. Speaking of writing to troubled people, there is another badly needed project which can be done best by our "active old-timers." That is to write to newspaper editors, magazine editors, mayors, councilmen, and congressmen whenever there is a matter which involves the Christian living . . . clean government . . . and public welfare. In the rush of these days, the older people have the most time to write. They also have the more experience through which to give advice to public servants and the public press. Therefore, their letters will have more influence on our leaders and our publications.

In the case of publications, our older people especially should write to editors and publishers when they run good religious articles or stories. For example, when the *Saturday Evening Post* published its interesting article on "Unknown Facts About the Bible," all our "over-6oers" should have written the editor or publisher thanking him for running this article of such great interest to the millions of religious people who read the *Post*.

3. One of the best ways for active old-timers to invest their time is to attend public hearings on problems and projects which concern public welfare, the church, young people, morality, etc. For example, they can and should sit in on local meetings on narcotics, juvenile

delinquency, etc. There they can make their influence felt. And the officials conducting the meetings will be encouraged by the presence of responsible citizens. Being better informed through their attendance, our older people will become valuable sources of first-hand information. By passing this on to their friends, neighbors, and relatives, they can be a direct force influencing public information and stimulating public action.

4. Many churches have found that they can get more young marrieds to attend churches by having "baby-sitters" take care of children while their parents attend the services. No group is better equipped to "baby-sit" in homes or in the church house than our retired men and women.

One of the best ways to organize the valuable services of the active old-timers is to make a survey of their talents. First make a list of the names and addresses of all members who are sixty or over. Then send them a letter, or call on them with a simple form to fill out. On this 3x5 card list the activities which each is willing to do. Wording for the card can be something like this:

ACTIVE OLD-TIMERS
          IN (*Name of Church*)

Name ....

Address .... Phone..........

          Will be willing to do the following:
              write newspaper editors ( )
              write magazine editors ( )
              attend public hearings ( )
              watch babies during service ( )
              baby-sit in homes ( )

---

5. The Lutheran Church of the Reformation in Rochester, New York, has a project which is ideal for active old-timers. The Rev. Alfred L. Beck tells us that they have a working Home Department in their Sunday School through which calls are made on over fifty sick and shut-ins, *several times a year*. The lay visitor brings a copy of the Sunday School quarterly and news about the church. Often they pray together. In between the regular calls these shut-ins are sent cards on their birthdays, Christmas and Easter. This is an ideal way to show your shut-ins that they belong to a church which really cares about them.

6. The older members of your church are just the ones to remind public office holders of the trust which the public has placed in them. This can be done by mailing the following prayer twice a year to all office holders.

A PRAYER FOR GUIDANCE IN OFFICE

Dear Lord, the people have elected me
To speak for them in things
Of state; to Thee
I come for help . . .
I shall be tempted by
Those men whose god
Is gain; may I
Be true to country, self and Thee!

Stand with me, Lord, each time
I speak, when godless
Men would make a mockery
Of righteousness.
At voting time touch Thou my lips,
For I would not bring shame
Or fear to fellow men—
Nor cast dishonor on Thy name.

And give me courage to defend
The weak; to work to ban
All things that would destroy
The dignity of man.
Knowing, Lord, that
Thou answerest prayer when
Humble knee is bent, I ask these things
   —but
Only by Thy will. Amen.

Herman S. Garst

It would be a good idea to mail this prayer (printed on a government post card, or typed on an 8½x11 sheet of paper) to *all candidates* in your fall election.

7. Dr. Frank Fremont-Smith, of New York City, suggests an excellent activity for active old-timers: *be a Foster Grandparent*. In that special magazine for older people, *Lifetime Living*, he spells out his idea in the following way:

"Many older people love to be with children, and 'have a way' with them which is particularly successful. Too often, however, older people can't have this kind of association, either because they live too far from their grandchildren or because they have none.

"A foster-grandparent movement might do much for both age groups. The proposal is very simple: Older persons can 'adopt' a foster grandchild or two, and a child can 'adopt' one or two foster grandparents.

"I know that this idea has been tried unofficially many times. What is needed is some promotion for the idea, perhaps a central clearing house or newsletter for the exchange of ideas and experiences.

"In some communities a church can start the project, give the plan publicity, and arrange contracts between prospective foster grandparents and foster grandchildren. The mutual adoption would be informal and voluntary, of course.

"Foster grandparents can take their youngsters on

expeditions, play games with them, teach them hobbies or skills. Foster grandparents can become godsends to parents by taking over a child for an afternoon—either at the grandparent's home or the child's—might baby-sit, or entertain the foster grandchild who is ill or convalescent.

"Groups of foster grandparents might meet occasionally to exchange ideas and might even form clubs. Once a year a grand picnic might provide some publicity and a lot of fun."

8. *Christian Herald* published a challenging article entitled "Smut on Our Newsstands." It told how filthy sensual paper-covered books are degrading the minds of our young people. These detective stories or whodunnit murder mysteries lure purchasers and readers through their front covers with partially nude drawings of oversexed girls. The stories mix sex, sin and murder in such a way that, according to Norman L. Hall of Houston, Texas, "this trash is contributing very heavily to the moral breakdown in our schools."

Legitimate book stores would not handle these degrading books, and many of the news dealers and other stores selling this paper-covered filth do not realize the harm they are doing.

Active old-timers are well suited to be a Committee, vigilantly calling the attention of the stores to the bad books on their sales racks. They should ask the store owners if they would like to have the minds and actions of their children or grandchildren influenced by this "Smut on Our Newsstands." Let's meet the challenge of this situation by calling on stands and stores, *continually*, until this filth is removed. You'll be surprised how few calls will be necessary because retail outlets value their good standing in the community. They don't want the ill will and bad regulation which can be given them by a Church Committee.

9. Our older fellow church members can lead a campaign to get Bibles placed in the reception rooms of

local offices. Bringing the Word of God near to visitors is already being done by leading companies like J. Walter Thompson Advertising Agency and Bridgeport Brass. The New Revised Standard Version of the Bible gives your active old-timers an extra reason to ask for this company cooperation. That's because most office visitors have heard about this new translation and will want to see how it compares with the Bibles in their homes. Reading the Holy Book while waiting for a business interview is one of the best ways to bring your religion into your daily business life, Lee H. Bristol, Jr., takes "Business-Bible-ism" one step nearer by keeping a Bible on his desk at the Bristol-Myers Company.

10. Local radio stations offer another opportunity for active old-timers. They can call on the station managers and program directors, asking their cooperation in broadcasting churchgoing reminders on Saturday afternoons and evenings. These include the playing of that inspiring and beloved song, "Let's Go to Church on Sunday Morning." If your station does not have the record, offer to buy it for them. It was recorded by the Capitol Record Co. and costs only 89 cents.

Other churchgoing reminders are station-break announcements (8 seconds between two recorded programs). These are worded as follows:

"Take someone to church with you tomorrow. You'll both be happier for it."

"Tomorrow be sure to worship in the church of your choice. You'll feel better for it *all week long*."

"Churchgoing families are happier families. Make yours happier tomorrow by going to church."

"Families that pray together stay together. Defeat divorce by praying together on Sunday."

"This week look through the windows of your church or synagogue from the *inside*."

11. The Nehi Corporation of Columbus, Georgia, and other leading companies open their sales meetings

with prayer. They know that taking God into their business sessions is one way to get the right guidance for their deliberations.

Your active old-timers can call on local companies that hold sales meetings and conventions, pointing out the good of opening the sessions with prayer.

12. The Holy Communion United Lutheran Church of Detroit, Michigan, has another activity which is suited for active old-timers. The Rev. Alfred G. Belles tells us that they hand-pick couples who are pledged to make at least three calls per month, on prospective or delinquent members. These callers have a meeting once every four months to compare notes, share experiences, and lend encouragement to each other. Why don't you try this proven plan in your church?

13. God bless the National Council of Jewish Women for their "New York Council Club for Older People." They organized meetings where men and women come together for fun and inspiration. This is a project for large congregations, downtown churches, or your local council of churches. After this older group is organized and functioning in your city, it can take on the projects in this chapter and many others which will occur to the active members.

14. *Protestant World* featured this story of how a New Orleans pastor gives a Special Service for shut-ins:

"The Rev. G. A. Schmidt, pastor of the First English Lutheran Church here, has taken a little leeway with one of the mandates of Jesus Christ and has come up with a new kind of church service which has proved very popular. The Rev. Mr. Schmidt, burdened with an exceptionally large number of sick calls one month some years ago, decided that Jesus's charge to his ministers to visit the sick need not be taken literally—if the 'sick' were actually infirm oldsters who could get out once in a while with a little help from their families.

"In short, the Rev. Mr. Schmidt thought that it would be a good idea—a real time-saver—if the 'sick' could come to visit him—in a group. He also figured—and has since been proven right—that these oldsters would be cheered more by the gathering than by a visit from one solitary minister.

"The Rev. Mr. Schmidt's idea resulted in a special monthly meeting and communion services for people who ordinarily are 'shut-ins.'

"The first Sunday of every month an unusual procession forms in front of the first English Lutheran Church, just before noon.

"Groups of elderly members, some of them in wheel chairs, many using crutches and canes, begin arriving for the special service. The youngest of the group is sixty-five years old. The eldest member is in his eighties.

"Relatives help most of them get to the church. The others, who are without families, get assistance from a group of volunteers who call for them and take them home.

"The service is held in the basement of the church, which is only a few steps below ground level, rather than in the chapel on the structure's second floor.

"For most of them, the trip to the church is their only journey outside of their homes each month. So, it's quite an event.

" 'They enjoy worshipping together and visiting together afterwards,' the pastor says."

15. The Welfare and Health Council of New York City has sponsored an older-person project which can be and should be duplicated by downtown churches, by larger older neighborhood churches, and by the local council of churches. This is an *Annual Hobby Show for 60-Plussers*. For six years this exhibit has been awakening the public's interest in the creative potentialities of people over sixty years old. Among the 2,500 exhibits last year was a model of a Normandy Synagogue carved by Herman Kasindorf, a bookkeeper and office manager.

You'll find the exhibits are so interesting that you

can charge admission to raise funds for some worthy local cause. Only be sure to announce your Hobby Show one year in advance so that the 60-plussers have plenty of time to work on their exhibits.

16. St. Matthew's Cathedral of Dallas, Texas, brings new life and new achievements to old-timers through its "Golden Age Club." This is a 60-plus, non-denominational organization which meets in St. Matthew's Church. There are no dues. At the Golden Age parties the old-timers have fun, meet new friends, and start on projects such as making small gifts for shut-ins. More than one oldster has begged to learn a new handicraft, "so I'll be accomplishing something again."

Incidentally, the "children" of Golden Age Club members are much happier, too. For in their homes, instead of having beginning-to-be-querulous old women whose discontent made them feel vaguely guilty, they now have lively little white-haired ladies who enjoy every minute.

Episcopal Churchnews credits Christ Church with organizing the first Golden Age Club in Dallas. Now there are four. So you can see you can have more than one of these helpful clubs in a city. They draw members like a circus draws kids.

Headquarters of this movement are on the grounds of St. Matthew's Cathedral in Dallas, Texas. Write Canon Edward B. Ferguson for complete details on how to organize and operate a Golden Age Club. And also say a prayer for E. D. Farmer, who financed the start of this project through his E. D. Farmer Foundation for the Aged.

17. Your active old-timers can also do a job in getting local newspapers to run more religious material. They can call on the editor and publisher and urge him to take the following steps:

a. Run a religious prayer on the Saturday church page, like the *Schenectady Gazette*.

b. Put a daily prayer above each day's editorial, like the *White Plains Reporter Dispatch*.

c. Use that basic religious theme or slogan "Church-going Families Are Happier Families" at the top of the church page, like the *Scarsdale Inquirer*.

18. In Larchmont, N. Y., Mrs. Roy E. Booth, organized the Genarians Club to rout loneliness.

"Early in January 1947, she went with her idea to the Reverend Dr. Floyd E. McGuire, pastor of the Larchmont Avenue Presbyterian Church. Dr. McGuire was enthusiastic about the plan. He helped organize the group—a club open to all persons, regardless of creed or church membership, who insisted upon remaining socially active and useful.

"The name of the club was suggested by the group's first chairman, Mrs. Katherine Lafitte. 'Since most of us are septuagenarians or octogenarians,' she said, 'let's call ourselves simply—*The Genarians*.'

"And then another member dubbed them with an appropriate nickname, *The Geraniums*. The geranium flower is now the club's official badge.

"The club was successful from the very start, for it fulfilled a universal human desire—*the longing to belong*. As one of the members observed, 'I had come to town a perfect stranger. The neighbors were very friendly, but I was anxious to associate with people of my own age. Now that I've found them, I feel as if I had received a new lease on life.' "

Journal of Living

19. Our last project is one that is near and dear to the author's heart. You dear 60-plussers will want to do something about it, too! It's the proved plan of organizing a religious service for plants and factories. It's being done successfully all over the country. One of the pioneers and leaders of this great movement is Rollin M. Severance, owner of the Severance Tool Company in Saginaw, Michigan. His story is so interesting we want you to hear it in his own words.

So take over, Mr. Severance. Tell the reader all about the services in your plant.

"Some may consider our devotional period as a church project, and I might say that we do not think of it as a church project in the usual sense of the word as promoting membership, etc., in a recognized church. It is strictly a spontaneous practice first instituted at a time when I only employed four or five persons. During the years since that time there have been various pressures exerted from one angle or another to change or otherwise modify this program. We have seen many things which are related to this little time together each day about the word of God which we feel are not to be valued in terms of the amount represented by that portion of payrolls in the time involved. All that we have is given to us of God and it is only appropriate that we unitedly take the few moments involved in devotion and recognition of Him at the beginning of our work periods."

The devotional services include: the singing of well-known hymns, reading from the Bible and prayers for the men, their families and their work. These morning devotionals ease tensions and bring feeling of kinship and good will. The men are paid for their time attending the services. The prospering Severance Tool Industries is today one of the best examples of what happens when faith hits the factory . . . when companies mix worship with work.

As the *Christian Herald* says:
"The National Safety Council recently reported that relief of strain and tension, especially in dangerous work, is an imperative statistical factor in keeping fatalities and accidents at a minimum. The Metropolitan Life Insurance Company has found that a worker doing perilous work is in much greater danger when troubled

by domestic discord, ill health in his family, or any recent emotional disturbance.

"Prayer, Eastman found, is the best antidote to the tensions that beset modern man. In actual practice, prayer soothes and invigorates the spirit and strengthens the tremulous and fearful.

"Daily worship is being practiced both at great plants throughout the country and at smaller, more humble places of endeavor. There is a citrus grower on the outskirts of Phoenix, Arizona, who conducts daily services for his workers amid the orange groves. At several factories of the gigantic Goodyear Tire and Rubber Company devotions are held daily for all who wish to attend. The company not only pays for the workers' time but supplies a suitable room properly equipped.

"At the famed R. G. LeTourneau Technical Instittute at Longview, Texas, and at all the LeTourneau plants, the meeting in daily prayer of students and employees has been a long-established practice. Is it mere coincidence that here, as at other plants which bring religion into the daily lives of the factory workers, statistics both for strikes and accidents show a remarkably low incidence? At the LeTourneau school, where qualified young men are trained in industrial operations, part of the curriculum lays emphasis on the need for prayer in the interests of harmony, higher production standards, and higher morale among employees.

The J. C. Penny Company, which operates several hundred retail establishments across the country, has promoted worship services in all its offices and stores. The same holds true of the Kraft Cheese Company, a mining company in Arizona, a dairy in Wisconsin, and a pop-bottling works in Arkansas.

In these organizations there prevails a spirit of contribution and good will that baffles their competitors. Employers and employees alike realize that they are working for more than just the profit and wages they receive. They find in their work a sense of dignity and a sense of belonging.

Chapter 9

86 PROGRAM &
PROJECT IDEAS

By Lee Hastings Bristol, Jr. *

IN YOUR PARISH organization does your program committee make a point of avoiding the "same old thing,"
or is there a deadly sameness about your events? Sur-
prises and a change of pace have helped save more than
one church group from going on the rocks. Instead of
speakers and routine discussion groups, why not more
debates, skits, role-playing? Even your business meetings, imaginatively planned, can be stimulating. And
just as it is wise to vary the programs you schedule, so
—don't forget—is it wise to vary the program committee
from time to time as well. Persuading some lukewarm
member to serve on such a committee may be the ideal
means of stimulating his or her interest in the group as
never before.

But projects are not an end in themselves. Your group
will want certainly to avoid pointless overbusyness which
obscures what your group really exists to do. The mission of the Church is to draw people to Christ and
change them. It is not to keep people busy. We will do
well to remember the wisdom of William Temple's
words that "To be is infinitely higher than to do."

Viewed in proper perspective, however, group projects
can be helpful in giving new vitality to your parish
group. Here are 86 ideas which may help "trigger" in
you and your colleagues still better program and project
ideas which can be useful to your committee in future
planning.

* Director of Public Relations, Bristol-Myers Products Division.

1. Why not schedule a brainstorm session on "New project ideas for our group"?

2. Why not organize a program of parish calling on newcomers, shutins, etc., by laymen?

3. Why not set up a file of babysitter names for the use of young parents who wish to attend your meetings?

4. Why not interest your members in sending local papers, church bulletins, and other material to parishioners in service—regularly?

5. Why not interest more restaurants in putting Grace cards on tables?

6. Why not make a practice of inviting foreign students at nearby schools and colleges to your homes and to parish functions?

7. Why not form a group of volunteers to call regularly on parishioners?

8. Why not sponsor extra weekday services in Lent?

9. Why not have some of these services led by laymen?

10. Why not put out a little book about the parish, giving its history, organizations, and work as a kind of "welcome" to people new to your community or to your church?

11. Why not emulate those churches which have successfully instituted "work pledge cards," getting volunteers from your group to donate so much time to odd jobs around the church each month?

12. Why not try setting up small prayer groups?

13. Why not place ads in the local paper, telling about the church, its history, Faith and Practice, etc., etc.?

14. Why not set up a vocational counselling service made up of laymen in your parish who are successful in different fields, to help your young people choose their careers?

15. Why not set up a parish lending library of religious books?

16. Why not set up subcommittees of volunteers, clearly identified with your church, who will make a

nearby veterans' hospital, home for the aged, etc. a parish service project?

17. Why not "adopt" some part of a project like the laymen-sponsored Kiyosato Educational Experiment Project (KEEP) in Japan and supply something they need as a gift specifically from the laymen of your parish? (For information, write KEEP, 243 South Dearborn Street, Chicago, Illinois.)

18. Why not have a carpenter on hand one night a week at the parish house to teach young couples how to make their own furniture?

19. Why not a toys-for-the-poor project at Christmas?

20. Why not a food-for-the-poor project at Thanksgiving?

21. Why not occasional guest night dinners at which people from neighboring parishes are invited over to hear a distinguished speaker?

22. Why not sponsor a community-wide effort to encourage family worship?

23. Why not sponsor a "Back to Church School" week each fall to encourage children to register for their classes?

24. Why not supply local papers and radio-TV stations with material they can use in "putting Christ back into Christmas" and giving the season a more spiritual tone in your community?

25. Why not schedule a series of evenings built around the lives of great Christian leaders and let different members speak about different phases of their careers?

26. Why not an evening on "A typical day in the life of a clergyman" led by parish clergy?

27. Why not a clergy-led series of discussions on the sacraments?

28. Why not a "Welcome Night" reception for newcomers?

29. Why not schedule a Christmas carol sing?

30. Why not a talk on vestments and church furnishings?

31. Why not an annual retreat?

32. Why not a series of talks by local clergy of other communions on the history of their particular churches?

33. Why not an evening devoted to hymns and hymn history?

34. Why not an evening on what seminary training is involved in becoming a clergyman?

35. Why not a discussion of family worship and how to begin it in the home?

36. Why not an informal lecture-recital by your organist at which he explains and demonstrates how a pipe organ works?

37. What about book reviews of old and new religious books of importance?

38. Why not a discussion on "What we hope Church School will do for our children?"

39. Why not a spring square dance?

40. Why not an evening devoted to how your national church is governed, etc.?

41. Why not a "Twelfth Night" party after the holidays?

42. Why not have a round-table panel discussion of race relations, family relations, education, etc.?

43. Why not break up your organization into smaller "interest groups" (e.g. lawyers, businessmen, housewives, etc.) to discuss the relevance of the Gospel to one's own work, be it law, business, running a home, or what have you?

44. Why not an annual picnic outing?

45. Why not a talk on "words of our worship," words often used in worship and seldom fully understood?

46. Why not a series of talks on church history?

47. Why not charades in which one team acts out some Bible story?

48. Why not get a few people to retell the parables using modern-day situations and see if the others can guess each parable? Follow, perhaps, with a discussion of the message each conveys.

49. Why not invite a Christian psychiatrist to speak on "Faith and Mental Health"?

50. Why not an evening at which a member of a religious community tells of his or her order, its work, its rule, etc.?

51. Why not plan an historical evening devoted to what was going on in the world at the time various familiar hymns were written? This "hymn-and-history" game makes an interesting program.

52. Why not set up a series of lectures on marriage for young marrieds in which local clergy and physicians take part?

53. Why not devote an evening to Christian symbols and their origins?

54. Why not plan an old-fashioned bazaar or fair for same specific cause, like building a church overseas (in some areas $500 will build a whole church!)?

55. Why not have a square dance as a "change of pace" or perhaps a parish benefit?

57. Why not have one of your clergy speak on God as revealed in the Old Testament and then in the New?

58. Why not a talk on the virtues and drawbacks of various Bible translations and how to go about becoming better acquainted with the Scriptures?

59. Why not a talk on the history of the Book of Common Prayer?

60. Why not a talk on particular services and their origins?

61. Why not conduct a course for laymen in non-directive counselling?

62. Why not organize a small devotional group and begin by asking members to write a few prayers (an excellent way to begin a devotional program)?

63. Why not encourage more local offices to put Bibles in their reception rooms or waiting rooms?

64. Why not interest nearby industries to sponsor "Clergy Days" at which clergy get to visit their factories?

65. Why not sponsor a much publicized essay contest for high school students on a religious theme?

66. Why not adopt an "overseas" war orphan?

67. Why not have an evening devoted to what a theological seminary is and what a clergyman has to study there?

68. What about an evening devoted to what life was like at the time of Christ and the early Christians?

69. Why not arrange for your clergy to go on the local radio or TV station regularly?

70. Why not a special service occasionally for those who are normally "shut-ins"?

71. Why not distribute books to veterans hospitals?

72. Why not a discussion of Christian Healing?

73. Why not observe Laymen's Sunday four times a year?

74. Why not a program on Christianity in the Fine Arts?

75. Why not a program on new teaching techniques and how they may be put to use in the church school?

76. Why not put on a few religious dramas?

77. Why not encourage nearby plants to schedule Lenten services as firms like General Electric have done?

78. Why not show a religious film?

79. Why not encourage parishioners to subscribe to religious periodicals?

80. Why not plan a one-week preaching mission?

81. Why not have a sale of old books for the benefit of some cause?

82. Why not tape record sermons and services for the sick to hear?

83. Why not have a competition sometime in the year for which each church school class makes up a little shadow box display showing some Biblical scene?

84. Why not schedule informal downtown luncheons for businessmen?

85. Why not an old clothes drive for Korea?

86. Why not organize a special "gardeners guild" to be responsible for new planting around the church (*not* mowing the lawn!)

Chapter 10

NEW AND DIFFERENT
WAYS OF
RAISING MONEY
FOR CHURCHES

J ESUS WAS INTERESTED in money. He referred to
money and its uses more times than to any other subject
—the Kingdom of God, heaven, hell, or salvation. The
use of money serves as a thermometer to indicate a person's interests. "Where a man's treasure is, there will
his heart be also."

The securing of funds is not an end in itself.
Money is but a tool whereby we may accomplish our
real purpose.

One of the best places to begin increasing the effectiveness of your church is in your church finance. Money
is not only necessary, but absolutely essential to the
success of your church program.

Of all the organizations and institutions, the church's
business should be conducted on the highest plane possible, because of the purpose for which it exists. Good
business is good religion, and good religion is good business.

Nearly two billion dollars were placed on the altars
of churches and synagogues by living donors in 1951.
This is approximately half the total amount given for
all tax-exempt religious, educational, and welfare causes.

While the amount thus contributed was approximately $100,000,000, more than that contributed in 1950, this increase of 5 percent was not enough to offset the increased cost of services dependent upon these contributions.

The income of the people in the United States, as measured by their expenditures for food, shelter, clothing, etc., doubled between the years of 1850 and 1920. Between 1920 and 1945 it doubled again. But much (?) small change is still found in the offering plates! Is the proportion of our income that we return to the Giver of all a worthy acknowledgement of our stewardship?

You readers who have the high responsibility of raising money for your churches know all the above facts. You are well acquainted with all those situations. You also realize that in many congregations the amounts raised through the annual pledge and every member canvass must be augmented by other money-raising activities.

Financially strong churches have found that new appeals, new and different ways, obtain new and added funds which otherwise would never have found their way into God's treasury. Here are some proved ones whose results justify their being adopted by many congregations.

1. The Reverend Gerald V. Barry of Christ Church, Riverdale-on-Hudson, in New York, found a source of new financial support by sending each member of the congregation a brand-new dollar bill the first week in June. The parishioners were asked to put "God's dollar" to work during the summer and bring back its fruit to the church three months later. The results were so satisfactory that we give you herewith the complete plan of three mailings:

To the Members of Christ Church: 6/4/51.

Are you surprised to *receive* a brand-new dollar bill

from the Church instead of being asked to *give* one? Well, there's no mistake; here it is!

This is God's dollar. It is being loaned to you. *We want you to invest it.* Invest it to the best of your ability, so it will grow and multiply many times over.

In order words, taking a lesson from the Parable of the Talents (which you will find in the Gospel according to Saint Matthew), here is your opportunity to put your talents to work for Christ Church.

Between now and September 15, let this dollar and the fruit it bears be your link between you and your Church. Whether you vacation in Riverdale . . . or spend your summer away from home . . . put your talent to work.

One dollar may make a cake that will sell for two.

Two dollars may make candy that will sell for four.

Four dollars may buy material that will sell for eight.

Here is a simple way to raise funds that can be practiced by children and adults alike. And as your talent (dollar) grows, and you see its earnings in a milk bottle, an old powder box, or an envelope, see how much satisfaction you will receive in knowing that this dollar you are working with is God's.

Frankly, Christ Church is badly in need of $2,800, with which to liquidate the debt on our Parish House. We don't want to ask you to give more than you can afford. That's why we are sending God's dollar to help.

Bring it back September 15 . . . with the talents it has earned.

Remember . . .

". . . and so he that had received five talents came and brought other five talents, saying, 'Lord, Thou deliveredst unto me five talents: behold, I have gained beside them five talents more.' "

The Rector, Wardens, and Vestry

9/13/51

THE MIRACLE OF THE BILLS
is soon to be revealed!

Sunday, September 23, is the homecoming date for those Talent Dollars entrusted to you during the summer.

Early reports indicate that most of them have been working overtime. How about yours? How many more will you have?

Please to bring or send them back by Sunday, September 23.

Thank you.

The Rector, Wardens, and Vestry

10/8/51

No one likes to be pestered. No one likes to be thought of as a pest—least of all, the senders of this letter!

BUT

—among the 159 Talent Dollars which have not yet come home to roost is the one that was sent to you. Maybe you lost it. Maybe you are using it as a bookmark. Maybe—well, whatever happened, won't you please send it on its way, accompanied by offspring?

The Rector, Wardens and Vestry

While this "God's Dollar" plan was done by Christ Church during the summer, it can be used during any three-month period.

2. *Presbyterian Action* magazine gives the outline for a "Sunday School Rally Day" which includes a special Rally Day offering to make Sunday Schools better:

Before a Church School can have a satisfying Rally Day (September 30), it must have an effective "Rally Month." The following four points are both the *requirements* and the *guarantee* of success in rallying your Church School:

(1) A RESTUDY OF YOUR CHURCH'S TOTAL PROGRAM OF CHRISTIAN EDUCATION—to find its weak points.

(2) A RESTUDY OF YOUR CHURCH'S RESPONSIBILITY LISTS—to find all the persons for whom you are spiritually responsible.

(3) A NEW PROGRAM OF VISITING—to bring into your Church School all the persons who need your Christian teaching.

(4) A NEW PROGRAM OF IMPROVEMENT—to strengthen your Church School for more effective teaching.

Workers' Conference

In carrying out the above fourfold program for "Rally Month," a Workers' Conference early in September will be of key importance. In this meeting the restudy of the Church School program can be begun, with the help of the check list, "Next Steps in Church School Progress." (Order from Presbyterian Bookstores, 10¢ a copy.)

The "Guide"

For a really thorough study of your Church School, the new manual *A Guide for Presbyterian Church Schools* is recommended. (Order from Presbyterian Book Stores, $1 a copy.) This *Guide* also serves as a handbook for the local Church Committee on Religious Education.

Responsibility Lists

During the first two weeks in September, every Church should thoroughly revise its responsibility lists —its list of persons who should be enrolled in the School's activities of study, worship, service, recreation, and fellowship. Every class and group, from the nursery up, should have such a list.

A few energetic leaders should head up the revision and enlargement of these lists, and the job should be completed by the middle of September. During the last two weeks of the month there should be an intensive program of visiting. Representatives of every class and group in the School should visit every inactive member and every prospective member before Rally Day.

The conscious purpose in the minds of the visitors should be to express the genuine friendliness of the class toward the inactive or prospective member, thus to draw him into the fellowship of the group and into active membership. Such visiting will pay rich dividends in Church School enlargement.

3. Every home should have one of the religious trivets made by the Garret Thew Studios, Westport, Connecticut. They read in cut-out metal letters, (1) "Give Us This Day Our Daily Bread," and (2) "Bless This House, O Lord We Pray." In fulfilling this need, one of your church organizations can raise funds in a new and painless way. All it has to do is get samples of these two metal trivets. Display them in the vestibule after church or in the church house at some large church gathering; then take orders from the congregation.

These trivets are ideal gifts for Christmas, Easter, or bridal showers. They can be hung over the front door, in the hall, over the mantel, on the kitchen wall, or used on the dining table. Your group can sell them for the regular price of $2.25 or add on 75¢ as a fair service charge for getting them for the members.

4. One of the most popular methods of raising funds is through church suppers. Yet the *Witness* magazine carried this interesting report:

Suppers a Poor Way to Raise Funds

Pastors generally disapprove church suppers as a way of raising funds, according to a survey made by rural church department of Drew Seminary. Reason: long hours for the women and small returns. The replies from 341 pastors showed that the money return on suppers was very low although the fellowship value was high. Church suppers in a single year netted $49,933 to the churches canvassed, with 7,840 women cooking, waiting on table, and doing dishes.

Perhaps if the church suppers were varied, had a change of pace, they would raise more money for the time and effort involved. One such variation is that used successfully by Trinity Church, Rocky Hill, New Jersey. This parish finds that more people attend when they have a Smörgasbord instead of the usual supper.

5. Just recently a new form of collection envelope has been developed which offers some new advantages for the giver and for the church treasurer. It is called an "Account-O-Lope" and provides a new plan for the every-member canvass. From the following illustration you will see that the "Account-O-Lope" is a completely new and different type of offering envelope.

Account-O-Lopes are put up like a BANK CHECKBOOK. They provide the contributor with a "stub" record of his contributions and a running balance of his PLEDGE just as a bank balance is provided in a checkbook—A CONSTANT REMINDER OF THE PLEDGED OBLIGATION TO THE CHURCH IN DOLLARS.

The Account-O-Lope System does not DEPEND upon "Sunday dates" printed on each envelope to REMIND the contributor of his unpaid pledge. Rather the system emphasizes the PLEDGED BALANCE IN DOLLARS, and provides an excellent record for the contributor's income tax report.

Consequently, "Sunday dates" are not printed on Account-O-Lopes, thus making it possible to use any Account-O-Lope on any Sunday or one for several Sundays. This feature saves the contributor and the treasurer the bother of handling the "several unused" envelopes which accumulate during the absence or vacation periods. After all the important thing is DOLLARS not "dates."

A complete set of 52 is just ⅔ the thickness of sets in cartons, and the Account-O-Lope sets may be mailed to contributors in standard mailing envelopes without getting damaged or crushed in the mail.

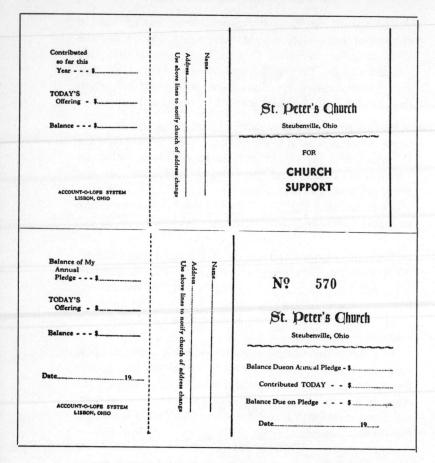

Contributed
 so far this
  Year - - - $................

TODAY'S
  Offering - $................

Balance - - - $................

Use above lines to notify church of address change

Address ....

Name ....

ACCOUNT-O-LOPE SYSTEM
LISBON, OHIO

St. Peter's Church

Steubenville, Ohio

FOR

**CHURCH
SUPPORT**

Balance of My
  Annual
  Pledge - - - $................

TODAY'S
  Offering - $................

Balance - - - $................

Date................19......

Use above lines to notify church of address change

Address ....

Name ....

ACCOUNT-O-LOPE SYSTEM
LISBON, OHIO

№ 570

St. Peter's Church

Steubenville, Ohio

Balance Due on Annual Pledge - $........................

Contributed TODAY - - $........................

Balance Due on Pledge - - - $........................

Date........................19......

The Account-O-Lope system does everything the old loose-envelopes-in-cartons can do. They provide a handy container for contributor's offering, a new, fresh approach to the problem of collecting pledges. The first church which used them reported that the new 25¢ Initial-Offering Account-O-Lope produced more than enough to pay for the sets—evidence that the people themselves really like the system. They also report that more people write the amount contributed on the face of the envelop than before, which saves the treasurer the trouble. A survey indicates that most of their contribu-

96

tors are using the "stub" and appreciate the opportunity to keep a record of their contributions and balances of pledge.

The Account-O-Lope was developed by John Taylor of Lisbon, Ohio.

6. For monthly articles on case histories of tested ways to raise money read *Woman's Day*. For example, one of these religious articles told exactly how the First Presbyterian Church of New Rochelle, New York, raised $4,800 on a bazaar. That's a great gift to God's work in any city, especially in a community the size of New Rochelle (population 60,000).

7. A student at Duke University developed a new way to collect money for the American Leprosy Mission. He has a piggy bank in his rooms. Any time a visitor uses profanity, he has to pay the piggy bank. Of course churches couldn't use this very same money-raising method because good members don't swear! But the piggy banks could be distributed to collect fines for losing one's temper.

8. Of course the surest method of balancing a church budget—of being able to carry out an expanding program of church and mission activities—is to follow the Bible's recommended plan for giving. Yes, you guessed it—that is tithing—giving back to the good Lord just one tenth of the monetary blessings he has given you.

One of the best case histories on tithing was written up in the *Presbyterian Survey* by Hugh B. Carter, Pastor of the Sunset Hills Presbyterian Church, Charlotte, North Carolina. Just read this for sheer inspiration and proof that tithing can be carried out even in the smallest of churches.

"Whether it is easier to say to the sick of the palsy, Thy sins be forgiven thee; or to say, Arise, and take up thy bed and walk? But that ye may know that the Son of man hath power on earth to forgive sins (he saith to the sick of the palsy), I say unto thee, Arise . . ."

Jesus raised the palsied man in order that men might know that the Son of Man has power on earth to forgive sins. For the same reason, I believe, He raised the Sunset Hills Presbyterian Church of Charlotte, North Carolina —a church which was as flat on its back as the palsied man.

Therefore, as you read this story of the miracle of grace at Sunset Hills, it should be remembered that these things were done in order that we may know that the Son of Man has power on earth to forgive sins.

Look at the palsied church as it was! Weeds were waist-high in the churchyard. The stairs that led to the choir loft were rotten and broken through. Doors needed replacing, outside and inside. A toilet and lavatory were needed. A new sink and cabinets were needed in the kitchen. These were the more obvious physical needs.

Financially, we had this report—that we had robbed God. The treasurer reported a bank balance of $19.24. This is an incredibly small balance for a church of one hundred members—a church receiving Home Missions aid amounting to more than $100 monthly.

Spiritually, the story is already told. The spiritual languor of the church was reflected not only in poor physical equipment and run-down financial condition, but in poor attendance at Sunday school and church. For six months a weekly average of fifty attended church and about forty-five came to Sunday school. During the same period we received nine new members. We had no evening service, no prayer meeting, and no men's organization. Behold the palsied church!

In the plight of this depressing situation our officers laid hold on the words in Malachi 3:10: "Bring ye all the tithes into the storehouse . . . and prove me now herewith, saith the Lord of hosts, if I will not open you the windows of heaven, and pour you out a blessing, that there shall not be room enough to receive it."

As a means of leading the other members to an active

acceptance of this challenge, ten of our twelve officers made a covenant with God to tithe for three months, October through December. On the last Sunday in September, almost half the congregation made a similar covenant. The next three months were known as "A Venture in Faith."

Now see what happened!

On the very next Sunday, there was an all-time record attendance at church with ninety-nine present. This surpassed even the Easter congregation. Mind you, there had been no campaign or drive for attendance. This just happened! Throughout the remainder of these three months, attendance showed an average increase of more than fifty percent. This was the first evidence of the promised blessing.

The Sunday school began to move along with the church. Attendance and offerings more than doubled. Interest climbed to new heights. As a result of the new emphasis, certain things came to pass, such as: (1) all rooms and floors painted, (2) nursery redecorated, (3) pictures, maps, books added, (4) a piano purchased, (5) a new class formed, (6) new teachers installed, (7) at least $100,000 in benevolences appropriated and disbursed, (8) scholarships provided to send two young people to Presbytery's summer conference with all expenses paid, (9) toilet and lavatory facilities purchased and installed, (10) and other minor improvements too numerous to mention. The Sunday school has pioneered in giving to benevolences, in physical improvements, in increased attendance, and in offerings received.

The church followed with the installation of new front doors, new back stairs, and a completely renovated kitchen. These items were costly, but they were necessary. A long-carriage typewriter was purchased for the church office. Ever since this period the church lawn has been cut regularly and kept in good condition. The entire church—outside and in—was beautifully painted and new light fixtures were installed on the front.

The Men's Club was revived, yea, leaped to its feet.

Regular monthly meetings were begun with splendid attendance and good fellowship. The club was further developed when the men entered a team in the church softball league. While runs batted in were not always sufficient for victory, no game was lost by default! The goal of the club is to include every male member of the church.

Two incidents in connection with the Men's Club are worth noting. In the spring, the men held a housecleaning in the Lord's house. They removed rugs and pews, washed and waxed floors as well as all the furniture in the sanctuary, and made the church shine. (The women washed windows, curtains, and venetian blinds during the same week.) The men put on a church supper for the women, asking only that the ladies be present to help eat.

Needless to say, the Women of the Church have prospered exceedingly, and God has worked through them to raise the church to new levels spiritually and financially. A new circle has been added and another is in view. It is not out of order to state here that the Women of the Church are dependable, responsible, and devoted servants to a gracious risen Lord through His church. During the months when our life was feeble it was the Women of the Church who carried the flickering torch and kept their feet on solid rock. It is the women who now lead us into new avenues through their weekly prayer meetings.

By way of extra blessings, a lady volunteered to do secretarial work at no monetary consideration. She has been as faithful as though she were employed under contract, working five hours a day, five days a week. A church secretary was more than our church was able to ask or think possible before.

The blessings have continued to pour in beyond the three months' "Venture in Faith," perhaps because most of our people did not withdraw their tithes. The covenant with God was continued by nearly all.

Within six months from the date that the church

2.1670

treasurer announced a balance of $19.24, Sunset Hills had assumed all its obligations and was no longer receiving Home Mission aid. This was not our objective in our venture of faith. It came as a gift from God, poured out as a blessing—a by-product.

Whereas our budget in 1949 was $4,000 and our people pledged only $2,700 (less than half the congregation made any pledge whatsoever), a budget was presented in 1950 for $6,000. The congregation approved this increased budget and gave proper evidence by pledging more than $7,000 on Every-Member-Canvass Day with ninety percent participation, and through the year the offerings went well over the pledged amount.

Gifts have come in almost weekly since we began this "Venture in Faith": a beautiful silver baptismal bowl, a silver flower bowl, linoleum for the Sunday school, indoor games for the Men's Club, a hot-water heater for the kitchen, an electric cooler for cold drinks, and over one hundred dollars in cash as special offerings. There have been others that cannot be named. No gift was solicited; each just happened!

Then we received blessings in adding new members. Since the first day of the period, the church has received an average of more than one person per Sunday, about one-third of whom are making professions of faith.

There is an evening service which is well attended and in which the people engage in studying the Bible, book by book. A midweek prayer service has come into being spontaneously. It is carried on by the Women of the Church, who meet informally during the afternoon in various homes in the community.

Our most thrilling experiences have been in the realm of transformed lives: members becoming interested and devoted to the church who previously were indifferent and cold, officers seriously assuming their responsibilities and keeping their ordination vows, noticeably with regard to church attendance and monthly meetings, broken lives restored and consecrated where previously they had been derelict, families reunited to

Lincoln Christian College

one another and then to the church, the abatement of physical handicaps as answers to prayer, and the like.

The whole story cannot be told, because our blessings cannot be counted. But this much is plain: Jesus has said to the palsied church, "Arise," and Sunset Hill has heard His voice.

All has not been accomplished. The church does not see itself as a model. We are not independent of God's grace. Our faith is still a frail thing, with all that we have witnessed. We do not say to others to follow us, but we do seek to point all to the Son of God who is able to give exceeding abundantly above all that we ask or think.

We believe that God has done these wonders in our midst, and not we ourselves. We believe that He has manifested Himself in order that we might know that this same Jesus who raised the palsied man is at work today.

Our message is that Jesus Christ came into the world to save sinners. And in order that slothful, disobedient, and selfish children of God might *know* that He has the power to forgive sins, He has worked a miracle of grace among us at Sunset Hills.

We know how the crowds must have felt when they saw the palsied man get up and walk; insomuch that we are all amazed, and glorify God, saying: "We never saw it in this fashion."

10. In the *Commission* magazine Frances McCaw Goldfinch writes about a Baptist church in Asuncion, Paraguay, where they "Tithe with Joy":

Deep spiritual power can be expected in a church when the membership practices Christian stewardship. The Ciudad Nueva Baptist Church, Asuncion, Paraguay, with sixty-nine members, has eighty-five regular contributors.

The church is mission-minded. It maintains eight mission Sunday schools.

The church has a praying membership. Five prayer

groups, divided according to age, meet immediately preceding every service of the church and the Sunday school.

The Ciudad Nueva Baptist Church was organized with fifteen charter members in 1946. It had its beginning earlier when preaching services were begun in an open-air tabernacle on a lot where a Baptist family had lived for many years.

Most of the charter members had been members of the First Baptist Church of Asuncion. The first pastor was Pedro Ruiz Diaz, a young Paraguayan who had been graduated from the Baptist seminary in Buenos Aires. Mr. Goldfinch and I continued as members of the church, helping with the Sunday school and other work.

Some pastors in the River Plate seem to feel that money shouldn't be mentioned from the pulpit because of the fact that they receive their livelihood from the church. But gradually our young pastor came to understand, through Bible study and contact with missionaries, that tithing and stewardship are truly parts of the worship of God and the privilege of every Christian. He began to preach and teach tithing, explaining it very carefully so that the young as well as the old might understand.

The pastor wrote ten suggestions with Bible references for the tither. He also prepared a pledge.

The Ten Commandments were memorized and said in unison from time to time. Each month when the envelopes were distributed, the pastor gave a message on stewardship. For the children, he drew diagrams, with decimals, and asked very simple questions, such as, "If you had ten cents, how much would you tithe?" The people came to feel that giving a tenth is a very natural part of becoming a member of the church.

We did not have canvasses or pledges of any specific amount of money. However, the church studied its budget carefully and accepted recommendations from the finance committee when changes were advisable.

The envelope system of giving was adopted, and immediately many who were not members of the church for various reasons wanted to tithe. The majority of the children in the Sunday school asked for envelopes. Many adult members of the Sunday school and many regular attendants at the worship service who could not be baptized due to irregularities in their civil status, etc., wanted to have a share in the financing of the church. Therefore, the number of tithers grew and became larger than the membership of the church.

11. Joseph C. Good and Dr. Fred V. Poag developed a successful flip-chart presentation which sold the tithing plan first to the canvassers and then to the congregation of the Shandon Presbyterian Church in Columbia, South Carolina. It enabled this church to meet its $44,314 budget.

12. I like the "you" and "shareholder" angle in the following appeal of the Traveler's Aid:

MEMO TO: You, owner of a share in our achievement

FROM: Edward E. Watts, Jr., President, Traveler's Aid Society of New York

Best thanks for your generous support during busy 1951! One hundred twenty-one thousand one hundred one persons found ready help and skilled counsel at the Society's lamps . . . beneficiaries of the friendly interest you displayed.

This is not the anniversary of your last gift, and the enclosed annual report is not an "extra" appeal. We do want you to see this record of how your 1951 contribution was used and how far we were able to s-t-r-e-t-c-h it.

Traveler's Aid counts it a privilege to number you among its members.

Both the you and shareholder appeal can be easily and successfully adapted to church appeals.

13. I simply cannot help but give you another outstanding example of tithing. Why? Because tithing is

God's plan of giving. And tithing makes for a stronger spiritual as well as a stronger physical church.

This example is the Lutheran Laymen's Movement for Stewardship. The members practice tithing, setting aside ten percent of their income for God. When they begin tithing, their faith invariably takes on new meaning. As one Lutheran put it, "Christians give not for special favors or for prestige but out of gratitude. Many believe that the reasonable first step in making offerings is the Christian tithe." No wonder they call these Lutherans "Men with a Mission."

We read recently an interesting item entitled "Church-Giving Rises" which went on to say:

Some 36,000,000 U.S. church members increased their annual contributions by an average of about two dollars apiece—and U.S. church-giving in forty-six Protestant Anglican and Eastern Orthodox communions reached an all-time high, topping the billion-dollar mark for the second year in succession.

Two dollars more apiece a year is an encouraging gain but it doesn't equal the increased cost of doing Christ's work. We must all give more . . . share more. So start raising some of the ideas in your church to increase its capacity for good works.

14. Every month *Woman's Day* magazine runs an article telling all about some proved way to raise church funds. For example, one monthly article explained in detail all the unusual ways through which the First Presbyterian Church of New Rochelle, New York, raised $4,800 at a church bazaar, in that small community. *Christian Herald* magazine also features many money-raising articles. You who have this problem should read both publications *regularly*.

15. One way to insure a better response to any financial appeal is to make sure that the givers or pledgers are adequately thanked. In too many drives, there is no

"thank you" sent to the givers. They never hear from the campaign committee, or the head of the institution, until they are asked to subscribe again. Although gratitude is the most fleeting emotion, there is no excuse for its not showing up in church financial matters.

One of the organizations which does an outstanding job of thanking its supporters is "Boys' Town." They go so far in their appreciation as to make each giver an "Honorary Citizen of Boy's Town," with an attractive card to visualize the recognition.

16. In *Building Up Your Congregation* we spelled out the reasons for . . . advantages of . . . and results from the *"Loyalty Sunday"* method of raising the annual budget. The Reverend Fred C. Wiegman is using a somewhat similar plan, called "Church Day," at the Trinity Lutheran Church in Akron, Ohio. Here is how he highlights their drive:

"Our Church Day, for the past twenty years, has raised eighty percent of our budget. At five Communion Services (preceded by three letters and one issue of the Parish Paper dealing with (a) the stewardship of tithing, (b) the world budget, and (c) the local budget, five laymen give talks on the needs of the church. Pledge cards are passed out and carried to the altar by the members. The twenty percent of the remaining budget is obtained by personal calls."

17. *Guideposts* magazine ran this money-raising idea, which can be duplicated by thousands of churches—try yours, perhaps.

"How can a church raise $10,000 for needed equipment? This problem faced the Reverend Harleigh Mood Rosenberger, Minister of the Baptist Church, Lockport, New York. Then he recalled an article in the November 1947 *Guideposts*. Adapting the project described in this article, Mr. Rosenberger distributed 230 ten-dollar bills to his congregation last May and told them to put the money to work. They accepted the challenge enthusiastically—sold baked goods at the church, hot dogs at the county fair; washed cars, mended clothes, and found other profitable turnovers."

18. The First Christian Church of Portland, Oregon, has developed an interesting and successful way of raising scholarship funds to help theological students. Once a year the church has a $25 plate Scholarship-Aid Banquet. The money from the project goes to help support students preparing for full-time Christian service. The need for more clergymen is so great, so many seminary students need help . . . that this is one of the most important activities mentioned in the entire book. How long since your church has raised money or sent a check to one of the theological seminaries of your denomination? This banquet idea is one proven way to do it!

Chapter 11

PROVED
DIRECT-MAIL PLANS
FOR ANNUAL
CANVASS

O NE OF THE BEST WAYS to remind people to support the church more regularly and more adequately is to send them some *useful* reminder. For example, this can be done with a blotter or a calendar. A blotter is good because it is used when people are writing out checks. It reminds them to write a check for the church.

Calendars remind parishioners of their needed financial support day after day, month after month. Trinity Church, Columbus, Georgia, sends out a handy calendar which costs only $6.50 per hundred.

1. One of the most attractive and effective money-raising calendars is that put out by the Henry Street Settlement House in New York City. Mrs. Stella A. Koenig, secretary of this outstanding settlement house, has written a most helpful book on raising funds. Entitled *How to Raise Funds by Mail,* her book contains dozens of tested ideas for increasing the returns from your mailings.

2. Blotters—A Constant Reminder

Do you have many executives and office workers in your parish? Here is a way to help them keep Christ's message at their fingertips.

Put out an ink blotter of a size suitable for mailing, with pictures or art work on one side. There are many ways of doing this and the cost should be small. Some-

one in your parish might possibly have contact with the
advertising-novelties field and could offer sound advice
as to style and cost, or perhaps could get a business firm
to donate them.

Religious pictures or drawings, or a short biblical
quotation applicable in the day-to-day pressures of the
business world, would serve to remind the user of the
church and the comfort of His ways.

To Raise Funds by Direct Mail

"Satisfactory results in the mail campaign are much
more difficult to achieve today than a decade ago. There
is widespread competition from the most expensive and
well-planned advertising of all types of business. Nearly
every individual who is able to contribute receives too
much mail to give serious consideration to any project
that does not instantly capture his interest." (From
How to Raise Money by William K. Gamble.)

Here are the questions to be considered *and answered*
before organizing an Every-Member Canvass by mail.

1. Can it be done?

a. Is there an adequate and sufficiently accurate mailing list?

b. Is there a potentially high enough percentage of
return to warrant such a type of canvass?

c. Do your parishioners have a normal interest in and
concern for the adequate support of the parish program?

d. Have you allowed sufficient time to create such an
interest and concern before you require a reply from a
contributor?

e. Will the necessary costs of a mail campaign be so
prohibitive that the net results are too small to meet
the need?

As a general axiom the most valuable function of a
direct-mail canvass is to reach parishioners that cannot
be reached personally.

2. *How much expert* experience and advice in preparing and distributing of the materials is available in
the parish?

a. Can your literature and material be expertly prepared?

b. Do you have the office help and equipment to handle the job?

Three stages of a direct-mail canvass.

1. Planning and producing the materials to be used and establishing an adequate mailing schedule. (Three mailings, each building up to a climax, is usually considered the minimum.)

This planning to include:

a. Selection of the type of appeal most likely to be successful. Appeal should be vivid, dramatic and important enough to stir the imagination. It should point up a specific need and be a "natural."

b. Literature and supporting materials should be highly readable, suited to the receiver, and emphasize the basic appeal selected. All materials should carry a demand for action.

c. Most direct-mail canvasses use a letter or a series of letters. These should be carefully written, follow well-recognized rules for obtaining a reading, and be signed by those who carry the most confidence.

2. Mailing

a. Follow a specific, well thought-out mailing schedule.

b. The timing of your mailing to reach receivers at the period of highest susceptibility is important.

c. Accuracy in enclosures and addressing is a must.

3. Tabulation of returns and follow-up.

a. A definite set-up to handle replies promptly and to check off returns is an essential.

b. A committee and the necessary equipment to locate and re-address non-deliveries is important in order that mailings will not be wasted uselessly.

3. Keeping in mind that the number of follow-ups directly affects the extent of the returns, it is advisable

to "stay with them" until sure that additional effort will not produce justifiable returns.

> Lord, grant us so to desire the things
> Which belong to our peace,
> That we may accept with quietness
> And with confidence the disciplines
> Which are their cost. Amen.

4. The Reverend Raymond L. Scofield, rector of St. Mark's Church, Jackson Heights, New York, with Walter Tibbals mapped out a direct-mail program to bring in new members, revive the interest of old members, and better the financial structure of his church. It worked out very well and the samples of the various mailing pieces are reprinted to aid you in planning a similar campaign.

Money-Saver for Churches

Third-class mail rating is a money-saving device for non-profit organizations and a time-saving one for their office staffs. It is a boon to churches, church organizations, diocese, and missionary districts, in mailing such material as bulletins and Every-Member Canvass material. A rate increase on third-class mail became effective on July 1, 1952, but churches and other religious organizations may be excused from the increase by making proper application.

This is how to get a third-class permit for bulk mailing, which is such an important part of a church's business, and also how to avoid the rate increase, as explained by Mr. R. C. Daffer, Senior Assistant Superintendent of Mails, U.S. Post Office, Washington, D. C.

First, apply to the local postmaster for a "bulk mailing permit for third-class mail." Be sure to specify "third class" since there are bulk mailing permits for other classes of mail.

There are three ways of mailing in the third class category (turn to page 204) :

RECTORY
33-40 81st STREET
NEWTOWN 9-7845

February
21
1951

PARISH HOUSE
33-50 82nd STREET
NEWTOWN 9-8893

My dear Neighbor:

Saint Mark's Church welcomes you to Jackson Heights!

We are a group of people who like the way the Episcopal
Church presents and interprets the Christian religion.
Some of us value its traditions, its history and the dignity of its Services. We pray together and play together.
Our aim is to adopt into our family all who will come to
us - regardless of their Church affiliation. We are an
Episcopal Church for ALL PEOPLE. We are a very friendly,
happy society standing for the best in Christian morality
and in American democracy.

You may have noticed our beautiful Church building and
the large well-equipped Parish House. The Parish House
is the center of our social activities for every age group
and for many interests . . .in fact there is something going on every day of the week. We believe the Christian
Church should be friendly . . . we try to be. If you are
unacquainted in this community and are not already connected with any Church, we shall be most happy if you will come
to us - make yourself known - and become a part of our busy
life.

Why not take a minute to fill out the enclosed card and drop
it in the nearest mail box?

Sincerely,

Raymond L. Scofield

Rector

P.S. Our Church is on 34th Avenue, between 81st and 82nd
Streets. The entrance to our Parish House is 3350 - 82nd
Street, adjoining the Church.

Saint Mark's Church

RAYMOND L. SCOFIELD, Rector

34th AVE., 81st TO 82nd STS., JACKSON HEIGHTS, N. Y.

RECTORY
33-40 81st STREET
NEWTOWN 9-7845

March 14, 1951

PARISH HOUSE
33-50 82nd STREET
NEWTOWN 9-8893

Dear Neighbor:

A short time ago we wrote to you about Saint Mark's Church.

This letter is to tell you a little bit more about what goes on in our busy life . . .because we think there is something to appeal to every one.

Saint Mark's Church, while Episcopal in denomination is open to ALL. We have lots of people coming to Church every day who have been raised in other Faiths. It is an Episcopal Church for EVERY ONE.

Some of these folks came to know us through the Cub Scouts, the Boy Scouts, Brownies or Girl Scouts, the Boys' Choir, the Girls' Choir, the Young People's Fellowships (two groups, one from 12 to 15 years of age and the other from 15 to 21). We think children need the training and association built by these Christian organizations.

If you have ever lived in a small town you know how nice it is to know your neighbors . . .well, we have sort of a small town here in Jackson Heights - it is a small town in a big city and you can meet your neighbors here at Saint Mark's. For instance, at the "Coffee Hour" which is held in the Parish House following the 11 o'clock Service. Here you may talk to those in charge of the various Church Committees, such as: Women's Guild - Sewing Guild (for St. Barnabas, St. John's Hospital, the Missions and the Annual Bazaar) - Young Married Couples Group (21-35) - Evening Branch of the Women's Guild - Altar Guild - Garden Group - Men's Fellowship Group.

The "coffee hour" also affords me the opportunity to personally meet and talk with my friends and neighbors - both old and new.

For your information and convenience we list our Services for Holy Week:

```
Palm Sunday - Holy Communion ...................8:00 A.M.
              Church School ....................9:30 A.M.
              Morning Prayer, Sermon, Process-11:00 A.M.
              ion of Palms (Boys' & Girls' Choir)
```

```
Monday........... Holy Communion ...............10:00 A.M.

Tuesday ......... Holy Communion ...............10:00 A.M.

Wednesday ....... Holy Communion ............... 7:00 A.M.
                                               10:00 A.M.

Maundy Thursday . Holy Communion ............... 7:00 A.M.
                                               10:00 A.M.
                                                8:00 P.M.

Good Friday ..... The Three Hours.....Noon to.. 3:00 P.M.
                  Evening Service ............. 8:00 P.M.

Easter Sunday ... Holy Communion ............... 7:00 A.M.
                                      (Choral) 8:00 A.M.
                                                9:30 A.M.
                  Morning Prayer, Sermon, Holy 11:00 A.M.
                  Communion
                  Children's Service .......... 3:00 P.M.
                  Presentation of Mite Boxes
```

If you plan on coming to the 11 o'clock Service on Easter Sunday
we suggest you fill out the enclosed card for tickets which will
assure you of seating in the Church.

I extend to you a personal invitation to attend at least one of
our Services during Holy Week to get acquainted with Saint Mark's.

          Sincerely,

        Raymond L. Scofield

          Rector

P.S. Don't forget . . .we have a Nursery School (free "sitter's
     service") for your young children during the 11 o'clock
     Service every Sunday. Call us at NEwtown 9-8893 for de-
     tails.

Easter

1951

My dear Members and Friends of St. Mark's:-

"And the third day He rose again from the dead"

Either we believe that statement as fact or we don't. If
we believe it, we must believe it all of the time. It is not
a pretty little fetish to be coddled on Easter and put away in
the hall closet the rest of the year. On it rests our alignment,
either with Christians who believe in the continuation of this
life, with its demand in the sanctity of the individual, and a
purpose for life, or with those who hold that 'this life is all
there is; therefore, let's make the most of it, forgetful of any
higher law' There is no middle course; there is no neutrality.

Some say 'What difference does it make'? Too many vital
questions are answered by that evasive reply. To believe that
I am undergoing a spiritual evolution in this world, 'a factory
where persons are made', steered by a God-given free will, inspires me to value righteousness, not motivated by fear of pun-
ishment or hope of reward for goodness. It instils a purpose
in my existence, otherwise purposeless. It makes me long to be
reunited with those whom I love and who have 'flown over the
hump' before me. It enfolds me in the rebirth of Spring, the
symbol of the Resurrection, and makes me certain of the victory
of goodness. It shows me the way to attain. It inspires me to
do good and to be good. It assures me that all men are the
temples of God. It raises me from the slave of man's economic
and political systems to be a Child of God.

So, we are a part of the Easter fact, on which our faith
is built. Jesus rose from the dead. His goodness is indestruc-
tible. By the same means we will continue our lives through
eternity.

I wish you a very happy, certain and joyful Easter.

Faithfully,

R. L. Scofield
Rector

P. S. Enclosed is a copy of a letter sent to new residents of
Jackson Heights.

Costs of materials and operation have gone up for the
Church as well as in other things. Please increase your Easter
offering.
.... *R.L.S.*

Saint Mark's Church

RAYMOND L. SCOFIELD, Rector

34th AVE., 81st TO 82nd STS., JACKSON HEIGHTS, N. Y.

RECTORY
33-40 81st STREET
NEWTOWN 9-7845

PARISH HOUSE
33-50 82nd STREET
NEWTOWN 9-8893

June 23, 1951

Dear Parishioner:

Now that the warm weather is here . . . we hope
you are going to take a vacation. Everyone needs
a rest.

Before you go away and while you're enjoying yourself will you give a thought to St. Mark's Church?

Over the summer, expenses at St. Mark's keep going.
They are just about the same as in winter . . minus
heat and coffee, but during each of the summer months
the Church revenues are less than half of what they
are during each of the other months of the year.

Here's where you can help. Won't you bring your
pledges up to date if they are behind, and further,
won't you keep them up to date if you are absent
from the Church. That way your Church won't have
to borrow from the Bank.

God's work is never done and we must function at full
strength, 52 weeks a year.

May you have a happy, pleasant and healthful summer,
and may the blessings of God Almighty be with you and
remain with you always.

Sincerely yours,

Raymond L. Scofield
Rector

116

Saint Mark's Church

8101-17 34th AVENUE, JACKSON HEIGHTS, N. Y.
NEWTOWN 9-8893

RAYMOND L. SCOFIELD, Rector
33-40 81st STREET, JACKSON HEIGHTS
RECTORY- NEWTOWN 9-7845

PARISH HOUSE
33-50 82nd STREET
Tel. NE 9-8893

November 5, 1951

Dear Friend:

Every year at this time your Church - Saint
Mark's - starts its drive for yearly pledges
and new members.

This year we are trying a slightly different
type of canvass. . . we will not call on you
at this time unless you ask us to, nor will
we pester you with telephone calls - or pop
out from behind the hedges and bushes while
you are on your way to church.

In a few days we will send you the facts;
you be the judge of what to do.

May the blessing of God guide you and be
with you in considering your pledge for 1952.

Sincerely,

R. L. Scofield

Rector

117

RAYMOND L. SCOFIELD, Rector
33-40 81st STREET, JACKSON HEIGHTS
RECTORY: NEWTOWN 9-7845

PARISH HOUSE
33-50 82nd STREET
Tel. NE 9-8893

November 26, 1951

Dear Friend:

Recently we sent you the facts on Saint Mark's
Church. Did you read them? They are most
interesting and important!

So far we have not heard from you. Will you
please return your pledge card filled out or
the enclosed card so that we may know you are
still a member of the Saint Mark's family?

Just check the card and mail it - no postage
is required.

                    Sincerely,

                    R. L. Scofield

                        Rector

P.S. Don't forget to attend Saint Mark's Annual
Parish Meeting on December 3, at 8:00 P. M. in
the Parish House.

✝

✝

HOW DO YOU VOTE? IT'S YOUR CHOICE- YOUR RIGHT TO

DECIDE

(FRONT COVER)

Direct us, *O Lord, in all our doings, with thy most gracious favour, and further us with thy continual help; that in all our works begun, continued, and ended in thee, we may glorify thy holy Name, and finally, by thy mercy, obtain everlasting life; through Jesus Christ our Lord. Amen.*

(BACK COVER)

Do you want GOD and this country the way you have built it?

HERE'S WHAT YOU DO

(PAGE 2)

Will you double your pledge to St. Mark's?

———

It would be great if you would— but we don't want you to!

———

Look at the table on the next page and

HELP ST. MARK'S

(PAGE 3)

if your weekly pledge in 1951 WAS	then please give IN 1952
$ .50	$ .75
1.00	1.50
1.50	2.00
2.00	2.50
2.50	3.00
3.00	4.00
4.00	5.00
5.00	6.00

THAT'S NOT TOO MUCH TO ASK TO...

(PAGE 4)

KEEP...

1 God in our homes

2 Peace in our hearts

3 The strength of Christianity in all of us

AND

4 ST. MARK'S CHURCH GROWING

(PAGE 5)

Proposed Budget for 1952
Estimated Receipts

COLLECTIONS	$ 4,900
Open offerings on Sunday mornings and other services, Easter, Christmas, etc.	
CHURCH SCHOOL PLEDGES	2,400
CONTRIBUTIONS AND GIFTS	5,100
From Church Guilds and Organizations, Bazaar, and from individuals for specific purposes.	
FOR WORK OUTSIDE PARISH	2,800
Gifts and subscriptions for Diocesan and General Church Missions Program, including Episcopal Charities Appeal, Church Charities Foundation, etc.	
RECEIPTS FROM PLEDGES	24,300
Owing to deaths, removals, etc., experience indicates that total pledges of $27,000 will be required to produce receipts of this amount	
Total estimated receipts	$39,500

Estimated Expenses

SALARIES	$15,300
Salaries and pension assessments of the Rector and Clergy assistance, salaries of office staff and Sexton	
MUSIC	1,900
Salaries of organist and choir, choir supplies, vestments, music, care of organ and pianos	
OPERATING EXPENSE	10,600
General expenses of maintaining Church and Parish House, including insurance, heat, light, gas, telephone, stationery & printing, postage, repairs and improvements, etc.	
CHURCH SCHOOL	400
Church School books and supplies (but not including permanent equipment and overhead items)	
INTEREST	2,500
Interest on Mortgage and Debentures	
DIOCESAN AND GENERAL CHURCH PROGRAM	4,600
For missionary, educational, social service and religious work of the Parish, Diocese and General Church	
ADDITIONS & BETTERMENTS TO PROPERTY	1,100
Purchase of Furniture & Fixtures, Extraordinary repairs	
REDUCTION OF DEBT	3,100
Amortization of Mortgage, Redemption of Debentures	
Total estimated expenses	$39,500

FILL OUT THE PLEDGE CARD ENCLOSED AND MAIL IT NOW OR

Drop it in the collection plate Sunday

(PAGE 7)

ENVELOPE NO._____

ST. MARK'S CHURCH (EPISCOPAL)
JACKSON HEIGHTS, N. Y.

I PLEDGE FOR THIS YEAR		MY LAST YEAR'S PLEDGE WAS	
PARISH SUPPORT $_____	☐ WEEKLY ☐ MONTHLY	PARISH SUPPORT $_____	☐ WEEKLY ☐ MONTHLY
CHURCH MISSION $_____	☐ QUARTERLY ☐ YEARLY	CHURCH MISSION $_____	☐ QUARTERLY ☐ YEARLY

Signature:_____

Dear Mr. Scofield:

☐　I am not at present connected with any church in Jackson Heights.

☐　I would like to learn more about Saint Mark's Church.

Mr.
Mrs.
Miss_____

Address_____

_____ Apt. #_____

---

1. With uncanceled stamps (ordinary uncanceled stamps cannot be used).

2. Postal meter.

3. Without stamps.

These conditions apply to all three of the methods that have just been listed:

1. Material to be mailed must be printed matter or form letters either in folder form or enclosed in unsealed envelopes. A folded church paper will be ac-

cepted without an envelope, saving not only the expense of the envelopes, but the time required to stuff them.

2. There must be at least 200 or more identical pieces of mail (or mail weighing 20 pounds or more) tied in bundles of about 50 for mailing.

The fee for a third-class bulk mailing permit is $10 and is only good for the calendar year or any portion of the calendar year remaining. In other words, if a church applied for such a permit in October or November, it would be required to pay another $10 at the beginning of the next year to renew its permit. The permit must be renewed before any mailings in each new year.

All third-class mail must have this endorsement: "Section 34.66 P.L. & R." This tells the postmaster that the publisher or sender of material agrees to comply with the postal regulations. Literally, the endorsement means: section 34, paragraph 66 of the postal laws and regulations.

The permit is good for all types of third-class mail at the rate of 14 cents a pound weighed in bulk with a minimum rate of one cent a piece. As much as eight sheets of mimeographed paper stapled together can be mailed third class.

Bulk lots of books and catalogs having 24 pages or more (including covers), 22 or more of which are printed, may be mailed for ten cents a pound weighed in bulk, with a minimum rate of one cent a piece.

Individual pieces—printed matter, circulars, pamphlets—may be mailed third class by authorized religious organizations for one and one half cents an ounce or each fraction thereof.

Effective July 1, 1952, the rate for third-class mailings were increased to one cent and a half of mailing. This applies to all except religious, fraternal, labor, philanthropic, and veterans' organizations. To avoid this increase a church must write a letter to the postmaster asking for exemption under the new law. Unless this letter is written the church will have to pay the increased rate.

The method of mailing without stamps under the third-class rates requires an additional $10 just for the privilege of not using stamps. This extra $10 (besides the annual fee) need not be paid every year but only once, and the privilege of mailing without stamps is effective always after payment of that initial fee.

The church may deposit with the post office at the time of mailing, or before, the money to cover postage cost, if stamps are not used.

Permits, but no fees, are required for use of pre-canceled stamps and metered mail.

The upper right-hand corner of a piece of mail requires this information which may be mimeographed, printed (might be done by hand), or metered:

Section 34.66 P.L. & R.

U.S. Postage

Paid

Name of city the post office used is in.

Permit number of church.

DETERMINING THE AMOUNT OF PLEDGE

One of the most difficult, yet important, pieces of writing in any annual-appeal literature is that which advises the member on how much he or she should pledge for the year . . . month . . . or week. One excellent way of solving this problem is found in the attractive and effective brochure which Robert Colwell (of Sullivan, Stauffer, Colwell & Bayles, Advertising Agency) developed for the Hugenot Memorial Church in Pelham, New York. It reads as follows:

"How to Determine Your Own Responsibility"

Many people ask how much they should contribute to Church Support and Benevolences.

There is no single answer. Each should give as the Lord has prospered him. A pledge of a thousand dollars a year might represent a heart-felt gift from one Christian. $78 a year—$1 a week for Church support and 50¢ a week for Benevolence—might be an equally sacrificial offering from another.

The Bible teaches us that all things belong to God. We are stewards, not owners, of his bounty. Some devout Christians give one-tenth of all their income, the Biblical tithe, for the Kingdom of Christ—the most important work in the world.

"Many cannot choose this percentage. However, your Church does urge you to plan your gift in terms of come definite percentage of your income. Above all, we ask that every member pledge something both to Church Support and Benevolence. We hope each Church member in your family will make his own individual pledge."

Mr. Colwell added a fine public relations note through this sentence on the back cover: "This booklet was printed without expense to the church."

The introductory page in this brochure is also worthy of being used by other churches in their annual appeals. Notice how the following sets a sincere religious tone or mood:

Acts: II, 45-47
(A description of the early Christian Church)

"And sold their possessions and goods, and parted them to all men, as every man had need.

"And they, continuing daily with one accord in the temple, and breaking bread from house to house, did eat their meat with gladness and singleness of heart.

"Praising God, and having favor with all the people. And the Lord added to the church daily such as should be saved."

Chapter 12

DETAILED
TRAINING
AND PLAN FOR
EVERY-MEMBER
CANVASS

By Ted Gannaway and Edwin Yowell

IT IS THE AUTHOR'S GREAT PRIVILEGE to bring you a tested and proven plan for an Every-Member Canvass which is used annually with success by a growing number of churches in New York State. This laymen's training program is the result of outstanding work done by Ted Gannaway, Director of Laymen's Work for the Diocese of New York, and Edwin Yowell of Christ Church, Tarrytown, New York.

We are sure that even the experienced organizers and workers on the Annual Canvass will get one or two new ideas or techniques from this outline. Messrs. Gannaway and Yowell also developed a successful plan for conducting an Every-Member Canvass by direct mail, and a plan for direct mail and visitation. You can get a copy by writing to either of them. Ted Gannaway's address is Synod House, Amsterdam Avenue, at 110th Street, New York 25, N. Y.

WHY EVERY-MEMBER CANVASS?

1. The plan is fifty years old with fifty years of successful history.

2. The plan deals constructively, simultaneously, and effectively with the three besetting problems of every parish:

a. Perennial waning of spiritual enthusiasm.

b. Constant lessening of a sense of corporateness and Christian fellowship.

c. Increasing cost of religious essentials.

3. The plan has the unqualified endorsement of all major communions in the United States.

4. The plan has successfully met parish crises such as:

a. A desperate need to extricate a parish from an accumulated deficit.

b. An awakened realization of the value of the parish to the community and dissatisfaction with the present status situation.

c. A conviction that the future security of the parish calls for an immediate attempt to broaden its basis of support from a few large gifts to financial participation by a majority of its membership.

d. A determination by the parish to go on a sound financial basis, i.e., full missionary quota and operating expenses covered by pledges using the duplex envelope and Every-Member Canvass.

e. Decreasing endowment income demanding wider membership participation in financial support.

f. Shifting population movements requiring rediscovery of parish manpower and new courses of financial support.

g. Parish recognition that the lifeblood of its growth and expansion is the missionary zeal of its membership, culminating in a decision to insist on active participation by all parishioners in the missionary program.

h. Physical condition of the parish properties requiring raising additional funds to maintain present plant and program of activities.

i. Unexpected emergencies that cannot be met with methods of raising funds previously employed.

TYPES COMMONLY USED

1. Personal Visitation
   A personal call by a trained canvasser on every communicant family (unit) for the purpose of:
   Explaining the Church's program and plans.
   Obtaining a valid pledge of payment of money toward the support of that program and those plans.

2. By Direct Mail
   A series of mailings designed to carry the story of the Church's program and plans into every home and including a pledge card and envelope for pledge or payment of contributions.

3. Direct Mail and Personal Visitation
   Loyalty Sunday
   A combination of the 1 and 2 above in which as many contributions and pledges are obtained by mail, and those *not* so responding are called upon by trained canvassers.

4. Experimental Donor Days
   A plan whereby the communicants are prepared by the minister through instructions from the pulpit on the plans and program of the Church, the missionary imperative of the Christian faith, and the necessity for adequate support. The minister then sets aside certain days to meet the families of his parish at the chancel and together personally present their gifts at the altar.

A Suggested Outline of the Basic Essentials
for a Successful
EVERY-MEMBER CANVASS
To Raise Funds by Personal Visitation

Personnel
   (*For each 100 communicant units*)
   One lay chairman
   Committee on special gifts

SUGGESTED ORGANIZATION FOR 100 COMMUNICANTS

CHAIRMAN
(Group)
Commander

VICE CHAIRMAN (Squadron Leader)	SPECIAL GIFTS COMMITTEE (Bomber Squadron)	VICE CHAIRMAN (Squadron Leader)

Team Chairman Flight Leader — Team Chairman Flight Leader — Team Chairman Flight Leader — Team Chairman Flight Leader — Team Chairman Flight Leader — Team Chairman Flight Leader

Workers { Pilot | Pilot } Co-pilots

TRAINING AND SUPPLY .... **TRAINING AND SUPPLY**

Literature and Mail | Parish Secretary | Rector and Clergy | Treasury and Audit | Arrangements | Publicity and Display

RECRUITING

General Chairman obtains { Two Vice-Chairmen
Special Gifts Committee
Three Team Leaders
Two Workers
One Co-worker

Vice-Chairman obtains

Team Leader obtains

Each Worker obtains

Six team leaders
Twelve teams of two each
(*For each additional 50 communicant units, add*) :
One vice-chairman
Three team leaders
Six teams of two each

CONFERENCES

1. Planning (Minister presides).... .. ..

INVITE: Minister and associate clergy, vestry and canvass chairman.

AGENDA (Allow two full hours) :
a. Establish campaign theme.
b. Determine objectives and dates.
c. Explain budget items.
d. Fix number calls to be made.
e. Appoint pre-campaign special gift committee and assign calls.
f. Develop potential worker list and allot names.
g. Nominate vice-chairman and team leaders and make recruiting assignments.
h. Set date for recruiting report meeting.

2. Recruiting Report Meeting (Canvass chairman presides)

INVITE: Same group as above plus vice-chairmen.

AGENDA (Allow 30 minutes) :
a. Install vice-chairmen.
b. Install team leaders.
c. Distribute worker lists to vice-chairmen and then to team leaders for team selection (As appointments are made, fill organization chart by phone call from team leaders) .

3. Workers' Rally (canvass chairman presides)

INVITE: Minister, associate clergy, vestry, general

chairman, special gifts committee, vice-chairmen, team leaders, workers and special guests.

AGENDA (Allow 3 hours if supper meeting; 2½ if not) :

a. Devotional service and prayers (in chapel). Commissioning of workers.

b. Invocation and supper. (See table set-up attached.)

c. (2 min.). Minister introduces canvass chairman

d. (5 min.). Canvass chairman declares objectives and theme, welcomes workers and exposes organization chart

e. (8 min.). Parish treasurer (or senior warden) covers budget items

f. Team leaders given call cards and report envelopes for assignment to teams at tables. (Pause 10 min. for distribution, discussion and questions).

g. (15 min.). Chairman briefs workers on campaign plans and procedures

h. (30 min.). Vice-Chairman conducts training conference on techniques

i. (30 min.) Inspirational address on parish and missionary program

j. Prayers and adjournment

4. Workers' Report Meeting (Canvass chairman presides)

INVITE: Minister, associate clergy, wardens, treasurer, and all Canvass personnel.

AGENDA (Allow one hour) :

a. Report of special gifts chairman and committee. (Team leaders should collect and tabulate returns during report of special gifts.)

b. Roll call by team leaders giving results.

c. Treasurer records results to date on organization chart.

d. Question and answer period.

e. Announce time and date of final report meeting.

f. Prayers and adjournment.

5. *Workers' Final Report Meeting* (Canvass chairman presides)

INVITE: As above in 4

AGENDA:

a. Prayers.

b. Team leaders report roll call.

c. Distribution of citations.

d. Treasurer gives final tabulation of results.

e. Service of thanksgiving.

f. Workers thanked and adjournment.

DIRECT MAIL

1. Minister's Letter (to be mailed immediately following Planning Conference)

FORMAT—for readability—four paragraphs of 5 to 9 sentences each. Sentences to consist of 17-21 words each. Words to average 1.8 syllables. All on one page, parish letterhead, personalized as much as practicable. For impact—a simple direct statement of the minister's expectations from each parishioner. (No apologies, budget explanation, pleading for attention, nor false optimism.)

For memory retention—start paragraphs with the pronoun "you" where possible. Speak in terms of the readers' interests, not the warden's, vestry's or minister's. Use simple non-ecclesiastical wording. Select sincere, colorful phrases that carry a punch.

2. *The Parish Folder* (to be included with the above). A four-page printed (where possible) illustrated folder. Suggestions: one page may be the simplified budget; one page, a carefully worded, short statement from the canvass chairman; one page carry the major items of the present parish and missionary program and essentials of the program plans for the coming year. Cover page, a picture of the church, the campaign slogan, and dates.

3. *Diocesan Missionary Folder* (to be mailed the day of the Workers' Rally).

4. *The National Church Folder* (to be mailed the day before the campaign opens). To be mimeographed or imprinted with a direct appeal and endorsement by the minister and the Canvass Chairman.

DUTIES AND RESPONSIBILITIES OF CAMPAIGN SERVICE PERSONNEL

The Minister

Call and preside at Canvass Planning Conference. Aid in selection of general chairman.

Meet with and assist the special gifts committee.

Assist in the assignment of call cards to vice-chairman.

Act as chaplain at all meetings.

Conduct worship services in support of campaign.

Assist the special service committees.

The Treasurer.

Prepare call cards for all communicant units.

Assist in selection of calls assigned to special gifts committee.

Receive all contributions and pledges.

Supervise audit and prepare campaign-progress reports.

The Chairman and Committee on Arrangements.

Arrange details of all workers' meetings, including meals, table arrangements, and decorations, etc.

The Literature and Mailing Committee.

Order, collate, and mail all literature, letters, and campaign materials on schedule agreed upon at the planning conference.

The Publicity and Display Director.

Prepare and send out press releases, set up displays at meetings. Arrange for photographs. Operate training equipment.

The Parish Secretary.

Prepare call cards for all communicant units.

Address and mail all literature, letters, and materials.

Operate a general information service for all workers.

Accept and record properly reports on workers recuited.

Notify or remind team leaders, vice-chairmen, and special committees of all meetings.

The Continuing Canvass Director.

TERM: Usually three to five years consecutively.

PURPOSE: To conserve the experience gained in each canvass; To know and use the best worker talent in the parish; To know and arrange the mechanics of conducting a canvass; To insure continual high standards.

QUALIFICATIONS: Young in spirit, tactful and capable of drawing out workers, thoroughly familiar with the parish and its budget, meticulous as to detail, ingenious in overcoming obstacles, alert to meet changing conditions and sharing the rector's or vicar's complete confidence.

SOURCES: Last year's successful canvass chairman, parish treasurer, parish keyman in laymen's movement, junior warden, vestry, advisory board, etc.

DUTIES: To recruit the annual canvass chairman; To organize the canvass preliminaries; To conserve the records of workers and evaluate them; To recruit possible new workers during the year; and such other duties as shall carry out the purpose of the position.

The General Chairman

Call and preside at all conferences and workers' meetings except the planning conference.

Recruit the vice-chairmen and brief them on duties.

Recruit qualified members of a special gifts committee and assist them in making the pre-canvass calls.

Confer with the minister, parish treasurer, and wardens on literature, posters, publicity, direct mail, displays, carding, meeting arrangements. Appoint chairmen to cover each above phase of the campaign.

Make five solicitation calls for contributions.

Conduct workers' training conference.

Supervise all phases of campaign.

Assign replacements when workers are unable to function.

Special Gifts Committee.

In cooperation with the minister and parish treasurer obtain the names and address of potential larger givers prior to the opening of the Canvass. Call upon each or enlist the aid of qualified people to assist in such a call and obtain as generous a contribution as possible prior to the Canvass.

Report such gifts at the meeting of the workers at the opening of the Canvass in such fashion as to provide the maximum stimulus to the campaign.

The Vice Chairman.

Recruit three well-qualified team leaders to serve as head of two workers' teams each.

Guarantee attendance of team leaders at all campaign meetings.

Divide call cards into packets of five according to address.

Issue call cards to team leaders.

Make five solicitation calls for contributions.

Collate reports of team leaders at workers' report meetings.

See that team leaders complete assignments as rapidly as possible.

Assist the general chairman in carrying out his duties, particularly in the conduct of the Workers' Training Conference.

Team Leaders.

Attend workers' rally and report meetings.

Recruit two teams of workers from workers' listings assigned.

Issue call cards to teams. Five calls to each team.

Guarantee attendance of workers at rally and report meetings.

Collate reports of team workers recruited by him.

See that team workers assignments are completed as rapidly as possible.

Workers.

Select and recruit a co-worker to assist in making calls.

Accept assignment of five calls, complete these calls and report results to team leaders.

Attend workers' rally, training conference, and report meetings.

PERSONNEL RECRUITING PLANS

In addition to the plan for recruiting canvassers given in the previous pages, the following have been used with success.

1. *The Area Plan*

The Parish is divided into geographical areas. A team leader is obtained for each area by the minister, the canvass director, or the annual canvass chairman. Each team leader obtains as many workers from his area as the number of calls to be made in his area requires. (For average canvassers no more than five or six calls per worker should be required. An exceptionally good canvasser can be given ten to fifteen calls to complete.)

2. *The Vestry Plan*

Each vestryman is automatically considered a team leader and given a quota of canvass workers to recruit.

3. *The Parish Organization Plan*

A varying quota of adult canvass workers is assigned to each major parish organization, and the organization recruits workers from their membership. (This includes team leaders and canvass officers if assigned.)

4. *The Men's Club Plan*

The organized men's group of the parish takes over the recruiting and furnishes the necessary personnel from among its own membership.

5. *The Open Selection Plan*

The minister and the canvass director cover the parish rolls and select six to twelve men to be team leaders. Selection is based on the proven ability of the men, and the number selected is dependent upon the size of the parish.

TRAINING OF CANVASSERS

By Edwin Yowell

Christ Church, Tarrytown, New York

The Training of Every-Member Canvasser

Any conversation regarding the *training of a canvasser* for the Every-Member Canvass presupposes three important factors:

1. A competent *general chairman* has been selected well in advance of the time the actual canvass begins.

2. A *general program* has been settled upon by this general chairman *and* the people he is responsible to.

3. *Accurate church records* are available. It is particularly important that the church roll be corrected prior to the time of the canvass.

Selecting the Candidate

In the past, many churches have had the unfortunate tendency to let the same old gang run all the church functions year after year. This is *not efficient, not smart, and not good* churchmanship. The general chairman and the minister should go over the church rolls and select, depending on the size of the parish, from six to twelve men to be *team captains*. The church's best team captains will generally come from people who have experience in dealing with people in their business lives. Lawyers, salesmen, engineers are always particularly adept in handling small groups such as a canvass team would comprise. After a man has obtained a certain maturity, necessary for effectiveness, of twenty odd years of living he has become, *potentially*, the greatest asset the Church has as an active worker. All that is necessary is effectively to direct his energy into the proper channels by the training we shall undertake today, and the Church will have a worker of far greater merit than the older man who has done the Church's chores for years through habit and what is sometimes called a "sense of duty." If the truth were known it would probably reveal that a great many of these men who have been asked year after year to make the annual Every-Member Canvass would be pleased if they were excused from their duties.

We are not selling the older men short; however, it is a well established fact that the young men of our churches are not asked to participate in many church functions because of what *Willard Pleuthner* so aptly called "Dangerous Dignity."

Religion is a living, vital thing. It is not necessary to be ninety-five, or even sixty-five, to properly appreciate its importance in everyday living.

Once the minister and the general chairman have selected the list of men they wish to ask to become team captains, the general chairman should personally contact each man and ask him to serve. The chairman should explain why it is important and why this particular person has been asked to head a team. The younger the person is who is asked the more honored he will feel for having been asked. This is the sort of captain we are looking for. The man who has worked on the canvass for twenty-five years will scarcely feel honored if he is asked again. He will more likely approach it with the "oh well" sort of attitude.

Training the Team Captains

Once a complement of captains has been arranged for (with one or two alternates, just in case), a meeting of the minister, the general chairman, and these team captains should be held in some appropriate church building for a general meeting. At this meeting the minister should formally turn the project of the yearly Every-Member Canvass over to the general chairman and from that point on exercise only what restrained control his own good judgment tells him is necessary.

At this general meeting the church secretary should be present, or whoever is responsible for the actual church budget. This functionary should attend all future meetings so that accurate, factual information will be available to the general chairman, the team captains and the workers. After the general program has been explained to the team captains and thoroughly discussed, the parish roll should be gone over and potential workers picked. Each captain should be given a free hand in picking the men who are going to work under him. Enough workers should be picked so that the captains will not have over six workers, and each worker will not have over eight or ten addresses to call upon.

As soon as the team captain is settled with his workers the actual training of the individual worker begins. This can be done either of two ways, depending on how many training meetings are to be held.

1. A general meeting, at which time a selected speaker could give a talk that would be generally related to the problem at hand, to be followed a few days later by a team meeting, which should be held at the team captain's home. Or (2) to reverse the above and have the team meeting first, followed by a general meeting, of the same type as mentioned before.

At the individual team meetings to be held in the home of the captain, the captain should explain in a give-and-take session just what, when, and how he expects his team to operate. I say "give-and-take" advisedly, however. Let the team captain be reminded that *he is* the captain and is responsible for the efficient function of his team and should not be stampeded or pressured into actions or methods which he does not approve.

The Actual Training of the Canvass Worker

The first and great problem of any representative, regardless of whether he is representing his church, some commercial organization, or simply himself in a discussion with his neighbor is to *know what he is talking about*. All sales managers maintain that there are three absolutes that the embryonic salesman must know. They are (1) know your product, (2) know your product, and (3) know your product. It is the responsibility of the team captain to see that each of his workers has a *workable knowledge* of the current budget and has an *intimate knowledge of the church organizations as they exist in his particular church.*

Do not try to make too many calls in one evening. It is better to make a single good call then ten poor ones. Before you get to the prospect's address, have everything in hand. Get out of your car and walk *purposefully* up to the door. *In front of the prospect's house is not the time to do your bookkeeping. Wear a hat.* It gives you something to take off in a show of courtesy (which all women like), and after you have it off, it gives you something to do with your hands. *Read the name off the card.* Ask the question: "Are you Mrs. Smith?" This gets the prospect into the conversation. Most people can't think and talk at the same time. If the prospect is talking to you she can't get her guard up and start to think of the different ways of saying "no." *Speak up.* Say: "I'm Ed Yowell, of Christ Church." Associate yourself with the church. To you, she can say "no," but it isn't quite so likely that she will cut you off if you mention the church. Remember when you introduce yourself to leave off the title. Your name is not "mister." It is Ed, Sam, Bill, or Joe—who knows, it may even be Clarence. *This is a friendly call. Be friendly.* You are not going to make much headway with the average American by giving yourself a lot of titles—especially when you are standing on his doorstep with your hat in your hand. Smile—establish yourself in that instant you have as a good fellow. *Those first twenty seconds are the most crucial part of your interview!*

If the prospect has a difficult name to pronounce, try saying it out loud before making the call. Most names are easy to pronounce if you give your ear a chance to hear them. *Stand on the side of the door that makes it necessary for her to open the door to talk with you.* If the prospect is talking with you from behind a partially opened door she is much more likely to tell you "no" before you get a chance to explain *who* you are and *what* you are. *Do not spill the beans on the doorsteps.* Ask the prospect: "May I come in?" Few, if any, people will tell you "no" to such a direct question.

Don't run over the prospect like a Mack truck with your sales story. There is always the business routine of your hat and coat. It must be placed aside. This normal routine places your prospect ever more at ease. After you are seated ask the prospect if she went to church today (assuming that it is Sunday). If it is not Sunday ask her if she went to church this past Sunday. This is your normal opening to discuss the business at hand. Lead easily into it by stating that "As you know, this is Loyalty Sunday." If she still looks expectant, continue: *"This is the one day of the year when the church solicits your financial support for its activities for the coming year."* Now the cat is out of the bag. At this point the individual canvasser must operate according to the ability, or the limitations, of his own personality. No amount of "canned sales talk" will make a person who is by nature tongue-tied into a glib, smooth talker.

The inexperienced should remember that his greatest asset is to be sincere, straightforward, and not to make the first call until he has all his basic facts down pat. You can cover up many things if you are clever but you can never cover up lack of knowledge when you are selling a product—and, gentlemen, *we are most assuredly selling our Church with its many blessings each time we ring a doorbell!*

When you get to the actual size of the pledge many people will ask you what *you* think. *Have a ready answer.* This should not be an off-hand answer. The general chairman of the canvass should furnish this information. Your average pledge must be the number of people divided into the amount of money you must raise on the canvass. This does not necessarily mean the total figure of the budget, as many churches have other sources of income. The only figure that the canvasser is concerned with is the figure arrived at by dividing the amount to be raised by the canvass by the number of people to be called on. Obviously you would not talk in terms of the average pledge with a couple with an income of twenty thousand a year any more than you would talk of an average pledge to the pensioner trying to get by on two thousand a year. *Discretion must be used.* It is the individual discretion used by the canvasser that will govern his effectiveness.

A great many people will want to make pledges much smaller than the church has a right to expect them to make. When talking to these people do not belittle the amount they have offered but dwell on the positive reasons why the church is essential in the community. If they talk in terms of a dollar a week, break it down to a daily pledge . . . this is only fourteen cents a day. A dollar may buy a lunch, but with current prices, fourteen cents will buy very little.

When the prospect says that he can't afford to pledge as much as he did last year or that the same pledge as last year is the best he can do, explain that the church's dollar too is buying less and less. *Do not passively accept the same old pledge.* Keep the conversation on the positive side. Don't sit around and agree that everything is going to pot. *Offer a solution, the church!* Tell the prospect this is something positive you can do! In describing the church do not use "soft" words. *Use words with positive meanings.* Do not say that it is *good* to have the church in the community. Say it is *vital* . . . say it is *essential* to have the church in the community. Since you are there to say something *get the most into what you have to say* so that your prospect *will get the most out of what you are saying*.

In discussing money there are two prime factors to be remembered: (1) be factual and (2) be relaxed.

Don't fluster, don't look away. Look directly at whom you are talking. Use the same tone you would use if you were talking about how blue the sky is. Do not apologize for what you are saying. It is a privilege to do God's work, and you have been honored by being asked to help. Do not be self-conscious, your embarrassment can easily be transferred to your prospect, and then you are really in a mess. Keep the canvass card in your hand. Tell the prospect that it is your only record. Don't let her put you off by saying that she will mail it in. You have two strikes against you if you do. If she tells you that she has not had a chance to talk it over with her husband, and you are not able to overcome this objection by explaining that he would probably leave it up to her good judgment anyway, tell the prospect that you will be working on other calls later in the week in this neighborhood and that you will call back. Don't let her put you off if it is at all possible, but let her know that you are perfectly willing to return at her convenience. On this score it is perfectly possible not to take "no" for an answer. If you state flatly that you *will* return there will be little she can do to try to stop you.

REMEMBER: Make all contacts personally. Do not use the phone. If you wish to pave the way by sending some literature and a short personal note saying that you will call at such and such a time it will be fine, provided that you actually follow up as you have promised. If you do not, you will have put yourself in a bad light to start with and everything you say will be properly discounted when you wish most urgently to make a point. Do not phone as a substitute for a letter. Some folks get very brave over the phone and will tell you anything just to get rid of you. Regardless of the attitude of your prospect, if you have him face to face you have a chance, but over the phone you haven't if he has really made up his mind that he doesn't want to see you. Remember: *Don't give him this chance.* Work for maximum results, not for time saved. Since you are not placing a value on your time, don't act as if you were on a piece-work basis.

Do not let the Worker take the canvass cards of his FRIENDS. *You simply cannot do business with your friends.* You will get a far more favorable relationship with someone you do not know. Your friends tend to take you for granted—either that or they will not take you seriously. A stranger will be sincere with you automatically, whereas a friend or neighbor can much more easily put you off.

A definite time limit should be placed on the time the canvass is going to take. There may be a few cards that are uncollectable by the time the canvass is over, and these few should be turned over to the church secretary for proper follow-up. In most cases the canvass should not exceed two weeks or three weekends.

In conclusion bear in mind the following facts.

When considering the qualifications of the individual worker watch out for the "know it all." The man who has stopped learning is going to be very hard to control. A man who will not take directions will hardly ever justify his existence in an organization. *This is essentially an organizational function.* There is *no place* for the *non-conformist,* the *rugged individualist,* or *the man who will not take directions.*

A simple yet comprehensive plan must be agreed on at the outset as to *responsibility, methods, and personnel.*

A *feeling of organization* will be achieved if the *general chairman* will make it a point to contact each of his *team captains* by phone at *least twice* during the actual canvass, and the *team captains* will contact their workers at least twice during the actual canvass and each time offer to help with any special problems. Remember, the captain who just goes along for the ride on the routine calls is wasting his time and is probably robbing his worker of a feeling of competence which is absolutely necessary for anyone calling on the public.

You do not want to work a man who feels he needs a crutch every time he makes a call.

The captain should give to the general chairman a record of every pledge card given his worker and the worker should be specifically instructed not to give the card to the prospective pledge-giver. A record of any additional pertinent information should be made on the back of the pledge card at the time the call is made. Later on there is a tendency either to let it go altogether or to put the information down in an inaccurate manner.

The captain should make it clear to his workers that he *expects* them to contact him if any special problems should arise. The general chairman should make it specifically clear at the first joint meeting of the minister, the general chairman, the team captains, and the workers that the lines of responsibility lie in this sequence and that for the sake of simplicity or organization they should not lightly be ignored.

A record should be kept by the general chairman of the effectiveness of each of his captains and he should require of his captains that they mark their workers at the end of the canvass as to degree of effectiveness and potential. This record should be kept confidential by the general chairman and the minister and should be used as a help in lining up the next year's canvass personnel when that time comes. After this has been done one or two years, the canvass personnel problem will be licked except for replacements of those who drop out or move away.

CAMPAIGN MATERIALS

1. An oilcloth streamer banner carrying the "Theme." To be displayed in parish house or meeting place during campaign.

2. A large flat of the canvass organization carrying the names of the workers and all personnel. Should also

provide space for writing in quotas and amounts reported if parish desires.

3. (Optional) A spectacular display portraying graphically the progress of the campaign (i.e., a detached model airplane on runway to be moved along as pledges are reported until minimum objectives are reached, then airborne as campaign totals are recorded).

4. Lapel name cards for workers—in colors to designate rank and to furnish an automatic attendance check at rallies and report meetings.

5. Parish activity and missionary exhibits around the sides of the meeting room.

6. Center pieces for card tables carrying team name and workers' designation as place cards. (See model table arrangement using model aircraft.)

7. Citations or awards for workers achieving goals. (Can be small silver "wings" in form of pins.)

8. National Council Missionary Posters and Every-Member Canvass posters. (Use in church vestibule and parish hall.)

9. Program film strips or motion pictures showing Church at work.

10. Workers' instruction sheets.

CAMPAIGN OFFICERS' MATERIALS

1. Recruiting report forms. (Used by vice-chairman and team leaders in reporting workers as they are lined up.)

2. Sample packets of all literature and campaign aids going out to all parishioners. (To be distributed to workers as recruited.)

3. Calendar of meetings showing time, date, place and purpose. (To be given to workers as recruited.)

4. Workers' registry for campaign officers giving name, address (home and business), telephone num-

bers, and special information on each, one copy to be retained by each officer to permit close contact with workers.

5. Report envelopes to collate and transmit cash and pledges.

WORKERS' MATERIALS

1. *Canvassers' Call Card.* Name, address, telephone number, and unit strength of each communicant unit to be called on. Grouped by fives by address; workers' card on top. Coded to indicate previous year's gift.

1A. *Workers' Code Card and Instruction Folder.* (Facts for canvassers.)

2. *Pledge Card and Envelope.* To be signed and, if requested, sealed in envelope provided.

3. *Report Envelopes.*
   Team Report.
   Workers' report.
   Vice-chairman's report.

4. *Treasurer's Tabulation Sheets.*

5. *Duplex Envelopes.* To include treasurer's card of thanks and indicating expected amount and serving as original reminder of pledge.

A new Every-Member Canvass plan has been promulgated by the Baptists. They have been getting unbelievable results with it. For full details I suggest that you write The Council on Missionary Cooperation, American Baptist Convention, 152 Madison Avenue, New York 16, New York, and ask for their manual entitled, *A Manual for the Every-Member Canvass Sector Project.* It may cost you a dollar or so.

Chapter 13

A TESTED METHOD
FOR
MODERN TITHING

CONFESSION TO THE READER: We originally intended
to have only three chapters in this book on ways to
secure church funds. That number seemed sufficient
and covered the main financial campaign, plus extra
ways of raising money for the church's work.

Yet when we tabulated the findings from the questionnaires sent out to 2,600 clergymen, we found that
many people asked for a discussion of tithing—the
oldest and surest way of raising money for our churches'
and God's work. In fact, we consider tithing so important that it was made a key chapter in our first
book, *Building Up Your Congregation.*

We were so encouraged by the "write-in-vote" of
request for tithing by so many of the clergy and laymen that we decided to add this chapter. We hope you
find it includes new material on tithing—new to you.

One of the most complete explanations and "sales
talks" on this original method for supporting God's
work which we found, was a talk given by Bishop Richard S. Emrich of Michigan. Here are the key thoughts
from this Detroiter's outstanding address.

Note: If you would like the full and complete discussion, just write the Bishop at 63 East Hancock Avenue,
Detroit 1, Michigan. Ask for a copy of the "1952
Reinecker Lectures," which includes talks on missions
and the ministry of the laity. The cost is $1 per printed
set of lectures.

THE PRACTICE OF
PROPORTIONATE GIVING

One of the tasks of a bishop is to form a policy and to make universal in a diocese those practices which are sound religiously and will help to overcome financial problems. There is one policy which I believe should be adopted by our whole Church because in many, many dioceses now people have gratefully adopted it, that is proportionate giving. It is not, of course, really new: it was tried and tested for many years by one of the larger parishes of Michigan, a parish which has the best record proportionately of any in the Diocese.

Many minds in many parishes, facing the same problem and the difficulties which we have been discussing, have arrived independently at the necessity of a standard—the necessity for the teaching of proportionate giving. This has the tradition of Scripture and of some of the Early Church behind it. It was the practice, as we all know, in the Old Testament to tithe—to give 10 percent of one's income to the Lord. This practice was undoubtedly supported by our Lord.

Let's list some of the reasons for this proportionate giving, or the Modern Tithe.

Let us sketch again the need for a standard and a guide. We tell people about the needs of the Church and of the community (and that's good), but we give them no guidance whatever in *how* to give. The results of this are clear—a giving, by the vast majority of our people, that bears little relation to their ability to give. There is a serious giving on the part of a small inner circle, but a wandering, confused ignorance on the part of most others. But if the law is a guide and is necessary to Christians, you do not think that we should show people what the love of God and man means as far as our pocketbooks are concerned? *Now*, when a sincere canvasser approaches a sincere new churchman, and the latter asks, "What would you suggest that I give? What

does the Church say?" The Church usually weakly answers, "Give what you can"—and that is no answer.

Since I have been in the ministry I have never gone
to any man and asked him for a specific amount. There
are rich men in my diocese but I have never said, "Give
$3 a week." I don't know enough definitely about any
man's personal affairs to ask him for a specific amount.
But I do not have the slightest hesitation in asking
every man to be responsible to God, grateful to God,
to remember his soul and his Maker, and to be fully
serious. I have not the slightest hesitation in asking a
man to give remembering what he has received. The
time has come to say with definiteness, and to suggest
without prying into details, what seriousness and gratitude mean. They mean 5 percent to the church and 5
percent to community charities.

Now, someone will say, "too much"; and here I can
only repeat something taught me by a layman. How can
any man say that 5 percent of his *net* income is too high
a standard when the government permits him to de-
duct 15 percent of his *gross* income? If the men in
Washington say 15 percent of gross income, you would
not respect the Church or its estate of the Gospel it
wants to preach if, apart from the traditional tithe, it
suggested a lower figure than 5 percent of net income.
There will be some people who will say that this is too
little, and I know some now; and there are more people
than you imagine who are already giving this, when
you think of building funds, special gifts, pledges, and
so forth. But this is a standard, a guide, and the real
sacrifices of the few will continue to go beyond it. And
the result of teaching this is an immediate raising of
pledges, as people turn and look at the percentage they
now give.

Once last year I talked with a man who tithes. He
is a fine person, admired by everyone, and I asked him
this question: "Why do people who tithe look with such
confidence at the future?" And he replied, "Because
they are the kind of people who tithe. They live for the

right things, and they know that tomorrow, no matter
what happens, love for the Lord will see them through."
The practice of tithing does bring spiritual rewards,
and, springing from the spiritual, leads to a stability
which brings material rewards. I believe this is true.
The only thing is that we must be very careful to keep
the thought of reward on a high Christian plane.

It is true to say that giving springs from faith: it is
just as true to say that faith is strengthened by giving.
And since this is so, we do our people a real injustice
when we do not hold before them a serious standard
which could lead them to deeper things. If you teach
this, you will find that people discuss it, that it becomes common knowledge in a congregation, and that
a new seriousness comes to the people. Is not one of
the problems of the Church that we have not asked
really serious things of men, specifically, which reveal
to them the full seriousness of the Faith and the necessity for important decisions? This is certainly only part
of what we should suggest to men, but its full seriousness should be welcomed by a Church that often plays
with Christianity.

Tithing is democratic, and fair. There are rich men
and poor men in the Church, and before God within
His Church they should stand on an equal footing. The
rich man should not feel that he is taking over; and the
rich man should not feel that he is the only one responsible, which sometimes happens. They should stand
side by side as friends, knowing that both are trying
to be responsible and that both are responsibly using
the talents God has given them. When a man dies and
his casket lies before the altar, God asks chiefly whether
with his particular talents he was a grateful and responsible man. There should, therefore, be equal and fair
standards for all men: a tithe—5 percent to the Church
and 5 percent to community charities.

And, speaking of fairness—and here, I believe, is
where the laymen have arrived at this theory independently—doesn't the fact of inflation drive us to the theory

of proportionate giving? In a day when the value of the dollar fluctuates, how can you finance a church unless when there are more dollars in circulation, the church receives more dollars, and when there are fewer we receive fewer? It would seem to me that proportionate giving is the only thing that will meet inflation.

The way to begin it is, of course, with ourselves. Revivals in the Church begin with groups of men who believe deeply and, because they know a thing to be true, can speak of it with power. The best teaching is not to exhort others to tithe, but to share with them your own experience and to give them the deepest religious reasons why *you* tithe. I can bear witness that it means much in my family and affords us, as we budget, an opportunity to show ourselves and our children that we are really trying *to put the Lord first*.

Two things I am afraid of, and I will close with these: 1. I am afraid of self-righteousness—the tithers may some day be looking down on the non-tithers. This is a possibility, I suppose, just as church attendance could lead to self-righteousness—anything can. I think the best thing is to teach the principle in all seriousness, and have laymen bear witness to its meaning, but leave to the Lord the final figures of those who tithe. In the last analysis it's between a man and his God. I have seen no self-righteousness at all, but this would do away with any danger of it. 2. My greatest fear is that men who do not understand the great motive of tithing—gratitude to God—will look upon it as a "money-raising scheme." It is not. It is, rather, a way of teaching all of us, a means to bring us to God, a result of serious faith. It teaches us what is important in life, brings home to our budgets the claims of God and the awareness of His Presence, teaches us gratitude, teaches us how to worship by giving ourselves.

The man who knows that God is the central fact of his life, who feels the daily nearness of God, who sees around him the evidences of God's love, and who gives himself to God in gratitude, is a transformed man. The purpose of tithing is to secure, not just the tithe, but the tither; not just the gift, but the giver; not just the possession, but the possessor; not the money, but each of us in a new way and a great way for the Lord.

NOTE: If you are interested in this Detroit plan of tithing, write Bishop Richard S. Emrich for copies of the booklets: *What Shall I Give for What God Has Given Me?* and *Don't Miss the Point.*

Being the general chairman of a canvassing program is not an easy job. If it were an easy job, you would not have been asked to do it. The same is true of your canvassers, for if theirs were an easy job, you and the general chairman could have handled the entire canvass by yourselves.

Because of the importance of the training work you are to do, we have asked a professional organization to write this training section for you.

Read it carefully and often between now and your Fall Canvass.

MEETING GUIDE FOR
EDUCATIONAL CHAIRMEN
1952 EVERY-MEMBER CANVASS
DIOCESE OF MICHIGAN

THE CANVASSER TRAINING MEETING

You must have ready for your canvass workers the following props and people to help you expertly to stage the training sessions. You will need a strip film projector, a suitable screen, a lectern, piano, tables, chairs, blackboard, canvassers' packages, the new tithing poster and the new tithing leaflet, and the slidefilm used in this meeting. (Also the motion picture on tithing if you need it.) Group the canvassers so that they can all see the screen and the lectern. You should have on display a copy of the poster, tithing literature, pledge cards, parish record cards. Provide pencils, scratch paper, ash trays.

You will need a projectionist, a pianist, and a man to handle lights. You should be at the door to greet all canvassers as they come in.

Before the meeting, be sure your projector is properly set up and tested—have the lectern and the screen in place—and arrange that the light on the lectern and projector do not go out when the house lights are dimmed. Run a trial meeting with the pianist and projectionist before the meeting is held.

The general chairman has arranged the meeting. Present at this meeting will be the general chairman, the rector, and the senior warden.

THE MEETING

At the exact moment which the meeting has been called for, call the canvassers to order. Seat them by teams. Lead them in singing a hymn—we suggest verses 1 and 3 of Hymn 535. Then, the rector should read two short collects—for the Church, on page 37 of the Book of Common Prayer, and then the fourth collect on page 49.

Let the rector talk—*three minutes*—on the Christian experience to be gained from Modern Tithing. The general chairman should talk—*three minutes*—telling the canvassers why they have been chosen and what a tough but satisfying job they have ahead of them.

LEADER—NOW YOU BEGIN YOUR ACTUAL TRAINING. WHAT FOLLOWS IS WHAT YOU TELL YOUR WORKERS. TRY NOT TO GIVE THE IMPRESSION OF READING IT.

"A man once asked this question of his friends, 'What do you consider the most satisfying human relationship in your experience?' The replies ranged all the way from religion to childhood. The happy smile of a child, the understanding nod of a friend, the firm handshake of another, the effect of prayer—all seemed to bring a deeper understanding of humanness.

"As canvassers you have the particular privilege of being able to meet with people who make up this parish, of getting from them an acceptance of their responsibility to God, to their church, and to themselves. To some of you this will be difficult, to others it will be an easy, pleasant job. To those of you who will find this work difficult, I can only say that the reward for doing good thorough jobs will be well worth the effort you put into it. And for those of you who will find easy enjoyment from the work, I urge that you spare nothing in your drive to bring into our parish the finest results that any canvass has ever made in the history of (name your church).

"As a canvasser you must do the following: One. Examine with us here at this meeting a list of those persons on whom you are to call. And select from that list those that you feel will be the most difficult to sign up on the Every-Member Canvass, and plan to call on them *after* you have called on those that you feel will be more easily persuaded by you. When you have had a chance to pick your tough prospects, discuss with the other people on your team, including, of course, your captain, the ways in which they would approach the difficult parishioner. We will at this time turn the meeting over to you individually at your tables. In front of you, at your place, is a list of those on whom you are to call. You are being asked to call on no more than ten parishioners, usually not more than five. Talk it over; there will be a limit of ten minutes on this discussion."

LEADER: DURING THIS TABLE DISCUSSION YOU SHOULD VISIT EACH TABLE AND DETERMINE IF THE VARIOUS GROUPS ARE HANDLING THE DISCUSSION CORRECTLY. HELP THEM IF THEY ARE NOT. THIS IS WHAT THEY

SHOULD BE DOING: EACH PERSON SHOULD BE QUIZZING
ANOTHER AT THE TABLE ABOUT ANY PARTICULAR FRIEND
THEY MIGHT HAVE. THEY SHOULD BE DETERMINING WAYS
AND MEANS TO GET TO THESE INDIVIDUALS AND FAM-
ILIES.

IN EXACTLY TEN MINUTES, CALL THE MEETING TO ORDER
AGAIN.

CHECK EACH MAN AT EACH TABLE. ASK HIM IF HE HAS
GONE THROUGH HIS LIST. ASK HIM IF HE HAS ANY PAR-
TICULAR QUESTIONS HE WOULD LIKE ANSWERED REGARD-
ING THE LIST OF PEOPLE ON WHOM HE IS TO CALL. THEN
GO ON AS FOLLOWS):

"We have gone over our list of parishioners, and they
have been segregated and discussed so that we are now
prepared to go out and talk to them as *individuals*. But
now we have to find out what we are going to talk to
them about. Your job as a canvasser poses a physical
problem of completing this canvass on 'C-Day,' or at
least within a week after 'C-Day.' And it also requires
that you know completely the subject you are going to
discuss with our parishioners. You must understand
that you have been selected to do an extremely important job for your church. It is as much the Lord's
work as kneeling in your pew on Sunday. As a canvasser today, you are the middleman in a revolution.
We are not launching the old type of canvass predicated
on underwriting a fixed operating budget. This is
rather the missionary work of spreading the basically
religious concept of Modern Tithing.

"A pamphlet has been prepared that tells the story of
Modern Tithing. We are not asking you to take my
word, the Bishop's word, but rather the word of hundreds of men like you: your neighbors. Today, we can
talk about what tithing *has done* and is doing for other
people, not what it could do nor what it might do. Let
me quote directly from the survey made by your diocese called 'What Tithing Has Meant to Me.' Before

we go into this survey, however, let's be sure we all agree on what Modern Tithing means.

"Modern Tithing means that the truly serious member of the church designates a definite portion of his income to church and charity—that five percent of his income goes for the support of his parish, the Diocese and the National Church. It represents the true realization that all we have has been gained through Another, and it results in a closer, more personal relationship between a man and his God.

"Maybe this sounds like a batch of fine-sounding generalities. Well then, let's read how your friends and neighbors say it. You have a copy of their statements before you. Let us take the next five minutes to read it."

EXACTLY FIVE MINUTES LATER, CALL THE MEETING TO ORDER.

"Let's read just this one introductory page again—

(LEADER READ):

" 'NOW WE KNOW.'

"During the past two years, the Diocese of Michigan —the Bishops, the Department of Promotion, and many of the clergy and laity—have talked about tithing in terms of what it would do for anyone who seriously gave it a try.

"The tone, up to this point, was, 'If you will try tithing, we *believe* this is what will happen to you.'

"Now, as we begin the third of our seven-year educational program, we come to a new phase of the discussion. No one need conjecture any longer. We can say, 'This is *what happened.*' Many people, in parishes all across the Diocese have tried it. We have seen tithing in action.

"We are on solid ground.

"No influence in life is more powerful than the influence of other people's actual experiences. No evidence is more conclusive.

"Here in this leaflet are verbatim quotations from people who have themselves been tithing long enough to tell you, first hand, how a tither feels—about Church, about life, about himself.

"The quotations printed here are taken from the results of a questionnaire sent to people in all kinds of parishes, and in 'all walks of life.' Here all sorts and conditions—mechanics, executives, housewives, lawyers, salesmen, teachers—tell you what has exactly happened to them as they practice tithing.

"We aren't talking theory any more.

"NOW WE KNOW!

"Now let's run through a few of the things these people said.

"One thing they said was that they no longer feel they are giving, but that now they are returning. What they mean is that they will remember that two years ago we started this whole tithing program with a pamphlet, the title of which was 'What Shall I Give for What God Has Given Me?' We are beginning to get results. People are realizing now that all they have has been given to them. It came from God—it belong to God. They are only *using* it.

"What I want to call to your attention is what it does to a man when he realizes that. It changes his whole outlook on life. He stops thinking of himself as sustaining himself by his own efforts, and as being a 'self-made man.' He's started to think of himself as what the Bible used to call a 'steward.' He has now become in his own mind the custodian of God's property, which is very different from being the frantic preserver of his OWN projects. An outstanding example of this is the Reformed Church of Spring Valley, New York. The congregation had to finance a new Sunday school building. But like most churches it did not have any money for it. One of the leading businessmen suggested that the members tithe for the new building. With the Reverend A. L. Wyckoff, the executive developed a most appealing and impressive bond certificate, to visualize and dramatize this proved form of giving. It was called a "Tither's Trust Bond."

As we cannot show the inside of the Bond, we give you herewith the wording which appeared at the top of the inside page:

THE TITHERS TRUST COUPON BOND

No._____   The Tithe

Taking Stock in your Religion
The Guarantee

Know ye all by these presents: "Bring ye all the tithes into the storehouse . . . and prove me now herewith, saith the Lord of hosts, if I will not open you the windows of heaven, and pour you out a blessing, that there shall not be room enough to receive it." MAL: 3:10.

This Is Not a Speculation: It Is an Investment.

Interest Payable Monthly: Principle Due at Death.

Do Not Expect To Draw Interest, Unless You Have Invested Your Principle.

This Bond Is Preferred as Assets, and Participates in Dividends.

Not Transferable
A UNIQUE AND UNPARALLELED FEATURE
OF THIS BOND

You, yourself, each month fill in the amount of interest you wish to take.

DIVIDENDS

There is also guaranteed to bearer, upon satisfactory fulfillment of the original conditions prescribed, which are: Bring ye all the *tithes*, bring ye *all* the tithes, bring *ye* all the tithes; an equal share in the undistributed surplus of benefits which have accrued, together with an equal share in those which have been accumulated by the Tithers Trust, also a blessing so great that there shall not be room enough to receive it—without our new building, also in the due process of time the New Sunday School and Recreational Building.

No limit is placed upon the amount of benefit allowed to one person, either in this life, or the life which is to come.

The consideration for this most unusual and remarkable bond is "The Tithe," that is, one-tenth of your income. It is offered on this sliding scale of cost so that it is within the reach of all. Five cents will buy it, if that is your tithe, five million dollars cannot buy it, if it is not a tithe.

Did the Tithers Trust Bonds pay off for the Church? You bet they did! They raised $50,000 for a church that had no money for the badly needed Sunday school building. Why? Because the unusual appeal and the Tithers Bonds reduced the irritation and embarrassment which some people in the congregation suffer when they start tithing.

If you have a similar problem and want to use Tithers Bonds, why not write the Reverend Mr. Wyckoff for a sample of the bond certificate?

We conclude this important *requested* chapter by reproducing the proven method which the Diocese of Michigan has developed for getting more members to make an annual pledge based on the biblical plan of tithing—but in a modern way. The following page reproduces the Tip Sheet which is followed by the mimeographed and printed material used by the general chairman and workers.

Now we reproduce for you the calendar used by the clergy and general chairman to schedule the various activities—all in relation to "C-Day" or Canvass Day.

THIS IS THE EDUCATIONAL CHAIRMAN'S GUIDE

Your job as educational chairman is to train canvassers, so that they make good calls, tell a convincing story, and bring back to the church results: modern tithing pledges.

This Meeting Guide will help you do this. Use it next fall with your canvassers as you see it used here today.

Two years ago the idea of modern tithing was to most of us a new idea. Some of us made progress the first year. More of us the second year. This year most of us

TIP SHEET

Your Job as General Chairman

1. You must first convince yourself of the importance to your parish, the Diocese and the National Church of the Every-Member Canvass. They form a spiritual as well as a physical viewpoint.

2. You must select, convince, and inspire a good group of captains and canvassers.

3. You must continually keep the prod under every one—minister, vestry, guild, team captains, and canvassers, until you are convinced that the canvass is complete. You must, in fact, be obnoxious in your pressure for the work of the Lord.

4. You must insist on and get reports and commitments when they are due.

5. You must help your fellow parishioners to enjoy a new experience in Christianity: MODERN TITHING.

will go out well prepared, especially if we follow the plan set forth in this guide. In the material supplied you for your canvasser instructions, you will find answers as to why people tithe and what we now know about the tithing situation in the Diocese. We have made a survey, and you will see it later in this meeting.

October

			1	2	3	4
5	6	7	8	9	10	11
12	13	14	15	16	17	18
19	20	21	22	23	24	25
26	27	28	29	30	31	

November

						1
2	3	4	5	6	7	8
9	10	11	12	13	14	15
16	17	18	19	20	21	22
23	24	25	26	27	28	29
30						

Steps

1 Determine C-Day
(write it in)

2 C-Day minus 30
Start your organization

3 C-Day minus 12
Personnel complete

4 C-Day minus 5
training sessions
C minus 3 - Make-up training session

5 C-Day plus 7
Report day

6 C-Day plus 14
End of canvass

7 C-Day plus 15
Start the clean-up

(THIS SCHEDULE GIVEN TO ALL PARISH CANVASS CHAIRMEN FOR THEIR OWN USE)

You have the job of taking men and women who have property.

"How would you like to help a man to change that way? How would you like to be the agent through which a man gets such a new outlook on life? Well, that's what you are! That's what this canvass is all about.

"Think what it will mean if you can plant this seed in the lives of the people in our parish!

"And do you see how different this is from the old-style canvass call, where you just went out and asked a man to underwrite a budget?

"A second thing they said was that they were relieved to be out of the hit-or-miss pattern in their pledging to church and charity. This is a valuable service you will be rendering as you go out on these calls. How many times have canvassers been asked the direct question: 'What shall *I* give?' and they have been unable to answer. Now you *can* answer: 'Five percent of income or as near as you can come to that percentage.' You can be definite, and at the same time impersonal.

"I think it will mean something to you if you can help take the confusion about giving out of the minds of some of the people of the parish.

"Do you see how different this is from the old budget calls?

"A third point: people said that tithing makes them feel that they are really IN the Church. Now they can call it OUR Church.

LEADER: SLOWLY, WITH EMPHASIS:

" *This is the biggest thing you will ever get a chance to do as a canvasser or in any other capacity.*

"For fundamentally, what is Christianity? Christianity itself is being a member—belonging, participating, being in a relationship—being in a Christian family.

"It isn't the clergy who 'save' people. People save each other—by *accepting* each other—by *belonging* to each other. Here in this survey are people telling us that this belonging—this 'salvation,' really—has come to them through tithing.

"There is nothing more important in anyone's life than that. Think what it will mean to you if you as a canvasser can bring that to some of the people in this parish.

"So you see how different that is from the old budget call?

"Fourthly: they told us they want their children to be taught to tithe. That they feel that it is unfair to the children *not* to teach them.

"Do *you* know how important this is?

"Ask a man what he wants for his children. Not what he wants them to have; not what he wants them to do— but what he wants them to *be*. If you ask him that, what he'll tell you will always in the end come down to the kind of relationship and the kind of inner living he wants for them.

"Here are people telling us that they have found such new relationships and such great inner change that *that* is what they want for their children.

"How would you like to be the agent through which that comes to some of the people in this parish?

"Do you see how different your job is from the old talking about a budget?

"Five. Some of them told us that since they began to tithe, they no longer feel some of the old inequalities that they used to feel in their relationship with other members of the church family. They have found that they are doing their fair share and the richest man in the parish can do no more. Do you see what this means? It pulls the parish together. It gives the parish family a chance to be a *real* family. Do you want to bring that to some of the people in this parish?

"Six. And in the survey, we found some things that indicate that we still have an information job to do. We found that people are not too clear on what the tithe really is. Some of them think it's duty; some of them think it's a device for raising money; some of them think it includes only the Church. They don't realize that charities are God's work, too. These are things that still remain for you to tell them. Minor things, perhaps, but part of the general education with which real tithing is to be undergirded.

"In all these things, certainly, you will see that your job has a dignity and a value that no canvasser could claim in the old days, when he went around asking people to support a budget. You are no longer a money-raiser. You are an agent of God with the wonderful job of helping people to a new richness of life.

"I don't believe a man here can help but feel the urgency behind Modern Tithing. And this brings us to another vital point of this session. Just what does tithing mean to you? Have you *personally* ever tried it? I charge you at this time to pick out your own canvass card and call first upon yourself. Think about this, because until you are convinced, you will have a hard job convincing others, and that is the great job the Church has asked you to do. If you can convince one person that they should enjoy the complete personal satisfaction of tithing, even though it be but yourself, you have performed a great missionary work for the Lord.

"We have asked you to make the first call on yourself. This should not be too difficult for you, as you are always available to yourself and probably enjoy talking to yourself. However, we have prepared for you a tip sheet and a number of suggestions on how most readily to handle calls on the other families assigned to you.

LEADER: HAVE A QUANTITY OF THESE TIP SHEETS AVAIL-ABLE—ONE FOR EACH WORKER.

TIP SHEET

"To assure a successful canvass, *you should plan to leave the better part of your next two weeks free.* It is important that you clear these arrangements with your family, so that they are not making appointments for you at the time when you wish to be out canvassing. On Sunday, immediately following church service, you will have a luncheon meeting with your general chairman and will receive your entire package of material. Having previously planned the order in which you intend to call on your people, you will be ready to start at the close of this luncheon meeting.

"To assure a brief and satisfactory call, first *contact the parishioner by telephone* and make sure that he and his wife will both be available to talk to you. In this way you can organize your time so that you are not contacting people while they are at dinner or have company. Before making the call you should study the family's church-record card. This will be available to you from the parish record card.

"With their record in your mind, you can *organize your call* and be prepared in advance for the points you can stress that will meet with a favorable reception.

"*Get there on time.* The very act of arriving at the time you stated you would be there is flattering to the person you call on. It also has the effect of giving you a good organization of your afternoon and evening.

"*Get acquainted with the family* if you do not know them. A few moments spent at this time can make the call easier, and you should have some familiarity with their interests from parish records.

"When you feel that you are on a friendly basis, you should *give them the tithing pamphlet to read*. It is a good idea to have the pamphlets available for all people who may be present. Being familiar with the pamphlet yourself, you can start a tithing discussion by mentioning certain statements which particularly appeal to you, or which you think might appeal to them.

"*It is important at this point that you endorse the tithing idea.* You can do this by explaining your stand on tithing. If you like the idea, but haven't yet reached the full goal, say so.

"Then be sure to ask the parishioner on whom you are calling if he has any questions to ask. Don't be afraid to say that you do not know the answer, but ask the parishioner if you can use his telephone to get him a true answer from someone who can, namely, his rector.

"*Then ask for immediate action.* Be sure you have a pen with you. Hand the man his pledge card, ask him if he wants one card for the entire family or separate cards for each member of the family. Also tell him that you have plain envelopes in which he may seal the pledge card if he so desires.

"If he says, 'I would like some time to think this over,' thank him and tell him you will *call back the same day,* and set a time. This procedure will very often result in his signing immediately or agreeing to have a signed card ready for you at a definite time later on.

"*Report every call.* This is extremely important. Immediately after completing a call you should spend the few moments required in recording on your parish card all comments made by any member of the family, whether these comments relate to tithing or are simply new items of interest about the family. It is through this important record that the clergy and the vestry can find out about points they are not now covering.

"If you have found it impossible—after repeated attempts—to see some person on your list, turn his card back to your captain, so that the clean-up squad can complete the call for you.

"We have here a film strip which we feel will tell the stoy of a not-so-good canvasser and another canvasser who had the right idea."

LEADER: AT THIS POINT HAVE THE LIGHTS TURNED OUT, AND AS YOU READ THE SCRIPT, SIGNAL THE PROJECTIONIST EITHER BY TELLING HIM TO ADVANCE THE PICTURE TO THE NEXT FRAME, OR BY RAPPING ON THE EDGE OF THE LECTERN WITH A PENCIL.

SHOW FILM

TIP SHEET FOR CANVASSERS

1. Clear the decks with your family.
2. Make dates with parishioners by phone.
3. Study the family's record.
4. Organize your call.
5. Get there on time.
6. Get acquainted with the family.
7. Give them the tithing pamphlet to read.
8. Endorse the tithing idea.
9. Ask for immediate action.
10. Call back the same day on slow signers.
11. Report every call.

MAKE YOUR FIRST CALL ON YOURSELF

WHY DO PEOPLE DECIDE TO TITHE?

There is apparently no single answer to the question of what leads a man or woman to try this way of giving. The incentives are many and various. Here are some of the reasons people gave when we asked them what made them decide to tithe:

"The way it was explained in church."
"Our Rector talked to us about it."
"We felt we were not getting as much out of life as we should."
"I heard another woman tell why she tithes."
"The Bishop told us about it."
"A Methodist friend told me about it."

"We want to express our gratitude to God."

"We realize that in not tithing we are not trusting God implicitly."

"I heard a sermon on the radio."

"As a lay reader, I couldn't urge others to tithe without trying it myself."

"The Diocesan literature convinced me."

"I heard a story about God's Acre on the radio."

"We talked about it in our discussion group."

THERE WERE PROBLEMS

No one goes into tithing casually. A profound reorganization of living habits is involved—for the individual and for the family.

Here is what people told us—about their apprehensions, and how it all worked out.

"I was afraid I couldn't afford it, but we manage to pay our bills and get along with plenty, thanks to God's generosity. We had a new home and many previous commitments, but as time goes on we are getting out of the woods."

"It solved all our problems in regard to budget, commitments, and—best of all—Church."

"The switch to a definite percentage was easy."

"Some luxuries had to be given up."

"One must cut other expenses."

"We don't give in order to receive, but actually the more we give the more we are blessed with."

"I don't feel as if I had given up anything. At first I did not know if I could work it—now it's easy."

"I just plunged in on faith, and reasoned about it afterwards. The only problem was that of giving up some of the 'things' which in the long run are of no importance anyway."

"A problem? Not when it's given freely from the heart, and to our best Friend. Since it all comes from God in the first place, tithing is the least we can do."

BUT HAVING TRIED IT THEY LIKE IT

Maybe it wasn't always easy, but when asked if they

now believe tithing to be a sound approach to Christian giving, here is what people said:

"It makes me feel I've been able to do a little for the One who gave me life."

"It takes the hit-and-miss out of giving."

"Yes—it helps to cultivate an attitude of mind in which giving is always present."

"It's the *only* way. No more doubts and worries about 'How much?' or 'Can we afford it?' Now we face only the positive question: 'Where can we do the most good with what we have to give?'"

"It gives one firm ground to stand on before God and man."

"It is a fair way. Everyone gives his fair share."

"It answers the all-important question: 'How much does the Church expect?'"

"It's systematic."

IT CHANGED THEIR RELATIONSHIP TO THE CHURCH

The tither sees things differently. That has been a constant claim of those who have been working with our parishes on the tithing concept.

One big difference in his outlook is in how he sees his church. Here is what people said about how that had been changed:

"It stimulated my interest in the Church's welfare."

"It has renewed my interest in working in and for the Church."

"The Church means more to me now. The Holy Spirit is always close to me."

"It makes me really a part of the Church."

"It makes it 'our' Church."

"It increases our interest in the Church, which automatically brings the Church into the center of our home."

"Your heart follows even one-tenth of your treasure."

"It has strengthened our relationship to the Church. There seems to be a more personal touch."

"There is a stronger bond."

"It helps us understand the Church's problems."

"Sure thing! Where you invest your money you want it put to good use. I find myself impatient with ineffective leadership."

"We have the satisfaction of doing this part of our job in the right way."

"It has made the Church a part of us."

IT CHANGED THEIR RELATIONSHIPS WITH OTHER PEOPLE

When God's world looks different, the people in it look different, too.

Tithers tell us they find friendships and family ties strengthened. Here is what they said:

"I have a personal responsibility now for bringing and training more people for God's family."

"There's a feeling of *belonging* you can't describe."

"It leads toward the Christ-centered family."

"It brings the whole family closer."

"You get real friendship out of your church."

AND IT CHANGED THEM INSIDE

The chief claim that has been made for two years has been that tithing will transform the tither. As first-hand evidence that this claim is true, here is what people said about how tithing affected them:

"Since we started we have never had a feeling of financial insecurity."

"I used to be distracted sometimes by the clothes of the obviously wealthy people of the parish. This no longer bothers me, because I know we are now supporting our church as well as they."

"The real fun is in the joy of being a 'rich man.' I find we can now give $50 where $5 was 'all we could afford' before we started tithing."

"It has brought us the warm feeling of satisfaction and accomplishment that comes of doing a job just right."

"Makes you feel much better."

"It is a good way of life."

"I realize now that to be the right kind of Christian I must give thanks to God in a practical way."

"It showed me the joy of knowing God."

"We grow in faith."

"I am much happier now."

SOME MATTERS WE MISSED

It never occurred to us to ask whether tithing was fun, or whether 10 percent seemed to be enough for a man to give. Enthusiastic tithers, however, told us all we wanted to know and a good deal more. Here are some of the "extras," the unsolicited information that came in:

"Giving does not need to be *limited* to tithing."

"I believe children should be taught to tithe when they are very young."

"Do start teaching tithing in the youngest Sunday school classes. Let the children grow up to responsibility."

"We are not giving—we are only returning that which we have custody of."

"It makes giving so very easy."

"The 90 percent now goes farther with us than the 99 percent did before we began to tithe."

"We would prefer to give more than 5 percent to the Church and less to charities. Our confidence in what the Church does with the money is greater than the confidence we have in some of the community things."

"If the one-tenth were followed by all professing Christians, Christianity would soon convert the world."

"Giving by tithing is fun."

Chapter 14

PRAYERS FOR USE
OF LAYMEN

W HEN A LAYMAN occupies the pulpit for the first time, or says his first public prayer at a meeting, he is naturally nervous. He knows he is not good enough to lead the congregation in worship. He realizes that some of those present may think: "What's that old sinner doing . . . acting as a holier-than-thou?' "

In this situation, the choice of prayers is most important. If the layman prays without a written prayer, or notes, he is apt to find himself stumbling through. His embarrassment may spread to the congregation.

If he reads a written prayer he may be more comfortable mentally, if he uses a prayer written in laymen's language.

Many readers of this book will find themselves in this situation. Therefore we give some prayers which lend themselves to use by laymen or laywomen.

PRAYER FOR PEACE

Come, Spirit of Peace, to an anxious world,
    Breathlessly listening, impatiently waiting
To hear the solemn music of thy majesty
    In all those strains of joyful promise,
That men have loved for ages—eyes straining
    For the vision of lasting peace; willing to endure
The stress for even the echoes of prophetic time!
    Peace, gently enfold thy peoples in prayer,
Grateful for the divinity of dreams the earth has known
    Nurtured in the soul of man, O, Spirit of Peace!
Despite the hate and fear that blinds to his sublimity,

Triumph, Oh Lord, in the very heart of man!
On the waves of the sea of human dream and thought,
 Bring us into harmony with thy ultimate glory,
  Dear Lord! Breathe Thy Word of Peace!

—Emily Barto

THE GOSPEL ACCORDING TO YOU

If none but you in the world today
Had tried to live in a Christlike way,
Could the rest of the world look close at you
And find the path that is straight and true?
If none but you in the world so wide
Had found the Christ for his daily guide,
Would the things you do and the things you say
Lead others to live in His blessed way?
Ah, friends of the Christ, in the world today
Are many who watch you upon your way,
And look to the things you say and do
To measure the Christian standard true!
Men read and admire the Gospel of Christ
With its love so unfailing and true,
But what do they say and what do they think
Of the gospel according to you?
You are writing each day a letter to men—
Take care that the writing is true;
'Tis the only Gospel that some men will read,
That Gospel according to you.

—Anon

Lord, Thou knowest better than I know myself that
I am growing older, and will some day be old.
 Keep me from getting talkative, and particularly
from the fatal habit of thinking I must say something
on every subject and on every occasion.
 Release me from craving to try to straighten out every-
body's affairs.
 Make me thoughtful, but not moody; helpful, but **not**

bossy. With my vast store of wisdom, it seems a pity not
to use it all—but Thou knowest, Lord, that I want a
few friends at the end.

Keep my mind free from the recital of endless details
—give me wings to get to the point.

Seal my lips on my many aches and pains—they are
increasing, and my love of rehearsing them is becoming
sweeter as the years go by.

I ask for grace enough to listen to the tales of others'
pains. Help me to endure them with patience.

Teach me the glorious lesson that occasionally it is
possible that I may be mistaken.

Keep me reasonably sweet; I do not want to be a
saint—some of them are so hard to live with, but a sour
old woman is one of the crowning works of the devil.

Help me to extract all possible fun out of life. There
are so many funny things around us, and I don't want
to miss any of them. Amen.

> —Written by a Mother Superior who
> prefers to remain anonymous

Dear Lord, it is not my will but Thine I seek to express in my relations with my fellow men. Thou hast
promised guidance, insight and strength, if I will but
follow Thy commands, as I best understand them. So,
with complete commitment and absolute trust, I shall
go forward this day, knowing that whatever Thou bring-
eth to pass shall in some way be for my good, and for
the upbuilding of Thy kingdom. In the Saviour's name
I pray. Amen.

MORNING RESOLVE

I will try this day to live a simple, sincere and serene
life, repelling promptly every thought of discontent,
anxiety, discouragement, impurity, self-seeking; culti-
vating cheerfulness, magnanimity, charity, and the love
of holy silence; exercising economy in expenditure,

generosity in giving, carefulness in conversation, diligence in appointed service, fidelity to every trust, and a child-like faith in God.

In particular, I will try to be faithful in those habits of prayer, work, study, physical exercise, eating and sleeping which I believe the Holy Spirit has shown me to be right. Amen.

—The Laymen's Movement for
A Christian World

THANK GOD

Thank GOD for little common things,
Small lovely things of every day.
Tree that is tall beside our door
And buttercups across the way.

Candles that flicker in the dusk
And fire-lit rooms where shadows play—
For silver fingers of the rain
Stroking a young tree's bending head.

For stars that blink thro' drifting clouds
And dawns that flame in gold and red.
Thank GOD for common lovely things
That are the spirit's daily bread.

—Anna E. Cunningham

"Grant, O Heavenly Sower, that as we tend and cherish the seeds we sow in our gardens, lest they perish, so we may tend and cherish the Divine seed of Thy Word sown in our hearts. May that seed never perish, but spring up and bear rich fruit in our lives. Help us so to increase in Thy Holy Spirit, that we too may sow seeds of truth and love wherever we go, which may bear fruit in the lives of others to Thy Glory." Amen.

—*Fellowship in Prayer*

A PRAYER FOR THE SOUL OF ONE
BELOVED IN PARADISE

O GOD, the GOD of the spirits of all flesh, in whose embrace all creatures live, in whatsoever world or condition they be: I beseech Thee for .... whose dwelling place and every need thou knowest. LORD, vouchsafe him light and rest, peace and refreshment, joy and consolation, in Paradise, in the companionship of the Saints, in the presence of Christ, in the ample folds of Thy great love.

Grant that his life may unfold itself in Thy sight and that he may find a sweet employment in the spacious fields of eternity. If he hath ever been hurt by any unhappy word or deed of mine, I pray Thee of Thy great pity to heal and restore him, that he may serve Thee without hindrance.

Tell him O gracious Lord how much I love and miss him and long to see him again, and vouchsafe him to me as a guide and guard, and grant me a sense of his nearness, in such degrees as Thy laws may permit.

If in aught I can minister to his peace be pleased of Thy love to let this be, and mercifully keep me from every act which may deprive me of the sight of him as soon as our trial-time is over; or mar the fulness of our joy when the end of the days hath come.

Pardon, O gracious Father, whatever is amiss in this my prayer, and let Thy will be done, for my will is blind and erring, but Thine is able to do exceedingly abundantly above all that we ask or think; Through JESUS CHRIST, our Lord. Amen.

—Mr. Griffen of The Church of England

MY PRAYER

Help me to live the Christian life in daring faith and humble trust, that there may be worked out in our congregation and even in me, Thy righteousness and goodness. May thy will be done by me in all I do and say and take and give, so that, through me and through the work of our Church, all men may learn to love Our Lord and Saviour Jesus Christ. Amen.

—Lutherans Laymen's Movement

TEN COMMANDMENTS TO HALT
JUVENILE DELINQUENCY

1. Thou shalt guard thy children in the home and on the street.

2. Thou shalt make thy home a sanctuary of love and devotion.

3. Thou shalt honor the teachers of thy children and teach thy children to honor them.

4. Thou shalt not condone the faults of thy children through a misguided sense of loyalty.

5. Thou shalt teach thy children respect for the law and keep them from the companionship of children who indicate a disrespect for the law.

6. Thou shalt not lead thy child into temptation by providing him with the means thereof: to wit—too much money, a car, and adult privileges.

7. Thou shalt enforce decency in the dress of thy daughters, and dignity in the dress of thy sons.

8. Thou shalt protect the morals of thy children from the indiscretions of youthful ardor and inexperience.

9. Thou shalt conduct thine own affairs in such a manner as to set an example worthy of imitation.

10. Thou shalt not permit thy children to bear arms except in the service of their country.

—Sam Levenson

PRAYER FOR BUSINESS EXECUTION

Our Heavenly Father, be with me through the coming day. Help me to be Christian in all I do, say, and think.

May I be able to ask Thy blessing on every plan I make. May I never take advantage of my position to hurt or hinder the welfare of my fellow workers. In all my relations with my associates and employees may I set the example of Christian living and Christian loving, in Christ's name.

—Willard A. Pleuthner

Chapter 15

BROADCASTING AND
THE LOCAL CHURCH

*By Charles H. Schmitz**

IN LANCASTER, Pennsylvania, a powerful, network affiliated *radio* station reports that its daily devotions by *local* ministers attracts a larger audience than they have for any other program, commercial or otherwise. In Syracuse, New York a pioneer, network affiliated *television* station reports that their daily *locally* produced religious program has a larger audience than the network produced religious programs aired on Sunday mornings. The local religious leader is a key person in the broadcasting field. He may do much to make religious radio and television truly effective.

The local religious leader needs to understand that the population of the world is increasing at the rate of 120,000 per day. The population of the United States is growing at a rate equivalent to a city the size of Omaha, Nebraska every month. About 30,000,000 people (mostly Protestant) change their address every year. How is one to reach the growing mobile population? What better way than by means of radio and television! These tools of communication have the possibility of reaching more people in less time than with any other tools. Broadcasting is never to be considered as a substitute for the church—it is to supplement and complement its life. Radio and television may bring the right kind of identification—personal, warm, friendly, quickly—at a time when it is needed most. The minister may make a pastoral call right in the home, visiting with the

* Director of Broadcast Training, Broadcasting and Film Commission, National Council of the Churches of Christ in the U.S.A.

people in his own community by means of these miracles of communication. This is really going into the world—but make sure it is with *the Gospel at its best!* It must be good radio and television, *and good religion.*

Purposes, Aims and Policies of World-Wide Christian Broadcasting

(with real meaning for local broadcasting also)

It is the mission of the Christian Church in fulfillment of her Lord's command to tell the good news of salvation through Jesus Christ to all people everywhere.

The urgency of the church's mission requires that every available means be used. Among the newer means of communicating the Gospel, radio and television offer the church a God-given means by which her voice can be heard by the millions still outside the Christian fellowship.

It is with a view to making the use of radio and television effective that we seek to clarify why we broadcast, what we hope to accomplish by means of broadcasting and what policies should govern our use of the media of radio and television for Christian ends.

I. Why We Broadcast

1. To reach the unreached. The urgency of the unfinished task of the church is such that we cannot afford to neglect the unparalleled potential of radio and television to cross every barrier and even to enter into minds and hearts hitherto closed to the Gospel. There are more millions who do not know Christ than there were fifty or even 25 years ago. We must accelerate and amplify the church's efforts to reach them. Other voices are being heard: the church's voice must also be heard.

2. To concentrate on reaching those whom it is difficult or impossible to reach in other ways.

3. To do for Christians what is not being done, or cannot be done as well by other means, such as bringing

spiritual nurture in the homes and areas from which people cannot readily come to Christian church and to encourage and enable them to spread the Gospel themselves.

II. *What We Hope to Accomplish*

1. To make Jesus Christ, Christian truth and the Christian way of life known, understood and accepted throughout the world.

2. To bring the judgment of Christ to bear upon our culture, and to speak to the condition of modern man.

3. To create a sense of responsibility and an awareness of the availability of spiritual resources adequate to meet modern man's every need and to better equip him for any task.

4. To stab awake, to disturb complacency and to create a tension between what is and what ought to be that can be resolved only by moving toward Christ and the church; and to hold before the world the concept, as expressed by Dr. John Mackay, that "the Christian lives a life of terrific tension, at the very heart of which there is abysmal calm."

5. To help the work of the Holy Spirit in the Christian and non-Christian and to keep alive an awareness that conversion is accomplished by God through human instrumentalities guided by the Holy Spirit.

6. To bring people into the fellowship of other Christians, in worshipping congregations that extend the leavening influence of the Gospel into the secular sphere, permeating every walk of life, every community relationship and all the institutions of modern society.

7. To deepen and widen the life of those already committed and to help them experience a oneness in Christ that impels them to take an active part in the evangelizing of others. In this regard, Christian broadcasting is to be supplemental to and not a substitute for the associating of Christians with each other in work, study and worship.

III. Policies

1. Christian broadcasting should be in the truest sense "communication."

2. The message presented must be given in the language and thought forms of the people for whom it is intended, and to this end indigenous persons should be used as far as possible in the interpretation and presentation of the Gospel over the air.

3. The gospel message as broadcast to non-Christians should be simple and positive, emphasizing those truths which are common to Christendom.

4. Christian broadcasting should be as relevant as possible to the actual needs of individuals and situations.

6. Careful consideration should be given to the extent to which the "non-religious" approach of many film, TV and radio programs can be made to bear fruit in a better understanding of the Christian concept of man's relationship to his fellow-man and to God.

7. We must keep before the leaders of the churches the importance of the use of these media and of the need to incorporate broadcast training in the preparation for the ministry and Christian overseas service; and to promote externally and internally attention to Christian broadcasting.

8. Continuous research will be necessary to ascertain the effectiveness of Christian broadcasting and should be encouraged.

These purposes, aims and policies from the perspective of world-wide Christian broadcasting hold equal weight at the local level and need to be taken seriously.

LOCAL RADIO-TV COMMITTEES

Through your local council of churches, or ministerial association, see to it that a radio and television committee is organized. This committee should consist not only of clergymen but also of interested laymen, women, a representative of a youth group and a representative from each of the local radio and TV stations. This committee should be given full power to act. This committee should be responsible for careful program planning. By planning is meant to study your own community to find out the number and type of stations and the number and kind (devotional, dramatic, news, interview, etc.) of religious programs they carry and the times these are on the air. Seek to discover the local needs in religious broadcasting of teen-agers, women, children, farmers, industrial workers, the aged, family groups, etcetera. Establish channels through which church members may register their opinions with respect to better broadcasting. This committee should provide broadcast training for qualified persons seeking to discover those with skills in writing, committee work, on-the-air talent, etc.

The committee should also take steps to promote and publicize the best in religious programs whether originating locally or nationally from the networks. Local church calendars and bulletins should be employed to call the attention of congregations to the excellent programs that are on the air, so that appreciation may be developed. Do not forget the religious emphasis in many commercially sponsored programs, and give these your commendation and support.

In all matters, enlist professional help where you can. There are a number of local radio and television station people who are also active loyal church members. Discover these people. You will find they are eager to help you to use these media in the wisest possible way. Write to the Broadcasting and Film Commission, 220 Fifth Avenue, New York 1, New York for program resources and broadcast training information.

FOLLOW-UP

The best in religious radio and/or television programming should have *follow-up*. This is a neglected strategy for the Christian use of thees media. Appropriate programs, whether produced nationally or locally, need to be *fitted* into the life of the local church. In an eastern city, a local council of churches put on a TV program called "Questions Children Ask," designed (with interesting giveaways) in a morning weekday hour to reach the mothers and children perplexed by such questions as "Why is Johnny a cripple?" "What is God like?" "Why is Good Friday good?" This was an ideal program to integrate into the life of the church, meeting a real need at the right time. The mass media are *points of contact* that need to be developed so that an audience reaction will be created, a kind of reaction favorable to the growth of the Kingdom of God. The local religious leaders are the key people in making best use of these points of contact.

More power to you and your associates in the full use of radio and television at the local level for the building of the local church.

The Broadcasting and Film Commission of the National Council of Churches of Christ in the U.S.A. has produced a most helpful book entitled "Television Do's and Don'ts." Its objectives are spelled out in its subtitle: "To Make our Words Useable . . . our Thoughts Real . . . Our Actions Meaningful . . . Our Faith Understandable." It shows Who, When, Where, Why, How and What.

Written by Dr. Charles H. Schmitz, this booklet covers these important subjects: Preparation, Still Pictures, Blackboard or Drawing Pad, Exhibits, Objective, Specimens, Demonstrations, Recordings, Interviews, Advice on Talking, Camera Presence, Make-up and Personal Appearances.

"Television Do's and Don'ts" is a gold mine of helpful advice and suggestions. You can get a copy for only 25c by writing the Broadcasting and Film Commission of the National Council of Churches of Christ, 220 Fifth Avenue, New York 1, New York.

Chapter 16

JOINT ACTION
BRINGS MORE SOULS,
MORE DOLLARS

By Joseph E. Boyle*

Hⓞw can the local parish or church compete these
days with the multitude of claims for the time, interest,
and money of laymen? That is a question which has
troubled clergy and laity alike. It is a problem which
many churches have had difficulty in solving, even with
worthy efforts.

It is unlikely that the pressure for the time, interest,
and money of the laity is going to decrease in the days
ahead; instead, it is more likely to increase and the
problem will therefore become more acute rather than
less.

What can be done about it?

More than 2,000 communities of the nation have in
the last four years found a new and at least partial solution to the problem. It is called the Religion in American Life campaign, nationally; locally, it goes by numerous titles. But whatever it is called, this new approach
to the community represents joint action on the parts
of churches and synagogues of many faiths and denominations. Let me add quickly that "joint action" in this
case has nothing to do with basic creeds and tenets; it
concerns itself only with emphasis on the importance of
religion to our American way of life and the importance

* Vice President in charge of public relations at J. Walter Thompson Co. Formerly Associated Press Correspondent and Director
  of Promotion, National Council of Episcopal Church.

of support—both personal and financial—for our institutions of religion.

The Religion in American Life effort has long passed the stage where it is mere theory; again and again communities which have used the plan for joint action have recorded these results:

—increased church attendance
—increased church membership
—greatly increased financial support

Here are a few sample reports:

Helena, Montana: "Many churches had the largest average attendance in the history of the community."

Crowley, Louisiana: "An average increased attendance of about 15 percent was reported, with many new members."

Worcester, Massachusetts: "Sixty-five churches secured $165,189 in new and increased budgets over the previous year."

One clergyman wrote: "It is like Easter every Sunday now," after the Religion in American Life plan had been carried out in his community.

What is it about this plan which makes it new and effective? It is simply the use of modern methods of mass communication on behalf of the Church. These modern methods can be employed to reach the people; the whole community. They include the newspapers, the radio, television, magazines, and outdoor posters. And the simple fact is that these media of communication cannot be used with the greatest possible effect by one local church or even one denomination or faith; they must be used on an inter-church, an inter-faith basis if they are to be used the way they can and should —and now have been used.

There is nothing particularly new about this method of approaching and influencing masses of the people. Ample proof has been provided by the Community Chests, the Red Cross, the Heritage Foundation, and other movements and "causes." But admittedly, organized religion has been slow to use a similar approach, because of the great differences in fundamental beliefs, terminology, methods of worship, and methods of finance. Religion in American Life compromises none of these individual characteristics: it merely provides a means for all the churches to talk to and influence whole communities, leaving to the individual to choose the faith or parish which he prefers to support.

Except for unusual events and occasions, the media of mass communication (newspapers, radio, magazines, etc.) long ago discovered that they could not give continuous time and space to the Church's message. At the same time, these media of communication realized that they should give continuous time and space to a limited number of efforts (limited primarily because of their own limitations of time and space) and, as a result, they organized what is called the Advertising Council. This Council is merely the joint agency of all major media of communication which screens and selects the causes to which these media will give concentrated attention during certain periods of the year.

The Religion in American Life campaign was organized to take advantage of these facilities, through the Advertising Council. A national committee of laymen, headed by Mr. Charles E. Wilson, supervises the campaign. This committee does not buy space and time in your local newspapers, on radio, television, outdoor posters, and in magazines. It pays only the mechanical cost of producing the advertisements and messages; the mass media *give* the space and time for the advertisements and messages.

But of course a local or community committee is essential to take full advantage of the materials and facilities which the national committee, through the Advertising Council, provides. Hence, in hundreds and hundreds of communities in all parts of the nation, local committees are organized to hold meetings, provide speakers and materials for attendance or financial campaigns. November is the period selected for this joint-action program on behalf of all the churches and synagogues. During November, on radio and television, in the newspapers and magazines and on outdoor posters, messages telling of the importance of religion; the importance of church attendance; the importance of taking the children to church or synagogue will be appearing.

If there is a community committee in your town or city, the individual pastor can get much help from it. If there is no community-wide organization, he still can use this period of religious emphasis to organize his laymen for calling on those in his neighborhood to interest them in church attendance and support.

No longer can there be any doubt that joint action by the churches brings more souls and more dollars. Again and again, the Religion in American Life effort applied to the local community has brought renewed interest on the part of the laity and increased pledges and contributions.

Religion in American Life is supported by this distinguished list of organizations:

The American Baptist Convention
The American Bible Society
The American Unitarian Association
The African Methodist Episcopal Church
The Augustana Evangelical Lutheran Church
The Church of the Brethren
The Congregational Christian Churches
The Disciples of Christ
The Evangelical and Reformed Church
The Evangelical United Brethren Church
The Laymen's Movement for a Christian World
The Methodist Church
The National Board of the Y.W.C.A.
The Presbyterian Church in the U.S.A.
The Episcopal Church
The Reformed Church in America
The Seventh Day Baptist Conference
The Synagogue Council of America

The United Church Men

The United Church Women

American business and the advertising industry provide nation-wide advertising during November through their public-service organization, the Advertising Council. The Volunteer Agency for the years of RIAL campaigns is J. Walter Thompson Co., New York, N. Y.

SEVEN STEPS
TO ORGANIZE YOUR COMMUNITY
FOR AN EFFECTIVE
RELIGION IN AMERICAN LIFE
PROGRAM

This brief guide outlines the SEVEN STEPS basic to a successful local Religion In American Life program. The guide is intended to provide tested methods for effective organization by a community in support of its churches and synagogues. It may be adapted or used only in part to meet local circumstances.

1. *Help "Spark" the Program*

RIAL can start in your community when one layman, one clergyman or the chairman of a "spiritual aims" committee of a service club believes that local action is needed to obtain full advantage of the RIAL advertising and publicity. Many successful local RIAL programs stem from the energy of one enthusiastic person. Will you start it?

2. *Enlist Every Interested Group*

After consulting with key clergymen, call a meeting by inviting one representative each from all cooperating churches and synagogue, *plus* the Y.M. and Y.W.C.A. Y.M. and Y.W.H.A., P.T.A., leaders of Boy Scouts and Girl Scouts, Boys' Clubs, Camp Fire Girls and other youth groups, General Federation of Women's Clubs, Business and Professional Women's Clubs, Chamber of Commerce, Junior Chamber of Commerce, American Legion, Knights of Columbus, Grange, Farm Bureau, and any other community groups with a religious interest who might desire to participate.

3. *Decide to Organize*

At this exploratory meeting, present the full story of RIAL—What it is. How it works. Who supports it. Its value and ways to get maximum results. (The RIAL story is contained in the theme folder, "SHOW THEM THE WAY—THIS WEEK.") Then, organize immediate action by getting commitments from delegates present to set up a General Committee. This is the over-all policy-making group and should consist of a key representative from each interested community group.

4. *Elect Officers*

From the General Committee choose the following officers: general chairman (preferably a layman active in religious and civic affairs) ; vice-chairman (a clergyman) ; vice-chairman (a layman who might become next year's chairman) ; secretary and treasurer. Also, select four able and experienced lay people to serve as chairmen of the following committees:

a. *General Publicity*— (For chairman, enlist the services of the person who directed publicity for your Community Chest, Red Cross, or similar efforts.) This committee will promote the use of RIAL advertising by local newspapers, television, radio and billboards; also, press coverage, window displays, and special events. Every newspaper will be offered free advertisement mats, every television station will receive two film strips, every radio station will be provided with a supply of spot announcements. The committee should encourage generous use of all this material.

b. *Promotional Literature*—for reviewing, purchasing, and distributing stimulating material to build up attendance in each of the *participating congregations*. Write to RIAL headquarters for samples, especially the RIAL kit.

c. *Telephone Invitations*—with an outstanding woman as chairman, to organize the women of the community to invite every family to religious services during November. This plan allocates the names of one page, or less, of the local phone directory to be telephoned by each woman. Example: In Marion, Ohio, every home-telephone subscriber received a personal invitation to attend worship services.

d. *Statistics and Records*—for setting up machinery to keep an accurate record of attendance each week in every cooperating unit during the month of November. Records might be tabulated and published in the newspaper each week or at the close of the campaign. Attendance-record reports are available from the national RIAL office for use in reporting (a) local church and synagogue attendance and (b) total community attendance.

5. *Set Up Time Table for Pre-Campaign Activities*

Establish a schedule of events timed to build up momentum during the fall months. Careful planning in advance will set up a timetable for a strong program of local promotion, simultaneous community events, and joint emphasis by participating groups. A full calendar of activities for November, or some other month, will increase the results of the local program.

PRECEDING MONTH

Publicity Committee plans local radio, TV, and newspaper coverage for November. Makes personal visits to radio and TV program directors and to newspaper editors to encourage consistent support. Example: In Paterson, New Jersey, daily sermonettes by layman and lay women on subjects like "What I Believe" were broadcast by the local radio station during the entire month; and both local newspapers carried front-page "boxed" sermonettes or talks by laymen every day of the month.

Have each cooperating church or synagogue send out first letter (second week) announcing plans. Enclose an attendance-builder leaflet such as "The Empty Pew" or "The Filled Pew."

Set up plan for weekly mention of RIAL in bulletins or calendars of each church or synagogue.

Arrange for special religious display in some centrally located business-house window.

Organize "telephone invitation plan."

Distribute posters to cooperating religious groups, business houses, and all others concerned with the effort for placement in windows or on bulletin boards.

Have each local church or synagogue set up a "welcome committee" for newcomers to services during November.

Appoint "attendance-record takers" in each local religious group.

LAST WEEK—place first newspaper advertisement.

Have each cooperating group send out attendance-reminder cards showing campaign theme—"SHOW THEM THE WAY—THIS WEEK."

Make sure every home has a RIAL sticker on the front door or window and that each car also carries one.

6. MONTH OF CAMPAIGN

Suggested outline, for each week in November, of special program, emphases, events, and other plans. Throughout the month it is especially important that all participating groups repeat each week the aim of the local program—to increase attendance and support for churches and synagogues. Constant repetition will spread the news of your RIAL program, and enhance its effectiveness.

FIRST WEEK Each clergyman of all participating bodies should announce through bulletin or pulpit the opening of the campaign as an intensive, month-long effort to increase attendance and support. Use the specially prepared RIAL bulletin or calendar from the national office.

Start telephone-invitation plan with a friendly invitation extended to every family in the community. Encourage everyone to "come to worship" every week during the month.

Place second newspaper advertisement.

Place notice in weekly calendars or bulletins.

Campaign chairman should check to see that all aspects of program are properly underway.

Mail Attendance Builder No. 1—"Your Spiritual Vote." Each church, synagogue, or group should mail these cards to every prospective newcomer to religious services.

SECOND WEEK Complete plans for a community-wide all (three) faiths "Thanksgiving-to-God" service. Where it is not possible for all groups to meet jointly, it is recommended that separate programs be set up for simultaneous observances. Suggested program: Two- or three-act play dramatizing the Thanksgiving period by local high-school or college drama group. This might be implemented by a community chorus or glee club using all Thanksgiving numbers.

Cooperate with United Church Canvass where such operates as a community project. Otherwise, conduct a campaign for attendance at worship services—a "go-to-church" emphasis.

Mail Attendance Builder No. 2—"By Proxy."

THIRD WEEK "Thanksgiving-to-God" community-wide service or program.

Designate this Sabbath or Sunday as "Service Club Day," "Youth Day," "Grange," "Legion," "Lodge," etc., and extend special invitations to all members of these groups and others in the community to attend.

Send letters of appreciation to local or national business groups who have contributed time (on radio or TV) or space (outdoor posters, bus cards, newspapers, etc.) for the RIAL campaign. *This is important!*

Mail Attendance Builder No. 3—"The Pattern You Set."

FOURTH WEEK Collect attendance records from each cooperating group, summarize totals and publicize.

Have newspapers, radio, television, and local clergymen announce results and general effects of campaign with a forecast of expanded efforts throughout the year leading to a greater campaign the following fall.

Mail Attendance Builder No. 4—"Real Security."

7. POST-CAMPAIGN SCHEDULE

A. Prepare and send complete record of local results to national RIAL office. Report full details of local RIAL campaign, showing statistics of attendance, week by week and for each church and synagogue for the month. Please use the RIAL attendance record form which will be sent to you. Also, please send to RIAL a complete set of newspaper ads, radio spot announcements, pictures of window displays, and other forms of local publicity. As a suggestion, a scrapbook with these various pieces of publicity is usually the best form of telling your local RIAL story.

B. Organize an "expression of thanks" letter-writing plan in appreciation of free advertising contributed during campaign. Encourage individually written letters to the radio and TV network presidents, your local newspaper advertising manager, your local outdoor-poster firms, local bus advertising companies and others who donated time or space. More specific details can be secured by writing the national office.

Although the annual RIAL campaign concentrates on November of each year, the work and activities of Religion in American Life goes on throughout all twelve months. At all times you, your church, or your local committee can secure from RIAL the following material for increasing church attendance . . . increasing church membership . . . and for increasing financial support:

	Rate Each
ITEM	
1952 RIAL PROGRAM KIT (includes samples of most items on this page). One copy free to a community. Extra copies	$ .10

SEVEN STEPS (A simplified manual outlining the basic seven steps which have been tested and found successful in the organization of an effective local RIAL program) .... .10

"SHOW THEM THE WAY—THIS WEEK" (Illustrated leaflet describing RIAL program, for distribution to clubs, societies, community groups). Limited quantities free. Extra copies........... .02

RIAL WORSHIP FOLDERS (Four-page folder, 8½" x 5½", with colored illustration on front cover, and inside pages left blank for local mimeographing or imprinting. Designed for use in local Sabbath worship or a community-wide union program or service)......................... .02

RIAL THEME POSTCARD (Postcard, 5½" x 3¼", carrying 1952 RIAL illustration and theme. For mailing to call local attention to your RIAL program effort to increase attendance and support) .... .01

RIAL ATTENDANCE PROMOTION POSTCARDS (A series of four postcards, 5½" x 3¼", each set in the series a different color, carrying RIAL illustration and messages urging worship attendance. To be mailed on each of four weeks in November or any other month, as a continuous direct-mail project):
No. 1. "Your Spiritual Vote" .... .01
No. 2 "By Proxy" .... .01
No. 3 "The Pattern You Set"................ .01
No. 4 "Find Real Security".................. .01

RIAL WINDOW DISPLAY POSTERS (16" x 28", heavy cardboard, in four colors, carrying RIAL illustration and theme. Designed for bulletin boards and store windows). Not included in kit.. .15
(Quantity prices: 25-99 copies—10¢ each; 100-499—9¢ each; 500 or more—8¢ each)

RIAL GUMMED STICKERS (3½" x 6" with RIAL theme and illustration in two colors, gummed on one side. Can be effectively used on auto, home, and business windows........... .01

THE EMPTY PEW (Successful leaflet for increasing worship attendance. Excellent for letter enclosure) .... .02

THE FILLED PEW (Campaign leaflet to "Empty Pew" with positive appeal. Good attendance booster for RIAL year-round emphasis)......... .02

Detailed information on radio, television, posters and other similar items relating to the localizing of the RIAL program will be found in one or more of the Confidential Bulletins issued periodically.

Note: Postage is extra on all orders. Material ordered cannot be returned for credit. Please allow at least 15 days for delivery.

Chapter 17

BRAINSTORMING . . .
THE NEW TESTED WAY TO
SOLVE CHURCH PROBLEMS

DOES YOUR CHURCH want to secure more new members . . . increase the size of pledges . . . or build up attendance? These are just three of the problems on which brainstorming has produced satisfactory results.

Now don't let the term brainstorming confuse or bother you. It's just another way of saying group ideation, or group dynamics, or thinking up ideas through a panel of people. It's called brainstorming because the participants storm a problem with their brains—commando fashion. The group drives for more and better ideas. It curtails everything that interferes with the development of problem solutions.

Started by Alex F. Osborn in 1939, brainstorming is being used by more and more churches, dioceses, and religious conventions. It differs from any other form of group activity mainly because of its four basic rules of procedure. They are as follows:

1. Criticism is ruled out. Adverse judgment of ideas must be withheld until later.

2. "Free wheeling" is welcomed. The wilder the idea the better; it is easier to tame down than to think up.

3. Quantity is wanted. The greater the number of ideas the more likelihood of good ones.

4. Combination and improvement are sought. Suggestions by others on an idea give better ideas. Combination of ideas lead to more and better ideas. These are

called "hitch-hike" ideas. You'll find them marked "HH" on the list of ideas starting on page 200.

The participants number from 10 to 15. They are given the problem at least two days in advance of the meeting. This gives them the opportunity of individual thinking, before the session. As a result most people come into the meeting with some ideas, to start the flow of thoughts.

Before the session starts its thinking-up period, food is served. This is either coffee and doughnuts or a simple lunch or dinner. This provides the relaxed or informal atmosphere which helps the group think up more and better ideas.

The meeting is run by a chairman who enforces the rules by ringing a bell when a brainstormer evaluates, uses judgment, or discusses an idea given by someone else.

A recording secretary takes down the ideas reportorially. She doesn't attach any name to the idea—just puts it down as he or she understands it—in one to four sentences.

The thinking-up period lasts from 30 to 60 minutes.

Here are some of the church problems which have been successfully brainstormed.

1. New things to do in connection with every member canvass.

2. Ways to make "Loyalty Sunday" more successful.

3. New and different ways to raise money.

4. How to get more members to participate in activities of church organizations.

5. New projects for the Men's Club . . . Ladies Aid . . . the Younger Married group . . . Sunday School.

6. Ideas for celebrating the 25th, 50th, or 100th anniversary of the founding of the congregation.

7. How can the church welcome new residents.

8. Ideas for getting more publicity for the church and its different organizations.

Here are some results secured through the use of brainstorming.

YOUNG PEOPLE FIND NEXT
YEAR'S PROJECTS

Lynne Pleuthner led a brainstorm session on what projects should be started by the young people's group of St. Joseph of Arimathea of Elmsford, N. Y. Several worthwhile activities were started as a result of this session.

FRENCH CHURCH USES 52
OUT OF 163 IDEAS

A Roman Catholic Church ran a brainstorm session on, "How to welcome new parishioners." The 163 ideas produced resulted in a comprehensive plan which included 52 of the ideas.

PRESBYTERIAN CHURCH ADDS
NEW SERVICES

The elders, trustees and deacons of Buffalo's Westminster Presbyterian Church brainstormed four problems. Over 100 suggestions resulted. One idea called for enabling office workers in the neighborhood to make better use of the church. This resulted in a new series of noon services during Advent, with an inexpensive luncheon following each service. These services proved so successful that a similar program was subsequently inaugurated for the Lenten season.

BAPTIST CHURCH PRODUCES OVER
100 USABLE IDEAS

Officers of the Greece Baptist Church in Rochester, New York, set aside a Sunday evening for brainstorming. Mrs. Virginia Shotwell, wife of the minister, reported that when 250 resultant ideas were passed on to

the proper committees and boards, they found that over
100 of the suggestions were helpful in setting up current programs and in formulating future plans.

ROCHESTER CHURCH DEVELOPS
NEW APPROACHES

A retreat of leaders of a Rochester, N. Y. church, the
elders and deacons and their wives brainstormed this
problem: "Ways to get more members to participate in
church activities." David J. Cull reported that the resultant ideas had "developed more participation and a
fund of new approaches in every phase of our church
work."

PARISH CHURCH ADOPTS 70 IDEAS
FOR COMMUNITY IMPROVEMENT

The Roman Catholic Church in Neuilly Sur Seine,
Paris, France, brainstormed the problem, "How to
make our community more livable." Fifteen panelists
produced 276 ideas. Through individual ideation after
the session, 82 more suggestions were added. Out of the
total of 385 ideas, 70 were found to be usable.

Recently a brainstorm session was held in connection
with the canvassers meeting of the Episcopal Diocese of
Newark. Bishop Stark reports that a panel of 16 men
and women produced 78 ideas in only 35 minutes.
Here are some of the ideas developed:

Note: "HH" indicates a "hitch-hike" idea, as developed in Rule 4.

I. *Materials*

1. Put more work and thought on material that goes
out before the canvass.
2. Be sure parish mission needs are clearly defined

in advance material not left to imagination of canvassers.

3. HH. Use a weekly leaflet sent to entire parish during active part of EMC. (Every Member Canvass.)

4. Do not be afraid to spend a little more money presenting and conducting canvass.

5. Supply canvassers with flip charts to use in illustrating objectives.

6. Seek out any existing professional fund-raising talent among your own parish to assist in guiding your own canvass.

7. HH. If no advertising people in your parish, solicit free aid from local advertising agencies.

8. Set a goal and keep parishioners posted (each Sunday) on how much has been received.

9. HH. Use thermometer chart to show canvass progress.

10. Use EMC slogans all-year round.

11. HH. Put book marks with slogans in prayer books and hymnals in church.

12. HH. Paste EMC stickers on your parish bulletin each month.

13. HH. Put EMC banner in front of church.

14. HH. EMC stickers on quota statements to pledgers.

15. HH. Have photo contest among children regarding church conditions.

16. HH. Show these pictures to congregation.

17. HH. Have prize contest for best picture of worst condition.

18. Insert dime or other coin with initial canvass mailing as an attention getter.

19. HH. Remind people to bring dime back.

20. Use film strip materials to show procedure on canvass.

21. Do whatever possible to make church look different during the EMC period (banners, tasteful decoration in parish hall, etc.).

22. In conspicuous place set up large display board.

23. HH. Include chart showing how pledges have grown over the years.

24. HH. Include pictures of similar sized churches showing their accomplishments.

25. HH. Borrow pictures from diocesan magazines.

26. HH. Borrow other EMC material from other denominations and communions.

27. Use material for National Council of Churches.

II. *Canvass Organization*

28. Have as many people work on canvass as possible.

29. HH. Call canvassers "visitors!" instead of canvassers.

30. HH. Ask canvassers to examine parish communicant list and select those who they would prefer to call on.

31. Have more than one chairman per canvass.

32. HH. Have a chairman for manpower, chairman for materials, chairman for dinners, meetings, socials, etc., connected with canvass.

33. Have two men and a child serve as canvass team.

34. HH. Use husband and wife teams.

35. HH. Use man and woman, not husband and wife as team.

36. EMC Committee should be appointed several months in advance of canvass.

37. Have a parish committee to work out mailing details.

38. Dinner meetings for canvassers should be open meetings to entire parish mission.

39. During canvasser training session, select more capable members of committee to give presentation of perfect pitch when canvassing.

40. Present award plaques at end of canvass:
    a. To canvasser who brought in greatest amount of money.

b. To canvasser who brought in largest amount of pledges.

c. To canvasser who brought in largest number of *new* pledges.

d. To canvasser whose pledges showed greatest increase.

41. HH. Announce the giving of awards at very beginning of canvass.

42. HH. Arrange for relief group of canvassers to fill in, in case of illness or other emergency.

43. Have each canvasser sign his/her pledge before going out to canvass.

44. Make lay visitations all-year-round affair after EMC.

45. HH. Have Canvass Committees to function all-year round.

46. No canvasser should have more than 4-5 visits to make.

47. Have more canvassers, so that entire canvass can be accomplished in one day.

III. *Church Organizations*

48. Officers of each Parish organization should be personally contacted by canvass chairman regarding EMC.

49. Encourage each church organization to have its own separate EMC meeting and make an organization pledge.

50. Use services, facilities and materials offered by the Department of Promotion of the Diocese.

51. Use Young People's Fellowship as part of drive organization.

IV. *In Calling and Soliciting*

52. Do not talk parish/mission budget to people being canvassed. (Known as pre-budget canvass.)

53. Stress missionary work is for Christ.

54. Describe parish expenses and give breakdown of share per person.

55. Give people idea of what proportionate amount their personal contribution represents of the total budget.

56. Make sure canvasser *positively asks for pledge.*

57. HH. Stress Christian Stewardship and the time is now.

58. Make all visits personally—none by telephone.

59. Make phone appointment prior to canvass visits.

60. Push church school all during canvass.

61. HH. Particularly canvass people who send their children to church school, but do not themselves attend church or pledge.

62. HH. Make people aware of the fact that church school budget is separate.

V. *Tithing*

63. Drive for more and more tithing.

64. Circulate reprints of *Reader's Digest* article on tithing.

65. Suggest that non-tithers start in as a "quarter-of-a-tither." (Two and one-half percent.)

66. Have rector/vicar lead and stress this concept of proportional giving.

67. HH. Special prayers to be said by clergy for tithers.

VI. *In-Church Activities*

68. Have a dialog sermon between rector and parish treasurer two or three Sundays before canvass as kick-off.

69. Give person idea of what proportionate amount their personal contribution represents of the total budget.

70. Suggest that non-tithers start in as a "quarter-of-a-tither."

71. Arrange for exchange of priests for the three Sundays prior to EMC.

72. During EMC have offering plate on the altar each Sunday.

73. HH. Have priest at the altar accept pledges and bless them.

74. Have each person go to the altar to deposit pledge.

VII. *Other Ideas*

75. Parishes and missions should conduct brainstorming sessions prior to their own canvasses to develop new ideas and approaches.

76. Have children fill out pledge cards of their own after they have been confirmed.

77. Have two Loyalty Sundays.

78. Get *new* people started on their giving before canvass time.

Would you like a free manual on how to start brainstorming in your congregation? Then write to Alex F. Osborn, president of the Creative Education Foundation. His address is 1614 Rand Building, Buffalo, New York. This manual tells you exactly what to do (1) before the meeting, (2) during the session, (3) the follow-up steps to take in the screening and developing the screened ideas.

Two notes of caution. Follow the tested procedures. They have proved successful in 20 years of practice. Don't use brainstorming as a substitute for anything your church is doing now to get ideas. It should be an additional, supplemental source of ideas from more church members on more problems.

Chapter 18

EXTRA IDEAS

T HE GLORIOUS PART about putting this book together is the use of the proven ideas sent in by clergymen and layworkers in all faiths—all denominations. They alone have made this book possible. We thank God for His help. May He bless all of you for your cooperation.

Just as in the case of our first book, *Building Up Your Congregation*, there are many good ideas for adding power to your church which do not fall logically into any of the regular chapters. So we put them all together in this last chapter. We pray you will find several ideas or plans which can be used in your church or synagogue. If you do not consider some of them "big ideas," remember that both morale and perfection consist of a number of little things done well. Likewise these little helps can produce big results.

1. Clergymen and devout church workers have long complained that business has overcommercialized our great religious feast days and celebrations. The comparison between the ways business and the Church observe Christmas and Easter would not be so unfavorable if we churchgoers would do more new and different things to call attention to these great religious festivals. One example is the Easter Parade held in the East Harlem section of New York City. No, it wasn't a showing of fashions and fabrics. This was a true Easter parade of

about two hundred devout worshipers, led by a crucifer with a simple wooden cross. It terminated in a recently cleared, open lot. There an Easter Service was conducted before a flower-bedecked altar, led by the ministers of the East Harlem Protestant Parish.

Churches which want to put up an impressive Easter Story panorama, 19½ feet wide by 7 feet high, on the church grounds, should write to William H. Dietz, 10 South Wabash, Chicago, Illinois. This reminds all passers-by of the Resurrection promise.

2. Here is how one growing church keeps track of its lost or missing members:

A simple, inexpensive way to "Save Church Members from Being Lost" is being used at Grace Church, Utica. At the back of the church there is a bulletin board which lists the names and addresses of the people who belong to the church, but whom the minister and leading lay people have not seen in church for quite a while. Then, as the regular churchgoers file in and out after services on Sunday, they have to pass the board and can see the names on it. It is their opportunity to volunteer to look up a certain family and invite them to church the next Sunday, or to report why they have been absent. By telling the minister's lay aide, standing beside him as he is shaking hands at the church door, the volunteer lay family can let their church know that they will try to save another family from being lost.

In Toledo, Ohio, "Go to Church" signs have been placed on benches at bus stops and other locations, as part of a local drive to increase church attendance. And there is choice aplenty, not far from where a new city bus bench is located along Collingwood Boulevard. Queen of the Holy Rosary Cathedral, Collingwood Temple (Jewish), and seven Protestant churches line the boulevard. Among them, and within a little more than a block of this bus stop, are the Collingwood Presbyterian, Washington Congregational, St. Mark's

Episcopal, First Unitarian, and Second Church of Christ, Scientist, Churches.

3. Has your church many golfers or sailors? If it has, here is a proved way to increase their attendance at Sunday services:

Few young people and summer visitors ever attended Sunday services at a little Long Island summer chapel. The minister, a 6 foot 2 former New England boxing champion, was puzzled by this as he began his first summer services. Soon he learned through interviews with the young people with whom his wife and he sailed or played golf on Sunday afternoons, that they never came to church on Sundays because it took away half their day. For the many who worked on Saturdays, it was obvious that they did not want to ruin their only day off which they could use for sailing and golfing. The young clergyman knew that he also liked to sail and play golf, but he wanted these good people to join their God first at the Altar each Sunday. Therefore, he moved the ten o'clock service up to 8 A.M.

His congregation grew from 12 to 65 and stayed there. He asked one of his young parishioners why, and he said, "Formerly I had to get dressed up for church, wait until 10 A.M. for church, and finally, at 11:30, I was in my sailing clothes and ready for the water. Now I can come to church in my sailing clothes. Our minister said, God primarily wanted us to worship. God didn't care what we wore as long as we were dressed. Then the minister served doughnuts and milk in the small parish room. After that all would go sailing together. The minister joined right with us, and that was good for all. No one had to go home again as the members were encouraged to bring their golf bags and sailing gear and leave them in the church vestibule."

A nationally known business leader, who for years has served as a leader of the Long Island Church, said in the 1930's, "That young clergyman will be a Bishop some day and lead thousands of people into the Church." His prophecy came true in 1950.

4. We like the introduction to that interesting, helpful booklet "101 Things a Layman Can Do" (10 cents a copy, from Presiding Bishop's Committee on Laymen's Work, 281 Fourth Avenue, New York 10, N. Y.). It inspires as follows:

GREETING . . .

Have you ever moved to a new community, knowing no one, feeling utterly lonely? It can be a dark day, indeed. Or, have you ever been stranded in a strange community on a week-end? There is nothing very uplifting about the four walls of a hotel room or a table for one in the corner of the hotel dining room. Or again, remember some of those homesick week-ends at school or college when a touch of home life would have lifted the pall of loneliness?

People are having just such experiences constantly. They crave fellowship. And they should be able to find it in the Christian Church, if anywhere. Sometimes they do. Sometimes they don't. Whether they find friendly people or not in a church may be the basis upon which they will judge the Church. A friendly church attracts. A cold church drives people away.

One way to carry out this Christian advice is to be on the alert for new families moving into your neighborhood. Do not wait to make a formal call, drop in right away, even when the moving van is still disgorging its precious load. After you introduce yourself, ask if you can run any errands for the newcomers, or answer any questions about local sources of food, drugs, schools, etc. Better still, take the new family something to eat and drink. A plate of sandwiches and a bottle of milk shows your Christian friendliness—it does it better than just a verbal expression of interest.

After you have given the new neighbors information about the neighborhood—shopping, medical care, schools—*then* say, "If you have no other plans for church *this Sunday* we would like to have you worship with us at (name of church) ." Should you find that the new people are of another faith or denomination tell them where the nearest church of the choice is located. And then be a helpful Christian by phoning the clergyman of their church, telling him about his new prospective parishioners. When we cooperate in this way with other churches and synagogues in our city, we prove the Brotherhood of Man.

Some influential churches organize this greeting of new neighbors on a basis of assigning neighborhoods and sections of the city to appointed lay greeters. This is a sure way to make certain that the calls are made as soon as possible. It is the way to help the clergy in this vital activity.

Experience shows that moving to a new city or neighborhood is one of the chief causes why people get out of the habit of attending church regularly. Let's all prevent this from happening by greeting new families just as soon as possible. Remember every unloading moving van is an opportunity for you to show your "love for your neighbor."

5. Here is how a minister extends the right hand of fellowship to newcomers:

When Mr. and Mrs. Milton M. Schneiderman and their son Laurence, 6, arrived in Saginaw, Michigan, from Arlington, Virginia, their furniture was hardly in place before the Rev. Howard B. Spaan, pastor of the Community Christian Reformed Church, rang the Schneidermans' doorbell. He welcomed them to Saginaw on behalf of the city's seventy-seven Protestant, Anglican, Orthodox, and Jewish houses of worship.

Spaan gave the newcomers a church directory, got in return a card stating their religious preference. He sent the card to Rabbi Harry A. Cohen of Saginaw's Temple B'nai Israel, who took over from there. The call on the Schneidermans was part of a new and unique interfaith visitation program sponsored by the Saginaw Ministerial Association. Twenty-four denominations and two local synagogues are cooperating.

Saginaw has been divided into eleven zones with a pastor assigned to each. The Ministerial Association receives a list of all newcomers from the local credit bureau, passes the information to the appropriate zone clergyman, who makes the first call. Dr. Don A. Morris, pastor of Saginaw's First Methodist Church, and Ministerial Association president, says ten to fifteen families a week are guided to the church or synagogue of their choosing.

Surprised and pleased, new Saginawan Schneiderman summed up his impression of the program in words which Dr. Morris said were typical:

"Sometimes you put off finding out about a new church in the bustle of moving. This makes it easier for us to join in the community."

6. *Pathfinder* magazine ran the following news story about an Oklahoma minister who finds sermons in comic strips and trains children to discover religion in funnies.

"When Charlie Shedd was a kid, he often sneaked out behind the barn and read the comics there—to escape the wrath of his strict minister father.

"By last week, memories of those juvenile escapades had led to a novel idea in young people's religious training: the 'God in the Funnies' program of the thriving First Presbyterian Church of Ponca City, Oklahoma.

"Now thirty-four, and the First Presbyterian's pastor, Charlie Shedd periodically sets aside one of his regular Sunday young peoples' vesper services for a discussion of who found what signs of God's work in the funnies the previous week.

"Sample discoveries:

"Rusty Manning, eleven, was impressed by a sequence in 'Terry and the Pirates' showing soldiers radioing for help. 'They just barely got their signal

through,' he reported, 'so God must have been with
them.'

". . . Nancy Ramsey, seventeen, noted that L'il Abner
fell in love with ugly Nancy O., 'which proves that real
beauty is on the inside, and everybody is beautiful to
someone.'

". . . One small girl, an 'Orphan Annie' fan, pointed
out that 'if Gramp had told God instead of Bancroft
he'd committed a crime, he would have gotten it off
his chest earlier.' "

7. The First Presbyterian Church of Sebring, Florida,
opens its 11 o'clock Service with chimes. This musical
opening provides an ideal background for the start of
one's worship.

8. The Western Massachusetts churches have a special service the Fourth Sunday in January, which other
congregations could adopt with real benefit. It is for the
reaffirmation of marriage vows. Standing before God in
the churches, husbands and wives repeat in unison:

"I have often failed to do my part in our life together," and chorused, in separate groups:

"I have taken you . . . to have and to hold, for better,
for worse, for richer, for poorer, in sickness and in
health, to love and to cherish, till death do us part,
according to God's Holy Ordinance, and today I gladly
reaffirm that vow."

In many churches, as in St. Luke's, Springfield, the
couples married the shortest and the longest time stood
before the priest at the altar, while others repeated the
vows in pews.

9. The Reverend Charles Allen of Christ's Church,
Atlanta, Georgia, writes a Sunday newspaper column
for the *Journal Constitution*. To find out if people were
reading his column he offered to send a color reproduc-
tion of Christ, billfold size, to anyone who wrote in.
More than ten thousand requests came in for nearly

60,000 copies of the picture. This is an idea which can be adopted by religious broadcasters, other religious columnists, and churches whose services are on the air.

10. A growing number of churches celebrate Family Week. This is built around the basic idea that "Faith is a Family Affair." Family Week develops rich dividends for the coming years. Here are a few simple things which help form a program for Family Week:

a. Attend church as a family, and sit together in a "family pew."

b. Read helpful literature on the family, provided by the Church and its organizations.

c. Listen to the good regular family radio programs and to special broadcasts, like "The Upper Room Family Week Series."

d. Develop some family recreation or hobby.

e. Establish daily family devotions, using a devotional guide.

All these help carry out the following truth: "The Family That Prays Together Stays Together." This is a slogan or truism that deserves a frequent place in your church bulletins.

11. Bass Hawkins of Lake Ronkonkoma, New York, likes to carry God's message to the hundreds of thousands who read the fine Saturday church page of the *New York Herald Tribune*; so he runs, and pays for, two column by five inch ads on this page. Each features a list of Bible readings which have to do with world events.

Mr. P. L. Norton is another devout Christian who is using a large share of his income to bring the Sermon on the Mount to the readers of newspapers. His full-page ad, "Can You Spare 9 Minutes to Read a Message 19 Centuries Old?" has appeared in the *New York Herald Tribune* and Washington newspapers. His Sermon on the Mount Project offers free reprints of the page and free mats which other Christians can use to

publish the Sermon in their local newspapers. All you
have to do is write Mr. P. L. Norton, Room 706, at
1790 Broadway, New York 19, N. Y. He sums up his
objective for this project as follows:

"WE BELIEVE there is no problem of any kind, concerning the individual or family, the community or
commonwealth, or of any 'ism,' or among the nations,
which would not yield to the intelligence, the courage.
and' the faith of free human beings, *if those who seek
solution* approach the problem in the spirit of the
Sermon on the Mount."

We who try to follow Christ's divine guidance in
The Sermon on the Mount are glad to know that this
secret of inspired living is now recorded. Yes, the record
is available for use in the home, school, hospital, prison,
and other institutions. Write H. C. Burke at 306 South-
way, Baltimore 18, Maryland, for complete details.

12. Stamp collector Arthur R. Von Wertheim decided to collect stamps which illustrated the Lord's
Prayer. The April 17, 1952, issue of the *New York
Herald Tribune* illustrated his collection. Each stamp
depicts a section of the prayer as follows:

(Portuguese stamp) "Our Father who are in heaven
. . . (Vatican City) Hallowed be thy name . . . (French
Somaliland) Thy kingdom come . . . (Brazil) Thy will
be done, on earth as it is in heaven . . . (Romania)
Give us this day our daily bread . . . (Croatia) And
forgive us our debts, as we forgive our debtors . . .
(Monaco) And lead us not into temptation . . .
(France) But deliver us from evil . . . (Austria) For
thine is the kingdom and the power, and the glory, for
ever and ever. Amen."

A stamp collector in your church could develop an
interesting exhibit for your Sunday school and vestibule
by duplicating Mr. Von Wertheim's collection:

    Portuguese—2½ Reis
    Vatican City—3 lire MCMXLIV
    French Somaliland—10c postes

Cote Française Des Somalis
Brazil—3.00 of 1934—Franchieta
Romania—3700-5300 Posta Lei
Croatia—16 + 8 kn. N.D.Hrvatska
Monaco—50
France—Postes 2,50.50
Austria—IS 40

13. Jack Garvin, of New York City, has an excellent idea for increasing church attendance. He points out that around 10 percent of the public is hard of hearing. Too many of these people dig up all kinds of excuses to play "hookey" from church services. They figure that if they cannot hear the sermon why bother going to church. One way to solve this problem is to install hearing aids in some pews. Then advertise this helpful service in your newspaper announcement and outside bulletin board. Another solution is for the clergyman to urge in his weekly announcement that the congregation tell their hard-of-hearing friends—their absentee friends—that they can enjoy the sermon, the same as everyone, by wearing a hearing aid in church.

14. If you have a dance instructor in your congregation she might be interested in duplicating the interesting project staged by the Oneonta Congregational Church of South Pasadena, California. This group took literally that part of the 149th Psalm which reads: "Let them praise His name in the dance." They interpreted the Lord's Prayer in a liturgical dance. This is quite proper, as dancing was probably one of man's earliest ways of worshiping his maker.

15. Herbert N. Morford, Superintendent of the Hospital of the Good Shepherd in Syracuse, New York, is a Christian who takes his religion into his everyday life. He helped re-establish the Huntington Chapel in this fine hospital.

Just after a patient is admitted he or she receives an

attractive card inviting the use of the chapel. This invitation reads:

"The Chapel, open every hour of the day and night, is for the hospital family, workers, patients, and friends. A place of spiritual refreshment, beautiful, intimate, restful, the Chapel seems to say:

" 'Whoever will, may enter here, of any creed or no creed. Whatever your care, your problems, your sorrow, your hope, yield your best self, make of me what you will, I am at your service.'

"In silence, in thought, in prayer, in search for fresh light and faith, in a few moments of reading, or of music, we gain courage and hope: we go out refreshed, strong, serene, confident."

This is a Christian service which should be available in more hospitals, for there we are often very close to our Maker.

16. The Reverend Harold J. Quigley has used most unusual methods for his unusual success in tripling the membership and attendance at the Central Presbyterian Church in Haverstraw, New York. The objective was to dramatize the pastor's search for a congregation—the search for *real* churchgoing Protestants among the passive stay-at-home Christians.

Pastor Quigley took a kerosene lantern in hand and went looking through the homes, stores, and banks of this conservative community of 8,000. He told people he was searching for the lost membership and vigor of his faith; not exactly lost, perhaps, but definitely mislaid.

He took a picture of a typical small Sunday congregation . . . enlarged the picture . . . and lettered over the empty pews: "Where are the others?" This home-made sign was publicly shown in the midtown window of the People's Bank. Because of no money for advertising, he made over large hair-tonic posters to carry challenges to the stay-at-homes and backsliders. To increase Sunday school attendance and interest youth in

Central Presbyterian, the Reverend Mr. Quigley turned the church's little basement into a roller-skating rink. Realizing that Rockland County is the home of many famous artists, this progressive pastor organized a three-day art exhibit at the church.

Yes, one would say that all of the Reverend Mr. Quigley's method's are dramatic. A few might say they are too "undignified." But these same people might say that some of Christ's miracles were also "undignified." We do know that conservative Haverstraw said they liked this search for a congregation. They said it with increased membership and attendance.

17. Rabbi Jacob K. Shankman has a service at Temple Israel in New Rochele, New York, once a month, called "Family Worship." Parents bring their children with them to worship. The service is abbreviated (easier on the squirmers) and the sermon is directed to the children, but planned to be of equal interest to the parents.

18. In another part of this book we have referred to the advantages of sending out blotters to members. The Reverend Frederick R. Ludwig, Pastor of St. Paul's Evangelical Lutheran Church, Postville, Iowa, uses these long-lived reminders in a most logical way. He sends them out a Lenten blotter containing the subjects of the sermons at his mid-week services. We like his basic theme (or slogan) used on his printed literature: "You Are Always Welcome At St. Paul's." We all applaud the Reverend Mr. Ludwig's use of the truism: "Christians Attend Church, Others Find Excuses."

19. Here is an ideal way to assimilate new members: When a new member joins the Men's Club of First Presbyterian Church, Bay City, Michigan, he is given a card listing all phases of the group's program. He chooses the activities in which he is interested and for which he is fitted before some enthusiast tries to influ-

ence him in the wrong direction. Youth groups and
women's societies use this device in other cities.

This plan is used by Christ Church in Tacoma, Washington, with equal effectiveness.

20. Has your church considered this growing means
of getting more people into a church service?

Last summer many churches experimented with outdoor Sunday services in drive-in theaters and parking
areas. All can hear and see while seated comfortably in
their cars. Some have called early services 'picnic spe-
cials' because they give picnickers opportunity to worship in their picnic outfits at an early hour.

Among churches which reported drawing up to four
times average church attendance last year were St.
John's Lutheran in Buffalo, Zion's Lutheran in Utica,
New York, and First Christian, Virginia, Illinois. All
plan to repeat. Early preparations and publicity are
recommended.

The Reverend George A. Rustad, State Director of
Arizona's Seventh-Day Adventists, and Elder Lawrence
E. Davidson have both pioneered in drive-in church
services.

A typical drive-in service begins at 8 P.M. after a
half-hour prelude of organ music. Elder Davidson opens
with a story for the children, then runs off a thirty-
minute religious movie, or a "family problem" movie
with such titles as *Love Thy Neighbor* and *Honor Thy
Family*. After a brief prayer, Davidson (or a guest
speaker) begins the half-hour illustrated sermon. Since
May, both drive-ins have been drawing steady crowds.
(Top attendance so far, for a visiting minister: 2,000.)
Says Adventist Rustad: "We live in a new age, and the
churches should keep moving with the times."

21. The influences that are desirous of destroying
Christianity are hard at work at home and abroad. The
challenge must be answered. The Heifer Program was
originated so that important groups of Christians, *the*

farmers, could help in the fight without leaving their farms.

Each farmer is asked to raise a heifer; the church will buy the calf and deliver it or will buy the calf direct from the farmer.

The farmer raises the calf until it is ready for breeding; then the Church breeds and sells the heifer.

If a farmer prefers to raise a steer, we will be grateful. If he prefers to donate a calf or older animal, we welcome and are thankful for his cooperation.

Most farmers take care of vaccination themselves in the course of having their own stock treated. The Laymen's Committee, however, agree to do this if the farmer doesn't wish to have it done.

If a farmer for any reason moves, loses his farm, retires, or any unforeseen contingency arises, the Laymen's Committee will remove the animal from his farm upon notice.

A directory of cooperating farmers is maintained at the Bishop's office. The Bishop will visit each farmer and give his personal thanks.

All placements should be reported to the undersigned so ear tags may be arranged for.

> Carl O. Hoffman, *Chairman*
> Bishop's Committee of
> Episcopal Laymen.
> "Broadfields"
> Chestertown, Maryland.

If you have a rural church, this project is one which is well worth considering.

22. The Community Synagogue of Rye, New York, believes in worshiping God outdoors during the summertime. Rabbi Samuel H. Gord places the Ark between the outside pillars at the front of the building. The service is held on the lawn in front of the Ark. There's a church down in Greenwich Village that holds Sunday night services outside. Worshiping out of doors is a change of pace that congregations appreciate and

that has many precedents in the Bible. Has your church
the grounds and the chairs to do this?

23. Minnesota has made at least two experiments in
using drive-in theaters for church services.

Reverend Morris C. Robinson of Grace Presbyterian
Church, Minneapolis, writes the City Church:

"Our Church sponsored a drive-in church service at
an outdoor theater some eight miles from the city and
just a few miles from Lake Minnetonka, which is a
heavily populated summer resort area. We had guest
ministers for three of the services and I conducted the
other four. Since we expected the congregation to be
made up of people of all denominations, we felt the
offering should go to the work of Cooperative Christianity and we are sending checks very soon to the local
Church Federation, Federal, and World Councils of
Churches.

"Our attendance varied from a high of two hundred
cars to a low of seventy cars. Our ushers estimated that
the number of people per car averaged three and one-
half to four. We had many expressions of appreciation
from people who, because of a physical handicap, could
not attend regular services. One elderly woman who
attended every service had not been able to attend
church for five years. A woman who suffered a stroke
two years previously and who had been unable to be in
crowds since, attended every service. Many young parents attended with children in arms or children of
younger years who played on the theater's playground
equipment.

Our session is planning on services again next year,
the first Sunday in July through the first Sunday in
September."

Advance reports that on July 2 Dr. Howard A. Ver-
non of the Congregational Church of Brainerd, where
the local theaters had carried a trailer for several weeks
announcing the "Church of the Open Air," found himself facing a congregation of 639 at a drive-in theater

six miles north of town. Some of these were local townspeople, old folks, and shut-ins, and vacationers. Later attendance passed the one thousand mark. "Come as you
are and remain in your car," ran the invitation—and
they did, "in cool, comfortable clothing." Local news-
men pointed out that this sort of service seems to throw
the members of a family unit into much closer relationship to each other. When some youngsters "acted up" a
bit in the back, others were not annoyed. A church previously closed for the summer discovered new family-as-
a-unit values along with large attendance.

Is this a modern equivalent of the old camp meeting?
Could your church organize and conduct an open-air
church? It would bring Christ's message to those who
might otherwise be unable to reach or be reached
frequently.

24. *The Gold In Your Backyard.*
"What we need is a talent committee in every parish
that can explore and find out what people can do or
what they would like to do."

These words are from a fine pamphlet written by
Bertram Parker, entitled, "I Am a Layman." (Available
at 3 cents each or $2.25 per hundred from Presiding
Bishop's Committee on Laymen's Work, 281 Fourth
Avenue, New York 10, New York.)

Check your congregation thoroughly; list the people
with skills and talents. Ask them, invite them, and use
them. They will be pleased and the church will prosper.

Form a committee and call the members "Talent
Scouts for Christ." They could send out and process a
questionnaire to be tied in with announcements from
the pulpit and in the church bulletins as to its intent.

25. *The Flying Deacon.*
Looking for a new and profitable idea for your
church fair or bazaar? Here is one that was fun for all,
those who worked in it and those who patronized it.

At a meeting of the college group in a Syracuse, New

York, church, their role in a forthcoming "fair" was brought up for discussion. With sighs and moans the young people said that the fair was the same every year and was a matter of Christian duty rather than a looked-forward-to event. Why couldn't it be both? The ministers called for ideas, new and workable ones.

A young man who was a professional photographer suggested that a photo booth with different backdrops could be worked out. The big thing was to deliver pictures on the spot and at reasonable prices.

Young college art students volunteered to paint several.comic backdrops, and amateur carpenters offered to construct the booth. A retired wooden horse from an old carousel was offered; others agreed to repaint and mount it. There would also be plain backdrops for "glamour" pictures. A polaroid Land camera was made available. This camera produces a 3 x 5 finished print sixty seconds after the picture is taken. Film and flashbulbs were obtained at cost helping to make low charge possible. By this time, every member of the young peoples group had a job to do and the group as a whole accepted other duties at the fair as well.

The photo booth was advertised in the church bulletins and programs. Displays were put up in the vestibule and Sunday school hallways. Parishioners were urged to bring entire families and friends to have their "picture took."

The booth was the hit of the fair and drew the largest crowds. Young cowboys had their pictures taken on the wooden horse, and the comic backdrops caused much amusement. A favorite picture was to have the church elders seated on the small horse with their coat tails trailing behind, hence "the flying deacon." It was fun, good public relations, because everyone, young and old, entered into the spirit of it. And the group raised more money than ever before.

26. *An Effective Hospital Ministry*

We all remember that well-known statement of

Christ's in St. Matthew's gospel, "I was sick and ye visited me, in prison and ye came unto me." Yet how few of us ever take on a planned Christian project of visiting people in hospitals or prisons. An inspiring example of service to hospitalized people is the dynamic program developed by the Los Angeles Baptist City Mission Society. Here is how it is described by Arnold S. Boal, Assistant to the Executive Secretary, in an issue of *The City Church Bulletin*.

"Many newcomers to the Los Angeles area apparently packed their church membership in mothballs when they moved West. In an effort to minister to the patients in the Los Angeles County General Hospital, one of the largest in the world, the Baptist City Society found that eighty percent of the patients who registered Baptist preference had no local church relationship. Consequently, a chaplaincy was instituted to provide double service. Patients are visited and aided while in the hospital. Then, in cooperation with local churches, there is a well-organized follow-up of dismissed patients.

"When patients are contacted in the hospital, they are provided with spiritual help, counsel, literature, and other services. Worship is conducted in the hospital auditorium, to which patients are brought in beds, wheelchairs, etc. Young people from churches in the area are enlisted to bring the patients from their wards to the auditorium. Those who cannot be moved are able to listen to the broadcast of the service by using earphones provided by the chaplain.

"A friendly call in the home following an experience in the hospital has produced amazing results in spiritual restoration. One staff member provided by the Woman's American Baptist Home Mission Society gives full time to this follow-up ministry and has the assistance of volunteer visitors in almost every Baptist church in the area.

"The magnitude of the work is indicated by the fact that over 1,600 Baptist-preference patients pass through the hospital each month. Scores of these patients are finding the joy of new or restored Christian fellowship in local churches.

"Baptists, with a burning sense of mission and foresight which anticipated this phenomenal growth, formed the Los Angeles Baptist City Mission Society in 1906. The Society has been the missionary arm of existing churches and the fostering agency for scores of new churches during the intervening years. For the past fifteen years Dr. Ralph L. Mayberry has been Executive Secretary of the Society and is largely responsible for its present program, which is outstanding in scope and effectiveness."

Most of our churches should have some organized program for calling on the sick at neighborhood or city hospitals. In addition to leaving inspirational literature, it might be possible to loan some of the patients a radio so they could listen to early-morning and Sunday religious programs. Some families in most churches have spare portable radios which can be fixed up at low cost for hospital loaning. In summertime, members with gardens could supply flowers for the "hospital visitors" to give out on their calls. A bouquet is one of the ways to remind us all of God's love for us, and the beautiful world of nature which he provides for his children.

Calling on Prisons

One group of inspired Christians who remember to call on hospitals *and* prisons is the Gideons. These businessmen have given hundreds of thousands of Bibles to hospitals and prisons. In the case of the prisons, their work just begins with the distribution of Bibles. The Gideons arrange and conduct religious services for the prisoners. As a result, hundreds who were lost in hopelessness are finding new hope in Christ. The prisoners join in singing their favorite hymn from the Gideon hymnal. Hundreds openly profess their faith . . . ask to be forgiven . . . and rededicate their lives to the Saviour. Some of the hardest and toughest prisoners have responded to these services arranged for both male and female institutions. God bless the Gideons! May they be given more strength and means to give out more Bibles . . . more hymnals. And may we fellow Christians follow the Gideons in calling on the unfortunate people in prisons. If we cannot arrange or participate in religious services, we can do some of the following:

a. Read the Bible to individuals or to groups of prisoners.

b. Pray with and for prisoners.

c. Take magazines and books to prisoners and to prison libraries.

d. Take flowers to prisoners, or for use on prison dining tables.

e. Help ex-inmates get work on release from prisons. This is vital to the rehabilitation of ex-prisoners.

f. Send Christmas cards to five or ten prisoners.

g. Arrange to send prisoners birthday greeting cards on their natal day.

h. Give games to prisons, such as playing cards, chess, checkers, backgammon.

i. Shut-ins or bed-ridden Christians can write letters to individual prisoners.

In working with prisoners and prisons, an excellent guide for us all is the experienced advice of Lt. General John C. H. Lee of York, Pennsylvania. He is now executive secretary of the Brotherhood of St. Andrew. From years of helping men in prisons, he can give you the right procedure. Why not write him this week?

Calling on prisoners is a most needed project for men's clubs, and Women's Auxiliaries. Let us all plan our spare-time activities, so that it can be said of us, "I was in prison and ye came to me."

27. *A Pastor's Anniversary Plus Wedding Anniversaries*

Special events are always newsworthy and create a great deal of interest. The Reverend Morris Robinson, pastor of the Grace Presbyterian Church, Minneapolis, Minnesota, observed his twentieth anniversary of service in the parish by underlining the place of the Church in the sanctity of the home. As part of the anniversary program, he read the marriage service, as fifty-five couples whom he had married renewed their vows. This drew the interest of the press, his congregation, and his community.

In a time of many divorces he dramatically showed that "Churchgoing Families Are Happier Families."

28. Don't drive to church with an empty rear seat. If you do, your conscience should bother you unless you have made an honest effort to take some friend or neighbor with you. To say, "Why don't you go to church?" is good. To say, "I hope to see you in church," is better. To do the right thing and say, "I'll pick you up on Sunday morning," is best. Try it!

Chapter 19

Wanted—More Exposures to Christian Ministry

PEOPLE today, more than ever before, need the teachings of Jesus Christ. They are faced with problems—gigantic, complex, and world-wide—which can only be solved through a Christian approach and an adherence to Christian principles. Whether the world travels the pathway to peace or takes the road to World War III will be determined by the number of people who follow the teachings of the Prince of Peace.

Today's problem of converting more people to the Christian way of life is history's greatest challenge to the Church. Only a phenomenal growth in the Church's influence and membership can save civilization from destroying itself. Only through Christians all over the world can we be sure that the new atomic power will be used to serve instead of destroy mankind. Therefore, we should all work unceasingly to live better Christian lives and to bring more people into the Church.

The basic objective of the clergy is the spiritual quality of the congregation. The primary questions in their minds are: "Is my ministry, my message, getting through?" "Is it building and lifting the souls of persons the way it should?" Churches should be interested *first* in the quality of their members' lives and only second in the quantity of their members. They should not be interested in mere growth in membership. Churches should not cater to the so-called "popular appeal" at the expense of deep spiritual growth. The seminaries and the denominational organizations are doing an outstanding job in helping the clergy to enhance the spiritual life and spiritual influence of their congregations.

To take the fullest advantage of the efforts of our pastoral leaders, as many people as possible should be exposed to their ministry and message. Isn't it difficult to influence a person unless that individual comes in close contact with the Church and Christ's teaching? Reading a newspaper report of a sermon is a poor substitute for hearing it at firsthand and sharing in the service. Even listening to the broadcast of a church service is not to be compared with attending the service personally. There is no exposure to Christ's teachings as effective and as complete as attendance at an inspiring church service. Therefore, it seems logical that to convert those outside the Church, we should make specific plans to get nonmembers to attend Sunday services. To influence a person you have to focus his attention on your message. In religion this takes place best in church. Thus in one way, the growth of a church depends on getting more and more individuals to attend more and more services. The more of these exposures to Christ's teachings, the more people will join and support His churches.

Naturally, these plans should not run counter to the feelings of the faithful, who are the backbone of church attendance. However, the plans in this idea manual have been carried out without disturbing regular congregations. In fact, most members welcomed those activities which brought into their church friends and neighbors who ordinarily did not attend.

Chapter 20

Dangerous Dignity of Church Boards

IS your board's dangerous dignity dwarfing your church's progress? That question combines dignity and progress in the same sentence. Seldom do these two words go together in actual life . . . at least in their extremes. Too much dignity usually means too little progress. An examination of the reasons why churches show so little progress often reveals too much respect for dignity.

Plans for aggressive action or progressive steps are often turned down by a church's board as being "undignified." The board members seem to forget that according to the New Testament, thousands of followers were attracted to Christ by what would today be considered undignified miracles—undignified acts of healing. Can you imagine the average church board being asked to approve such miracles as the turning of water into wine, or feeding the multitude on two fishes and five loaves of bread?·

Deacons, elders, trustees, or wardens forget that the most dignified thing in the world is a corpse. One of the most undignified is a growing baby. Too many churches are like the former and too few like the latter.

One reason for the dangerous dignity of many church boards is found in its membership. On the boards of urban churches there are often too many bankers, lawyers, doctors, and retired businessmen, and too few sales managers, advertising men, and active business executives on the way up the ladder of success. As a result, there is little aggressive salesmanship-thinking to "season" the conservatism of men who have to be conservative to succeed in their nonselling professions. Yet, today our churches need aggressive selling leadership more than any organization in the world. The yearly gains in membership show that many churches are not keeping abreast of national growth. They are being by-passed by competing activities which grow bigger and bigger through successful methods of selling.

Another factor in the dangerous dignity of some church boards is their self-perpetuating membership. An inner clique stays in power continuously A few leading families monopolize the officerships. Yes, a certain degree of continuity in trusteeship is a good thing. However, to be truly democratic, members should be elected for three- or four-year terms.

The more progressive and open-minded churches realize that their church board is not complete, is not truly representative unless it includes at least one representative of Labor. Like sales and advertising executives, labor leaders are usually conspicuous by their absence. This tends to make the church seem like a "one-class institution." One of the best places for management and labor leaders to get to know and trust each other is on a church board. You may not have a labor leader in your congregation. However, any member who belongs to a union or is a "shop steward" can bring to the board the benefits of Labor's point of view.

Right now you may be saying, "What's wrong with successful bankers, competent lawyers, and professional men? Why are they responsible for the church's dangerous dignity?" The answer is obvious. Most of these board members achieved success by having people come to them for help and not by going out and selling their services to people who needed them. Today, most churches cannot grow unless they stop waiting for people to come to them, and take a more progressive attitude toward getting new members and increasing church attendance.

Churches should go out and sell their exclusive God-given advantages to the general public. The Church has more happiness, more peace and contentment, more true joy and satisfaction to offer than any merchandise or service advertised in full-color pages in national magazines.

Yet the average church shuns most of those successful forms of planning, selling, and advertising which have made business grow bigger year by year. They are classed as "undignified" by the conservative members of the church's board. Well, let's turn our backs on this dangerous dignity and take a look at some of these proven ways to grow, to attract and influence more people.

Chapter 21

Establishing a Yearly Goal of Growth

MOST of the methods of building larger congregations fall into the following three classifications:

1. Establishing a yearly goal of growth in church attendance and membership.
2. Organizing definite plans for achieving the desired yearly growth.
3. Maintaining accurate, comparative records showing whether or not the goals are being achieved (and how quickly or slowly).

Now let's look at the problem of "Yearly Goal of Growth" through the eyes of a business doctor. How would your church answer these clinical questions?

(a) Have you a yearly goal for increased church attendance?
Yes ( )   No ( )

(b) Have you a yearly goal for increased church membership?
Yes ( )   No ( )

(c) Are these objectives explained to the entire church?
Yes ( )   No ( )

(d) Are any definite plans made to achieve the goal?
Yes ( )   No ( )

(e) Who makes these plans and sells them to the members and organizations?
Professional men ( )   Salesmen ( )

232

Where denominations have considered these questions, and have worked out plans to increase their membership, the results have been tangible. If your church has not set up its individual goal for yearly growth, this should be done at once.

The Baptists are one of the denominations that establishes definite goals of yearly growth. Their local congregations have been told how these objectives will be obtained. The Roman Catholics also establish a progressive program for increasing their parishes.

The Presbyterian Church (Northern) is another denomination that has set up definite goals for its evangelism. Under the fine title of "New Life Movement," the Presbyterians have established the following objectives for a three-year period:

300 new churches
1,000,000 new members

More than 100,000 laymen are being recruited and trained as evangelists. Through their efforts, the invitation to attend church has changed from a general, "Come worship with us soon?" to a specific, "This coming Sunday we have a special service. Will you join us?"

The successful sales executive is constantly comparing the growth of his company's business with that of competition and the industry as a whole. He is not satisfied unless the percentage of yearly increase for his concern is as large as any competitor, and is larger than the industry as a whole.

Many businesses aim for a 10% increase in normal years. Of course, this gain is not secured by every business in every year. Yet most successful businesses have found that unless an organization works for a definite increase, it doesn't stand still—but slips backward. It is better to aim for a 10% gain and only obtain a 6% increase than to coast along with the status quo.

Shouldn't the clergy and their boards take the same constructive and progressive attitude as these successful businessmen? Shouldn't each church want to attract new members in at least the same proportion as the national average for the denomination? Parishes with unusual advantages and unusual growth opportunities should not be satisfied with just the average national growth. They should want to better the average year after year. How can your church measure its growth? All you do is find out the number by which your 1956 membership was greater than 1957. Next figure the percentage gain over your 1956 membership. Then compare that percentage with the national gain for your denomination or faith, and with the others.

Thanks to the cooperation of Mr. Fletcher Coates of the National Council of Churches in Christ in the U.S.A., we can give you the following statistics.

Religious Bodies With Membership over 100,000	Members 1956	Members 1957	Percent of Gain
7th Day Adventists	283,140	291,567	2.98
Assemblies of God	470,361	482,352	2.55
American Baptist Convention	1,528,210	1,536,276	0.53
Southern Baptist Convention	8,700,481	8,956,756	2.95
American Baptist Association	600,000	630,000	5.00
Conservative Baptist Assoc. of America	250,000	275,000	10.00
Free Will Baptists	163,619	172,683	5.54
General Association of Regular Baptist Churches	129,100	122,038	−5.47
National Baptist Convention of America	(2,668,799 for 1956)		
National Baptist Convention, U.S.A. Inc.	(4,557,416 for 1954)		
Church of the Brethren (German Baptists)	197,290	199,936	1.34
Church of God (Cleveland, Tenn.)	147,929	150,227	1.55
Church of God (Anderson, Ind.)	127,395	131,420	3.16
Church of the Nazarene	277,618	281,646	1.45
Churches of Christ	1,700,000	1,750,000	2.94
Congregational Christian Churches	1,379,394	1,392,632	0.96
Greek Catholic Church	100,000	100,000	
Greek Archdiocese of No. & So. America	1,150,000	1,150,000	
Russian Orthodox Greek Catholic Church of America	755,000	755,000	

Serbian Eastern Orthodox Church	100,000	150,000	50.00
Syrian Antiochian Orthodox Church ('55 figure)	110,000	110,000	
Evangelical & Reformed Church	784,270	800,042	2.01
Evangelical & United Brethren Church	742,537	746,460	0.53
International Church of the Foursquare Gospel	110,568	112,706	1.93
Jehovah's Witnesses	189,517	208,260	9.89
Jewish Congregations	5,500,000	5,500,000	
Augusta Evangelical Lutheran Church (1954 figure)	549,604	576,189	4.84
Evangelical Lutheran Church	1,021,058	1,058,722	3.69
United Lutheran Church in America	2,174,500	2,235,455	2.80
African Methodist Episcopal Zion Church	761,000	761,000	
The Methodist Church	9,422,893	9,543,245	1.28
Pentecostal Church of God of America, Inc.	103,500	105,000	1.45
United Pentecostal Church, Inc.	125,000	135,000	8.00
Polish National Catholic Church of America	250,000	267,418	6.97
Presbyterian Church of the United States	829,570	848,735	2.31
Presbyterian Church in the United States of America	2,717,320	2,775,464	2.14
United Presbyterian Church of North America	251,344	257,513	2.45
Church of Jesus Christ of Latter-Day Saints	1,289,581	1,339,638	3.88
Recognized Church of Jesus Christ of Latter-Day Saints	142,480	146,076	2.52
Lutheran Church (Missouri Synod)	2,076,550	2,150,230	3.55
Evangelical Lutheran Joint Synod of Wisconsin & Other States	339,106	(no figures)	
American Lutheran Church	(no figures)	910,011	
Protestant Episcopal Church	2,852,965	2,965,137	3.93
Christian Reformed Church	211,454	221,969	4.97
Reformed Church in America	208,999	213,544	2.17
Roman Catholic Church	34,563,851	35,846,477	3.71
Salvation Army	247,964	250,156	0.88
International General Assembly of Spiritualists	164,072	(no figures)	
Unitarian Churches	101,549	104,914	3.31

Even if the one-year gain of your church equals the average for the denomination, you should not be satisfied. For the average of the denomination includes the small gains of many churches which are not progressing as fast as they should. The average gain in some denominations is too low because the total figures contain parishes which have ceased to exist actively, but must be counted until the property is sold.

There are some churches that have shown abnormal gains because of unusual growth in their city or neighborhood population. Other congregations have a small population on which to build. In either case, churches should use every sound and tested method to build up their congregations to the greatest possible percentage of their local population potentials. By having church services which satisfy and inspire the souls of men, by properly promoting these services and activities to members and the unchurched, they can obtain "S.R.O." congregations. Yes, there is every reason why successful churches, like successful plays, should have "Standing Room Only" attendance. Certainly Jesus had many occasions when his listeners were so many that they stood and forgot any physical fatigue.

Chapter 22

Why People Get Out of the Habit of Attending Church

SUCCESSFUL businesses learn to avoid losing customers by finding out why customers stop buying. Then they correct the adverse conditions. Churches can use the same technique to stop losing members to other churches, or losing the regular church attendance of members.

What are some of the "reasons" why some people say they stop going to church regularly?

1. Too many requests for special funds—too many tickets to buy.
2. Too many requests to attend or join church social activities.
3. Regular members "kid" or "roast" the irregular member when he or she appears in church. Remarks such as the following annoy the irregulars and keep them away: "You must be sick or afraid you are going to die." "What's the matter? We only see you on Christmas and Easter."
4. The hymns are unfamiliar.
5. The church gives no special reason for attending most services. There is no special personal appeal to specific groups of people to attend on definite Sundays.
6. The minister fails to keep up his calls on families in the church.
7. Overhospitable churches put "greeters" at the end of every aisle and at each door. To get out of the church, each visitor must be welcomed and "greeted." Some people dislike this. So leave one door, one aisle free for them.

After reading this list, you will see why quotation marks were put around "reasons." For some of them seem to be quite superficial, in fact, just plain excuses. However, it is true that many of these nonmembers like the Church—try to follow Christ's way—but just got out of the habit of attending Sunday services.

Looking at the situation from another viewpoint, many people do not attend church regularly because they cannot, by themselves, reconcile religion with present-day secular life. Or they find the ritual meaningless. Both of these real reasons can be changed by an inspired minister, a devout congregation, and church services which give people something specific to live by in their week-day world.

The above reasons do not apply to all churches. There may be special local or parish reasons for nonattendance. The best way to find out the facts on this problem is to make a local study. Have trained survey reporters call on a cross section of nonattenders. The local newspaper can put you in touch with men or women who have experience in making surveys. In these calls, a questionnaire should be used. In addition, valuable information will be uncovered in the miscellaneous comments made by the respondents. Naturally, the interviews should be made among both men and women.

A good basic questionnaire for this study has been developed by Robert N. King, in charge of research for Batten, Barton, Durstine and Osborn, Advertising Agency. Mr. King's questions are as follows:

1. In what church or faith were you brought up?..............
2. Have you attended a local church of that denomination?......
    Yes ( )   No ( )
3. About how many times per year do you attend church?.......
4. How does it happen that you do not attend more frequently?
    ....
5. What could churches do to make you want to attend services
    more frequently?..
6. Miscellaneous comment..................................

Local conditions will suggest additional questions. The sex and approximate age of respondent should be recorded on each interview.

The above questionnaire is designed to be used in interviewing people who are known to be infrequent churchgoers. They include the perennials who attend only on Christmas and Easter. When this survey is done on a house-to-house basis, the same questions are logical. In this case, the survey could be done under the local council of churches, or a group of churches in the same neighborhood. The prospective respondents could be found by getting a house-to-house list of telephone subscribers and then crossing off the names of regular churchgoers. This survey should be followed up with a recruiting drive for church attendance and church membership.

There is another reason for nonattendance or infrequent attendance which does not apply to most churches. That is the small amount of missionary work done by or sponsored by the parish. In this case, some people give as a reason (or an alibi) for their nonattendance the fact that the church spends too much of its time, energy, and funds on its own members and is not spreading the gospel to foreign lands or helping the poor within the city. Right or wrong, these churches are considered more of a religious club than an organization carrying out God's work at home and abroad.

Chapter 23

Know Your Congregation as Business

Knows Its Customers

SUCCESSFUL business firms have grown by finding out everything they could about major factors, such as the following:

1. Present customers
2. Past customers
3. Why new customers are won
4. Potential customers
5. Statistics on increase or decrease in customers
6. Frequency of customer purchases
7. What satisfied customers like about the company
8. What dissatisfied customers dislike about the company

This same type of information can help a church grow and become more successful in influencing its members and the community as a whole.

In many churches the vital statistics on church membership have not been properly audited. The parish lists are woefully padded. People have left the church to attend other churches without asking for a formal transfer. Hence their names usually stay on the former church lists and membership rolls. A good time to correct this false situation is in the summer months when the church office generally has less to do. A letter should be sent to all borderline nonattending members from the minister. This letter should express the desire to keep the member's name on the parish roll, but should state that the church wants to make its list 100% accurate. Therefore, would the recipient please sign an attached post card stating that he or she desires to have his or her name retained on the official membership list? Wrong addresses and lack of information on the family can be corrected at the same time. People who do not fill out the stamped self-addressed post cards are then removed from the parish rolls. Through this checkup, some churches have discovered that up to one-third of their membership list was deadwood.

Here is the information which every church should have and should review at regular intervals:

1. Comparison of each Sunday's attendance with the same Sunday of the preceding year.

2. Accumulated attendance at the Sunday services for the year. This accumulated attendance figure overcomes the discrepancy caused by the fact that the date for special church days like Easter varies year by year. Individual Sunday attendance and accumulated attendance figures for the year to date should be given to the minister every Monday.

3. Sunday school attendance compared with same Sunday last year.

4. Year-to-year comparison of number of people who have joined the church.

5. Year-to-year comparison of people who have left the church and joined other parishes. Why did they leave your church?

6. Year-to-year comparison of average pledges. If this average is standing still or going down, something is radically wrong and should be changed.

7. Breakdown of congregation by these age groups:

Number	Group	% of Total
. . . .	Sunday School Pupils	. . . .
. . . .	16 to 20 years old	. . . .
. . . .	21 to 30 years old	. . . .
. . . .	31 to 40 years old	. . . .
. . . .	41 to 50 years old	. . . .
. . . .	51 to 60 years old	. . . .
. . . .	61 to 70 years old	. . . .
. . . .	71 and over	. . . .

The percentage of the total congregation in these age groups will show a minister and the board whether the church is growing enough in younger members to more than overcome deaths of older members. It will indicate whether the church is converting its teen-age Sunday school members into regular church members. It will show whether the Younger Marrieds are staying in your congregation or going to some other church.

If the statistics for your church indicate a loss of members in any age group, have someone ask a representative number of that age group why they left the church. Then make plans to correct the conditions which caused their leaving. If your congregation is not showing a 5 to 10% gain each year, find out what is wrong. A church must grow to stay alive. A church which is just standing still will sooner or later start shrinking in membership and influence. No progressive church should be satisfied with its attendance unless it has two well-attended services every Sunday. Reuben Youngdahl, the outstanding pastor of the Mount Olivet Lutheran Church in Minneapolis, has built up the congregation so that three identical services are held every Sunday. One strength of the Roman Catholic churches lies in the fact that each parish has enough communicants to support several morning services every Sunday. There is no reason why Protestant denominations should not achieve similar growth.

It is sound planning to have a meeting of your minister and board regularly (not less than every four months) on ways and means to build up your church attendance. At the time, review the comparative statistics and plan special events to bring more people into your church more frequently. That's the same technique which successful businesses use to grow bigger year after year. Detailed suggestions for attendance-building special events are given in chapter 7.

For example, you may find the boys and girls who go away to school do not come home regular "attenders." This is a serious problem. These boys and girls represent the potential leaders and future strength of your church. You can help assure the church attendance of youth by supporting some organization like the "Church Society for College Work." Chapter 8 explains how this society works to maintain church attendance of away-from-home students.

Some churches have attendance statistics compiled by a special committee. The report is presented to the minister and board twice a year. Any activity which is not producing the desired results or does not have a satisfactory following is carefully examined. Where necessary, special committees are appointed to make a study of the situation and to develop recommendations for its correction.

An outstanding example of knowing your congregation is the survey planned and directed by Bishop G. Bromley Oxnam, head of the Methodist Church in New York City. Bishop Oxnam's study included all the people in Brooklyn. The revealing figures showed the membership of all faiths and how much they have increased or decreased. Population trends by races were charted to indicate the changing potential. Sunday-school attendance was analyzed; congregations were broken down into age groups. The pledges and total church support were also shown by age groups. This comprehensive study gave Bishop Oxnam, his ministers, and their boards a complete detailed picture of their problems and opportunities. Other denominations and/or city councils of churches could make similar surveys to the great advantage of all concerned.

The Lutheran Laymen's League conducted a survey of people who listen to their radio program, "The Lutheran Hour." Filled-out questionnaires were received from 9,678 persons. Those listeners who wrote that they did not attend church regularly were asked to give the reason. Here is the summary of the replies.

Distance	492 or	5%
Work	495	5%
Illness	973	10%
Nonmemberships	57	.59%
Other reason	520	5.61%
No reason given	7,141	73.8%
TOTAL	9,678	100%

Note that the biggest percentage, 73.8%, did not give any reason. Among this large group are your fellow-townspeople—your friends and neighbors. Most of them are just waiting to be asked—waiting to be sold on worshiping with you—in your church.

NOTE:

On the following page you will find the first of a series of plan sheets. Similar plan sheets follow other chapters in this book. They are designed to make it easy and convenient for you to start right away to carry out in your church, the ideas and suggestions about which you are reading.

Plan sheets are more fully discussed in the last chapter of the book, and you will find that there is a duplicate of each plan sheet at the back of the book, perforated so that you can tear them out.

Don't delay in taking this important "first step." Get a pencil right now. Be ready to write in your plans for using these tested methods.

PLAN SHEET

Essential Information on Congregations

1. Official Number of Contributing Members

Year	Number of Members	Gain or Loss over Preceding Year
19	....	....
19	....	....
19	....	....
19	....	....
19	....	....

2. New Members of Congregation

Year	Adults	From Sunday School	Total Gain
19	....	....	....
19	....	....	....
19	....	....	....
19	....	....	....
19	....	....	....

3. Members Lost to Congregation

Year	Deaths	Transfers to Other Churches	Members Who Stopped Contributing	Total of All Losses
19	....	....	....	....
19	....	....	....	....
19	....	....	....	....
19	....	....	....	....

4. Size of Sunday School

Year	Registered Members of the Schools	Gain or Loss over Previous Year
19	....	....
19	....	....
19	....	....
19	....	....

5. Attendance at Church Services

Year	Average Attendance at Sunday Services	Gain or Loss
19	....	....
19	....	....
19	....	....
19	....	....

Chapter 24

Special Services
How They Help Increase Attendance

THERE are several plans which can help your church increase its attendance at regular services. This new set makes a special appeal to definite groups of members or nonmembers. These new special services are to be in addition to the church's regular services on Christmas, Easter, or during Lent. They increase attendance in between major church Sundays of the year.

Right here some readers may ask: "Why suggest some *new*, special Sunday services when our church already has so many?" This is a logical question, and naturally some congregations will prefer just to follow the regular liturgical calendar of their own denomination.

The special Sunday services about to be described were developed from the techniques used by successful and growing businesses. Like business promotions, they have a *specific* and *understandable* appeal to definite groups of prospects . . . prospective churchgoers. Their appeals are basic, everyday ones which do not require an understanding of church Holy Days or ecclesiastical celebrations. In using these special Sundays to invite nonchurchgoers to attend your church, you don't have to explain at length the meaning of the special Sunday service. Like successful business promotions, no involved explanations are necessary.

Just like business-building campaigns, these special Sunday services will bring new faces into church. These services will definitely expose certain people to the ministry of your church who otherwise would not have attended. Experience shows that a definite percentage of these "special guests" at these special Sundays will attend your church again and again. A definite percentage of these repeat-attenders will become members of your congregation. Exactly what percentage of special guests will come back again, and exactly what percentage join the church depend on many factors, including: the music, how guests are "greeted," the atmosphere of the church, their impressions of the congregation, the depth of feeling created by the service and sermon. No special promotion takes the place of these basic factors.

The primary function of these special Sunday services is to expose more people, more souls to Christ's Way of Life and to the ministries of His church. This exposure is made acceptable by using approaches easily understood by the prospect. This strategy is like that of medical and agricultural missionaries who influence people by first appealing to an interest which is already part of their lives, and, then, after this bridge has been set up, use it to transmit new ideas.

Following is a discussion of some such special services. Church groups may think of others which would serve various needs.

FOUNDERS' DAY SUNDAY: Why not honor those families that founded your church? The Sunday nearest the official beginning of your congregation would be the best time. It's easy to build up a "Standing Room Only" congregation for this service. Personal letters go out to all living descendants of the founders, inviting them to attend Founders' Day Service. A section of seats in front of the church should be reserved for the Founders' families. This special service gives you the opportunity to have an *exhibit* of early church pictures in the vestibule or in the parish house. The more your congregation knows about the history of its church, the more interested and loyal it becomes. *Why wait for the fiftieth and seventy-fifth anniversaries of the church when you can celebrate Founders' Sunday every year?* Naturally, you will plan special music and an appropriate sermon for this special service.

Department stores have found that Founders' Day and Anniversaries are tested promotions for getting people to come into the stores. How much more worth-while it is to use these activating events to get people to attend services in your church.

GOOD NEIGHBOR SUNDAY: Here is a "natural" for practically every church. This special service stresses and takes advantage of that true Christian virtue—neighborliness. To Good-Neighbor Sunday service are invited all the people who live right around the church. A friendly letter carries the following invitation:

Dear Neighbor,

We, at (name of church) are proud of our neighbors. We believe your neighborhood and our neighborhood is one of the finest in the entire city.

This Sunday (date) we will have a special "Good Neighbor" service at 11 A.M. At that time, we will pay tribute to you and our other neighbors with special music and a special sermon.

If you have no church plans for this coming Sunday, we cordially invite you to join us in "Good Neighbor Sunday."

Sincerely yours,

(Hand-signed by minister)
MINISTER, NAME OF CHURCH

A notice should also go to the congregation. Here is suggested wording for a government post-card mailing to all members:

Dear Parishioner,

Sunday is "Good Neighbor Sunday" at (name of church). We honor your neighbors, and the church's neighbors.

The sermon pays tribute to good neighbors. Our fine choir will sing special music.

You will want to attend Good Neighbor Sunday at (name of church). So invite, and bring with you, some neighbor who does not attend any church regularly.

Yours faithfully,

NAME OF MINISTER

Notice that each invitation to neighbors is worded to attract those who do not attend any church regularly. Some church choirs are so informal they sing that lovely song, "Love Thy Neighbor."

As an extra attraction, you might collect and display in your vestibule pictures of your neighborhood in its early days. A picture committee would ask the congregation for exhibits. This feature exhibit should be mentioned in all announcements of the service. The local newspapers should be sent an advance publicity story on the service. An annual Good Neighbor Sunday is a proven way to increase church attendance and expose nonmembers to the comfort and inspiration of your services.

Good Neighbor Sunday is also an excellent opportunity for an annual combined service sponsored by a group of churches in the same neighborhood. It should be given on Sunday evening or during the week so it does not interfere with the regular Sunday services of the individual churches. The churches and ministers take turns in being hosts and preachers at this group service.

CHURCH SUNDAY SCHOOL: Each church should have at least two Sundays per year when the Sunday school attends the regular services —and takes part in the regular service.

BOY OR GIRL SCOUT SUNDAYS: These two services are growing in popularity and importance. Attending a special service in their honor, in their scout uniforms, makes an effective appeal to most boys and girls.

Properly planned and publicized, these services will attract attendance from the parents and families of scout members. The National Headquarters of both organizations usually designate a certain Sunday for these services. Front seats should be reserved for the scouts and their leaders. Having the church troop march in together is very effective.

A service in honor of the Campfire Girls is also worth-while.

MEDICAL SUNDAY: Why not have a special service to honor those men and women who keep people well, who help bring the sick back to health? Reserve the front pews for families of doctors or nurses. Send special letters of invitation to the heads of local hospitals and medical organizations. Ask them to send representatives to the service.

FLOWER SUNDAY: Hold a "Flower Sunday" in spring when due tribute is paid to God for His gift of flowers to our world. A special décoration committee would solicit donations of flowers and plants. These would be distributed to hospitals after the service.

MEMORIAL SERVICES: Some churches have an annual memorial service for families whose loved ones have died in the past year. This is a real comfort to the bereaved families, and assures attendance that Sunday from some who would otherwise not attend the service. The families can become a part of the service by contributing to the church flowers for that Sunday.

CHURCH DECORATION NIGHT: This is a beautiful service for some week-day night before Christmas. The congregation and neighbors are invited to decorate the church with Christmas greens. A Decoration Committee is formed to obtain the necessary material. Wire-screen forms and garlands are used as far as possible so that many amateur decorators can participate. The service starts at 7:00 P.M.; when the decorating is completed, a lighted star is raised and the choir (in regular week-day clothes) leads in singing "O Star of Wonder." This is followed by other familiar carols. The singing is closed with a prayer. Then all adjourn to the parish house where coffee and cookies are served.

GO-TO-CHURCH SUNDAY: Attendance at individual churches can be increased through a city-wide "Go-to-Church Sunday." Shown (p. 32) is

YOUR CHURCH IS CALLING
You!

"I am the best friend you ever had,
I am hung about with sweet memories . . .
Memories of friends . . . memories of mothers . . .
Memories of boys and girls . . . memories of angels.
I am blessed with loving thoughts . . .
Crowned by happy hands and hearts.
I safeguard man through all his paths.
I lift up the fallen. I strengthen the weak;
I help the distressed; I show mercy, bestow kindness, and
Offer a friendly hand.
I am good fellowship, friendliness and love.
Sometime . . . someday in the near or far future,
You will yearn for the touch of my friendly hand.
I am your comforter, and your best friend.
I am calling you now.
I AM YOUR CHURCH."

—Selected.

Heed this call in person!   Lead the way for others!!

- The church represents the unseen "eternal lifting force" that is to save the world from destruction.

- The church through its leaders conceived and sponsored most of the great reforms.   The social order of today is undergoing a change that challenges the church . . . the challenge to bring order out of chaos.   Our children need this guidance and direction of the church to meet the situations they must face.

- Few human beings worship or labor alone.   The church offers the strength of organization.   It gives the urge of leadership, supplies encouragement when despondent, and offers rebuke when selfconfident.

- The church is the best place to share our abilities and resources.   Presence is the evidence of accepted community responsibilities.

"To say that I do not need the church is mere bravado. I needed it when my
father died. I needed it when we were married, and when our babies were
taken from us, and I shall need it again sooner or later, and need it badly."
—Edgar A. Guest

CHURCH GOING FAMILIES ARE HAPPY FAMILIES!

Prepared by T. H. Stanley

the type of city-wide campaign material which can be used by all churches and produces good results. It was prepared by Mr. T. H. Stanley for the "Go-to-Church" Sunday in Columbus, Georgia, sponsored by the Junior Chamber of Commerce.

EDUCATIONAL SUNDAY: At this service, the church pays tribute to the fine work being done by the local school authorities and teachers. The date for this service is three or four weeks after school opens in the fall. It is best to arrange the exact Sunday with the principal of your neighborhood school. Explain the purpose of the service. Get from him the names and home addresses of his teachers and/or his entire staff. Show him the letter you plan to send these people, inviting them to the service. Plan to enclose a small but attractive card which introduces the recipient. This card enables the ushers to seat the school guests in the seats of honor, reserved for them at the front of the church.

Make sure your congregation is informed in advance of Educational Sunday. Urge them to attend and, by their presence, to honor the great contribution which the schools make to the training of youth. Suggest that their children ask the teachers to attend. Where possible, the members should phone and see if they can bring the teachers to church with them in their cars.

Churches that have this service report an unusual increase in attendance. As in the case of all special Sundays, some of the honored guests do not have a church affiliation. Therefore, a definite percentage of guests come back again and again to the church. And eventually some of them become regular members—active members.

LAYMEN'S SUNDAY: It is a known fact that most people take a greater interest in church attendance, and in Christ's Way of Life, when they are given special responsibilities. Thousands of churches of all denominations use "Laymen's Sunday" to build up this special interest on the part of key members, and to build up attendance on the third Sunday in October. In 1949 over 30,000 laymen spoke in their churches on "Laymen's Sunday." They discussed the application of Christian principles to everyday living and business affairs.

For a full outline on how to arrange a "Laymen's Sunday" in your church in connection with the national observance in October, write to: The Laymen's Movement for a Christian World, Room 1402, 347 Madison Avenue, New York 17, N.Y. You will be sent a free plan and all the necessary details.

NOTE ON GUEST CARDS: The success of all these special Sundays is increased when the letter of invitation includes a guest card of identification. It is possible to have these printed and filled in for the various occasions. Such a standard card can be as follows:

```
┌─────────────────────────────────────────────────────────┐
│                                                           │
│            INTRODUCING OUR HONORED GUEST                  │
│                                                           │
│   ....................................................    │
│            (Name to be written on above line)            │
│                                                           │
│     For whom a special place is reserved at our services on │
│   ....................................................    │
│                 (Date to be filled in)                   │
│                                                           │
│   Name of Church.................. Church Address.............. │
│                                                           │
└─────────────────────────────────────────────────────────┘
```

Chapter 25

Keeping the Away-at-School Crowd

Going to Church

TO grow in size and influence, every church should have a continuing procession of boys and girls who will be future leaders in church activities. Some of these leaders should come from the youth who go away to school. It is tragic, but true, that colleges and out-of-town schools are not developing anywhere near their share of church leaders.

This is due to the fact that many boys and girls enter college with weak enough Christian convictions and entirely get out of the habit of going to church when they go away to schools. Many even lose their faith or become agnostics. No church can afford the loss of these potential leaders. When they come back home, their continued nonattendance is a serious influence on their contemporaries. Moreover, as more and more college-trained students assume most of the key positions in the industrial and professional worlds, their continued nonsupport of the church is a contributing factor to the financial difficulties and low salaries which afflict many churches today. Here are some ways to help prevent this happening to the away-at-school crowd of your church:

1. Find out the addresses of the boys and girls who are away at school. Then write the minister of a good church in each city. Most churches have annuals which list the college-school clergy. Ask him to call on the students and welcome them to the church services and activities. The home-town minister should also write the student and urge him or her to attend the school-town church.

2. Three or four times a year, send the students a copy of the church bulletin or some other news of their home-town church. In the accompanying letter, tell them you are looking forward to seeing them in church when they return for vacations.

3. Hold a tea or dinner for the away-at-school crowd during Christmas, Easter, or spring vacation.

4. Have a special service the first Sunday in September for students and their families.

5. Work with your denominational students' organization. The one I know best is the Church Society for College Work. You'll be encouraged and inspired by the fine job this organization is doing to keep school youth going to church, to help students keep and strengthen their faith, and to help local church groups better meet their school and college work. It brings leading ministers to school-town parishes. The Society helps provide funds to bring more and better chaplains into college centers. Like Army chaplains, college chaplains work among all groups. They provide friendship for the fearful, a mature guiding hand for the confused. They conduct chapel services, hold discussions on religion and present-day problems, and teach the Christian faith. They work closely with the college authorities and local ministers. They bring understanding and security to those who seek it.

This is not an experimental undertaking, but has been worked out successfully during the last ten years at Harvard University, Amherst College, University of North Carolina, Smith College, University of Wisconsin, and many other college centers.

Chapter 26

Building Attendance
Through Better Singing

THERE is another way to increase church attendance which at first may seem of minor importance. Yet experience shows that improved congregational singing can improve the regularity of the attendance of existing members and even attract new members. This is because most people like to sing.

The singing at luncheon clubs, rallies, and social gatherings is evidence that most individuals enjoy being a part of the program. The ministry of music at any church is more effective when the congregation actually sings out instead of mumbling the words. Church services at which the members really participate in the singing give all a spiritual lift. For this lift, people will return again and again. It is one of the surest ways to make visitors feel at home in church and want to attend frequently.

Improved congregational singing is not dependent upon increasing the expenditures for the choir or organ. There are other successful methods which can be used by any church. Here are some of the most popular.

1. The best first step is to find out the favorite hymns of your congregation. The idea back of this is based on sound psychology. It lies in the fact that most adults like to sing the old familiar hymns they sang in childhood. They do not want to learn new hymns no matter how beautiful the choirmaster considers them. When people get together and sing in private homes or at service-club lunch meetings, or church-group get-togethers, they always go back to the old favorites. The radio "hit tunes of the week" are disregarded. Hymn singing is no different—the old familiar ones get the greatest response.

It is very easy to determine which hymns your parishioners like to sing. All you do is put little mimeographed slips in the pews with the following request at the top—"Please write below the titles, first lines, or numbers of your favorite hymns." This simple survey form can also be included in your church bulletin. On the Sunday you make the survey be sure that pencils are put in the pews. Then make an explanatory announcement of the survey from the pulpit. Simply explain that you want to have the congregation's favorite hymns included in all Sunday services. In order to do this, you want to find out which hymns they like best. Then give the congregation five minutes to fill out their survey slips. The slips can be placed on the collection plate, collected separately, or left in the pews for collection after the service is over.

Recently the Capitol Records people contacted several thousand churches throughout the country. Trained reporters asked the congregations to vote on their favorite hymns. Careful tabulations showed that twelve beloved hymns led all the rest. When you glance over the following titles, you'll agree these winners are a fine group for congregational singing:

"Abide With Me"
"For Thee, O Dear, Dear Country"
"He Leadeth Me"
"Holy, Holy, Holy"
"Jesus, Lover of My Soul"

"Lead Kindly Light"
"Now the Day Is Over"
"O Love That Wilt Not Let Me Go"
"O Paradise"
"Onward Christian Soldiers"
"Saviour, Again to Thy Dear Name"
"The Church's One Foundation"

The above hymns, are listed alphabetically, and not according to the voting of the congregations. All twelve have been recorded by the famous St. Luke's Choristers. This group needs little introduction as their voices are called upon by almost every motion-picture studio in Hollywood when church choir music is needed. Remember them in *Going My Way* and *Boys Town?*

This Capitol Album of Familiar Hymns should be owned by every church which has a phonograph. The records are excellent for your Young People's meetings. This album should also be in every home. For hymns are not just for Church on Sunday—they take on new meaning and increased beauty when brought to life in the home. Here are the old friendly hymns that the homemaker will enjoy on a quiet afternoon. Here, too, are the fine majestic hymns that will inspire the whole family in the cool of the evening. And what a lovely thought to have these masterpieces where growing youngsters can hear them often . . . learn to enjoy and love them in the old-fashioned way.

Other evidence on the relative popularity of different hymns was found in the fan mail received by the General Electric Company in connection with one of their Sunday radio programs. The radio audience was invited to vote for their favorite hymns. These favorites were high in the voting:

"Softly Now the Light of Day"
"Dear Lord and Father of Mankind"
"God Be with You Till We Meet Again"
"Love Divine"
"Eternal Father"

"Be Still My Soul"
"Faith of Our Fathers"
"Come Ye Thankful People Come"
"Rock of Ages"
"America the Beautiful"
"In the Garden"

No minister or choirmaster should ever worry about repeating the old favorites at frequent intervals. That's what congregations want and will respond to. If in your church, the ever-popular "Onward Christian Soldiers" is sung once a month, you'll get no complaints except possibly from the choirmaster or some professional singer. Please don't let that bother you. The basic objective of congregational singing is to get as many people as possible to join in the service with their voices. Experience shows there is nothing like old familiar hymns to inspire the congregation to sing out their praises, instead of mumbling through a beautiful but new song. To increase congregational singing, the St. Joseph of Arimathaea Church in Elmsford, N.Y. sings six hymns each Sunday.

2. One of the surest ways to increase singing and start the service on a high note of congregational participation, is to have the choir come down the main aisle singing the processional. This entrance always stimulates greater volume. It is not fair to either the choir or the congregation to have the choir enter from a door near the altar. To get the greatest inspiration, the processional should be sung as the choir proceeds through the congregation along the middle, main aisle.

Some churches are built so the choir cannot come down the center aisle during the winter. But in fair, warm weather, it is possible to have the assembled choir walk outside to the main door and then come down the main aisle singing the opening hymn.

Other churches have the choir come down the main aisle only at special services or on special Sundays. They admit this is a more effective processional but feel it should be reserved for special occasions. When any arrangement stimulates greater congregational singing, it should be used regularly.

3. The Christmas carols and Easter hymns include many of the favorite songs of churchgoers. Therefore they should be sung one or two Sundays preceding and following the day itself. Successful radio programs have found that Christmas carols are especially popular. So why shouldn't the Church which fathered the carols, offer this popular feature several times during the Christmas season?

4. Many churches have a Sunday school choir of boys and girls in addition to their adult choir. Where this is so, the youth choir should sing at the main service at least once every other month. Young voices are a delightful change and will attract increased attendance from friends, relatives, and neighbors.

5. Many churches make their procession more colorful and inspiring by including the church flag and the American flag.

6. The better the singing of the choir, the better the congregational singing. So here are two ways to stimulate your choir to even better singing:

   a. Once a year have a "Choir Sunday" at which the minister and church pay tribute to the fine support of the choir. Have front pews reserved for the families of choir members. Send out letters of invitation to all past and present families of choir members. Before the sermon, read a tribute to the choir and choirmaster.

   b. If you have a boy or girl choir, you have an unusual opportunity to show appreciation and stimulate even greater efforts. That is to provide crosses for the choir to wear at each church service. Silver crosses hung on red or purple ribbon make the choir feel more like a part of the church staff. Each boy or girl who has been in the choir one year or longer is given the right to wear the cross. This stimulates the new members to stay in and win their crosses at the end of the first year. When a member leaves the choir, he or she is presented with the cross as a token of appreciation and as a remembrance of choir days. Presenting the crosses to the entire choir should be done at a special "Choir Sunday."

If the choir or church budget does not permit the purchase of crosses and ribbon, some leading member of the church will be willing to provide the funds. For instance, the choir crosses make an ideal gift in memory of a loved one. Sterling silver crosses measuring two and one-half inches long can be obtained for a low cost. The choir mothers can get the ribbon locally and sew 24 inches of ribbon on which to hang each cross.

7. Another scheme which works wonders with the young married group is to organize a volunteer choir from the young married women and their husbands for some series of Lenten or Advent services in the evening—this group to meet after work for a six-o'clock supper prepared by the group. The rector, the choirmaster, and the rector's wife are included. After supper the group rehearse simple music for an hour, then have a prayer, and march into church for the service. This gives the choirmaster an opportunity to teach the group how to sing properly. He explains what he is trying to do and the part real devotional music should have in the service. Here is the most important advantage. After the series is over, the choirmaster gets this group to scatter themselves around in the congregation at the regular services. Then they become focal points for good singing and bring their neighbors in the congregation into the habit of singing well and energetically.

8. A leading downtown church holds "congregation hymn practices" in connection with the regular service. Led by the choirmaster, these practices help the members sing the hymns better and easier. This plan is even more successful in a neighborhood church where the congregation is the same "family" each Sunday.

Chapter 27

Preparing the Annual Appeal

THE need for greater support of the church and its activities is seen on every side of us. Mortgages are not paid off as promptly as they should be Sunday schools do not have adequate equipment. Ministers are not paid enough to compensate for their ability, high calling, and continuous devotion to duty. Most important of all, too many churches receive so little support from their members that they cannot do their share of foreign and domestic missionary work. They are also unable to contribute their quota to the denomination's national organization.

Two other facts indicate the seriousness of this problem. The first is that only about 17% of all Americans have been sold on the plan for making an annual pledge of financial support. The rest are content to pay-as-they-attend or pay-as-they-use the various church services.

The second fact is the division of national expenditure expressed in the chart (page 50) made by the Golden Rule Foundation of New York.

These figures tell a story which should arouse every member of a church board. This comparison should be used in literature sent to members and used by canvassers. The churches can never fulfill their constructive mission on this earth *completely* until they are supported by expenditures which equal United States budgets for the Army and Navy.

Here are tested ways which many churches have used to increase the support of their members at their annual financial appeal.

1. Prepare a report, in folder or letter form, on the services of the church during the past year. This report should include:

    a. Number of Services
    b. Number of Weddings
    c. Number of Funerals
    d. Number of Baptisms
    e. Number Who Joined the Church
    f. Total Annual Church Attendance
    g. Attendance at Sunday School
    h. Total Number of Contributors

   This same report should give a breakdown of where the past year's money was expended. This breakdown of expenditures should be done with simple diagrams, using either pie-charts or bar-charts. These take the place of a lengthy, wordy report which few people read or understand.

   The facts illustrated through pie-charts or bar-charts should include the following:

   Total Income..
   Pledges...
   Plate Collection......................................
   Donations from Organizations..........................
   Salaries..
   Amount of Endowment Fund..............................
   Report on Special Gifts...............................
   Money Spent in Domestic and Foreign Missions..........
   To National Denomination Headquarters ....

   Then you should outline the objectives of the coming year and how much money will be needed to carry them out. Some churches find it helpful to put down the average pledge for the past year, and what the average pledge should be in the coming year, in order to achieve the new financial goal. Then the can-

ESTIMATED INCOME OF TYPICAL CHURCH

Pledges	$14,150.00
Plate Collections	1,400.00
Special Collections	2,500.00
Miscellaneous	150.00
Legacies	500.00
	$18,700.00

ESTIMATED EXPENDITURES

Pastor's Salary $4,300

Parish Office Workers $2,968

Music $2,320

Janitor
Treasurer } $2,170

Heat $1,400

$1,200   Printing, Publicity

$1,100   Share of Conferences

$700   Upkeep of Property

$600   Insurance

$556   Foreign Missions

$500   "Herald" and Calendar

$450   Electricity, Gas, Telephone

$286   Radio

$150   State Council

vassers can urge "less-than-average supporters" to increase their pledges to an amount equal to the average or more, if possible.

At canvass time, put up a chart in the vestibule containing the figures on points a, f, g, and h.

A letter from the bishop or head of the church urging a generous support of the financial campaign is always helpful.

In developing this report, get the help of a member who has advertising or sales experience. He will know how to make the report more interesting and readable. He will use pictures if possible and will put effective selling into your appeal.

2. Appoint as head of your canvass committee a sales executive experienced in training and directing the efforts of salesmen.

Mail the church report to members so it is received two or three days before the canvasser calls. In this report *first* thank the member for his past year's pledges. Point out that the church's record of service was made possible only through his support.

3. On the Sunday of your drive, have a prominent and well-liked member of the church give a ten-minute talk on the church's needs. In his talk, he should point out the church's opportunity to be of greater service to its members and to the community. He should ask the members to compare the amount of money they give to the church with the amount of money they spend for other activities including the following:

> entertaining   movies and theatres
> golf and social clubs beauty parlors

This should be graphically shown by taking total subscriptions in a year divided by total membership, divided in turn by fifty-two weeks. In most cases the amount will equal the price of a couple of popular magazines or less than the car fare to get to work.

He could ask if the members were really proud of the amount they put down on their income tax as a church pledge, compared with the total amount of money received in salary and dividends.

4. Be sure that each pledge is acknowledged with a personal letter of thanks, signed by both the chairman of the drive and the minister. This helps develop "repeat pledges." Too many organizations only write the giver when pledges are due, and never write a "thank you" note.

Here is another example of a successful annual appeal. This "Every-Member Canvass" campaign was developed for the Congregational Church of Portland, Oregon. The creative and business programming of the soliciting was sparked by Lawrence A. Pierce, a top-flight sales executive, experienced in selling and motivating people.

Among the complete program of material were the following:

1. Opening the campaign with a government post-card mailing. This card carried the following message:

MEMBERS AND FRIENDS OF
FIRST CONGREGATIONAL CHURCH

PLEASE WATCH

for a letter, with enclosures, from the Division of Business relative to the Every-Member Canvass in behalf of the year's church budget! This should reach you next Monday.

SUNDAY, NOVEMBER 27TH

is Annual "Dedication Sunday" and you will, this year receive only ONE LETTER prior to the campaign for underwriting the year's expenses and benevolences. PLEASE READ THIS LETTER CAREFULLY AND HELP US MAKE THE CAMPAIGN A GREAT SUCCESS!

R. T. Titus, Chairman
Division of Business

2. The next mailing was a complete report and solicitation. It included a letter from "The Division of Business" (a good name for this part of church work), a fact folder, a stewardship folder, and a pledge card. Notice the splendid wording and tone of this letter.

To Members and Friends of First Church:

Sunday, November 27, is the IMPORTANT DAY when we underwrite the new budget of church expenses! It is always a happy day, for our people are enthusiastic about the Church. High-pressure, money-raising methods are out of keeping with the spirit of devotion and loyalty characteristic of First Church folk.

Again, this year, on "Dedication Sunday" we ask that pledges be brought or sent to the Church. In the Morning Service these will be collected and dedicated in a lovely ceremony. There will be no pulpit appeal for funds. There will be no pre-Dedication Sunday solicitation. This letter, with fact folder and pledge card, goes to all our people, presenting our needs. You are urged to give careful thought to your responsibility and privilege in sharing the underwriting of the forward moving program.

If you find it impossible to be present Sunday morning will you kindly mail your pledge to the Church office or send it by someone else so that you may be represented in the service of dedication AND SO THAT WE MAY QUICKLY COMPLETE OUR EVERY-MEMBER CANVASS. We do hope that you will be present.

The plan is very simple. People bring their pledges or send them on Dedication Sunday. Members of the Church from whom we do not hear, will be contacted personally as soon as possible after Dedication Sunday.

All pledges and contributions will be acknowledged by the treasurer and weekly payment envelopes provided those who desire these.

With appreciation for your co-operation in this important task.

Sincerely yours,

THE DIVISION OF BUSINESS

R. T. Titus, Chairman

The fact folder was an attractive, easy-to-read report with the title, "You and Your Church." The copy on the cover contained this line sure to step up reading:

READING TIME: 10 MINUTES

but please read it twice!

The most interesting section of this folder was the second page containing an interview with Mr. Titus, chairman. It read as follows:

A LITTLE TALK WITH MR. TITUS

YOU: Mr. Titus, may I ask you, as chairman of the Division of Business of our Church, for a few facts? How much is the 1950 budget?

MR. TITUS: $39,045.00. See the next page for a breakdown of this total. $30,270.00 must be obtained in gifts and pledges from individuals; other sources of income care for the balance.

YOU: Does the $39,045.00 include benevolences?

MR. TITUS: It does. We have set $9,050.00 as our share in the wider Christian program, and $8,000.00 of this is for the "Christian World Mission" of our own denomination.

YOU: How was the budget prepared and who set the amounts?

MR. TITUS: The Executive Council, consisting of officers and division heads, received "askings" from the various departments, co-ordinated these into a budget and recommended the same to the Church at a special meeting —a very democratic procedure.

YOU: What is MY share of the $30,270.00 to be raised in pledges?

MR. TITUS: Well, that is for YOU to say! Giving should be part of one's religious experience, a matter for careful thought and prayer. The amount should be determined by one's own ability to give, not by what others do or do not do.

YOU: Well, what is the AVERAGE contribution?

MR. TITUS: 1949 pledges, not counting children, number 492 with a total of $25,767.00, an average of approximately $52.00 or $1.00 per week. But if no one gave more than the average, of course, the budget would never be raised! Many cannot afford to give that much.

YOU: Is the budget larger for 1950?

MR. TITUS: Yes, and we are proud to say: the largest in First Church history! To cover it we must have more people giving and people giving more. We shall need approximately $5,000 in new money.

YOU: That's an increase of 20% in pledges. Can we get it?

MR. TITUS: Surely! There are few of us who couldn't give more than we do.

YOU: What of people who, because of uncertain income, feel that they cannot pledge a specific amount?

MR. TITUS: They can pledge a percentage of their income—whatever it may be. The Bible tithe is 10% but most of us give much less.

YOU: On what basis are pledges made?

MR. TITUS: Most people pledge an amount WEEKLY, others monthly or quarterly and some give a lump sum. Weekly or monthly payments mean a stabilized income for the Church, but terms of payment are always left to each individual.

YOU: What are the plans for underwriting the budget?

MR. TITUS: Please read our letter regarding the Every-Member Canvass. A copy is enclosed.

This folder, like any good direct mail piece, was printed in an attractive color. It was printed in brown on a canary yellow paper stock. Too many church mailings are always black, the color of mourning.

The stewardship folder enclosed was "Givers are Likest God." It was obtained from the Commission on Stewardship and the Missions Council at 287 Fourth Avenue, New York (10), New York.

Chapter 28

Loyalty Sunday,
A Stimulus to Generous Support

THE newest and most successful plan for increasing church support is "Loyalty Sunday." This is a method developed and perfected by Austin Pardue, now Bishop of the Pittsburgh diocese of the Episcopal Church. He discovered that most churchgoers would rather express their loyalty by pledging at church in their pews than waiting at home until a canvasser called. In addition, Loyalty Sunday always results in pledges from people who attend the church more or less regularly but are not listed on the rolls as members.

Records prove that pledging in church is more conducive to increased contributions than canvassers calling at the home, for the nearness to God felt in church is not usually equalled in the home. Pledges signed in church can be gathered by the ushers, presented on plates to the minister, and then blessed by him at the altar. Funds devoted to God's work are so important they should be consecrated to God's work in front of the givers.

A well-filled church on Loyalty Sunday is a great stimulus to generous support. In itself, it develops loyalty and increases the congregation's pride in the parish.

Another big advantage of Loyalty Sunday is the saving of time. Canvassers do not have to call on loyal members who pledge in their pews. Letters mailed to all members the week before Loyalty Sunday increase attendance and thus reduce the follow-up calls. In the advance letter, the member is given a report of the church's work for the past year (see page 52). Here is a letter used by Bishop Edward R. Welles of St. Paul's in Buffalo, New York, when he was Dean.

Dear Mr. and Mrs. . . . . (hand-written by the Dean)

You and I belong to a church with a great spirit of loyalty and service. For 128 years St. Paul's has loyally served God and man at the very heart of this growing city. During all those years loyal men and women have given gladly to make that service possible.

Today St. Paul's stands open and accessible to the thousands who come to worship, to be quiet, and to seek personal help. They come from every walk of life, every part of the city and the world, every race and creed and color and age. They do not come in vain.

In a very real sense the Cathedral serves two congregations: the whole community, including transients; and the 3,704 persons on our parish list. For the latter group, St. Paul's provides additional strength and inspiration by hundreds of pastoral calls on regular members and newcomers, on the sick, the shut-in, and the bereaved—and by Christian education in the largest Episcopal Sunday School in western New York.

Loyalty Sunday will be held on November 19th. Make every necessary sacrifice to be present and to pledge on faith for the new budget. In due proportion to your faith you will be blessed.

A year ago not a single home solicitation was necessary. In my first year as your Dean, I am counting on you to back me to the hilt. I need the power of your prayers, your presence, and your pledges.

Come and make November 19th a real Loyalty Sunday!

Affectionately yours,

(Signature hand-signed)

The church bulletin for St. Paul's on Loyalty Sunday carried the following message:

OFF THE MINISTER'S DESK

Once again we come to a high spot in our year at St. Paul's—
Loyalty Sunday. It is truly a high spot because it is our annual
opportunity to express in a tangible financial fashion our deep sense
of loyalty to St. Paul's and to Almighty God and the work of His
church throughout the whole world. We have the chance to come
and offer in the privacy of our pew. There is an extra satisfaction,
it seems to me, in being able to give voluntarily and freely, without the pressure of a personal solicitation.

May I make three suggestions for your expression of loyalty?
First, offer the maximum when you fill in your pledge card. Second,
do it on faith. Don't hold back through fear of what may happen in
the future—you will be blessed in proportion to your faith, and
remember that any pledge made to St. Paul's may be changed
(either increased or decreased) at any time by giving notice to the
treasurer. Third, if you are ill or out of town and cannot come to
the Loyalty service, please let me know immediately, sc that I may
send you a pledge card and return envelope for your convenience
in sending in your pledge by mail.

THIS IS LOYALTY SUNDAY—COME AND OFFER

At the service on the week following Loyalty Sunday, members
or guests who did not attend the preceding Sunday are given an opportunity to pledge. Then the remaining members who have not
pledged are contacted personally by canvassers. Loyalty Sunday reduces
the job of canvassing by 70 to 90%. It is a proven method of increasing
pledges and getting new additional pledges. It merits a trial in nearly
every church.

As a personal build-up to the church's pledge-making Sunday, the
Reverend Robert W. Anthony (Minister of the North Presbyterian
Church, Flushing, Long Island, New York), staged a most successful
telephone roll call of the entire parish. One Saturday at 10 A.M., he sat
down with a list of phone numbers of every member.

During each call, he told the family about the special talk which would be given at the Sunday service by Philip Everest. He explained that this leading layman, a member of another congregation, was going to talk on the subject of church finances and church support. At 5:30 P.M., the Reverend Anthony stopped, worn out by constant phoning and talking. The reward was apparent the very next day when the church had a "Standing Room Only" congregation. As a result of the unusual turnout, plus Mr. Everest's talk, and the great loyalty of North Church members, pledges for church support were tripled and pledges for benevolences were quadrupled. So, when planning a Loyalty Sunday, don't forget the effectiveness of phone calls by the clergy and lay workers. The build-up and persuasiveness of the human voice are hard to equal.

The canvassers of the North Presbyterian Church say that they were helped by the excellent "Turnover" presentation prepared for the Presbyterian Church by the Jam Handy Organization of Detroit, Michigan. Other churches could use this businesslike presentation to good advantage.

A "Turnover" presentation is a modern, successful way of selling ideas, merchandise, and even organizations to prospective customers. It is a loose-leaf binder of "selling" pages which, when open, sets up like a pyramid. Each page is turned over, from front to back, of the pyramid-hinged top. Each page carries a separate selling idea or message. These ideas flow logically to a conclusion page which requests the "audience" to do something. Thus the user of a Turnover presentation has the advantage of a planned, pretested interview. A Turnover on church support helps make the average volunteer a better salesman and solicitor. The pages can be almost any size. While these Turnovers cost a little money, they can pay for their costs in a greater number of increased pledges.

Chapter 29

Reselling a Church to Its Members

WHEN the Reverend William Kirk went to St. John's Church in Buffalo, New York, he assumed spiritual leadership of a parish which was about to celebrate its 100th anniversary. Instead of having just the usual centennial celebration, the St. John's board decided to include one continuing basic objective in their anniversary plans. That was to embark on a campaign to resell St. John's to its members and friends.

To do this, a series of letters was written by a successful insurance salesman. Here are some of the letters. They are well worth editing and adopting by other churches. Thanks to the low cost of direct mail, these letters are an economical way to build up enthusiasm, interest, and loyalty.

Says a Layman to a Layman:

A CHURCH FOR SALE

Dear Member,

It may be news to you but as indicated by the caption we are going to sell St. John's Church. At least, we are going to try.

We are going to sell the grounds, the building, the traditions, the services, the choir and, yes, even the bell.

If this statement has caused you to feel a little twinge of regret somewhere down deep within you—don't let it, because we are going to sell St. John's Church to you.

This letter is not intended for those loyal men and women and young people of our church who for many years have given generously of their time and effort, but is primarily intended for members such as I, who, year in and year out, have taken the church for granted and have done so little to help those who have worked so hard.

We go to church on Easter come hell or high water and again we grace the pews at Christmas (because we like the carols) and we sing lustily and we put a dollar in the collection plate and we go home feeling quite content now that we have discharged our duties to the church and Christianity for another year.

Oh yes, it's true we sign a pledge card when called upon during the "Every-Member Canvass," usually for an amount much less than we should (and we know it) and it's true that when some hardworking member calls us on the telephone and asks us to be present "Please" on Loyalty Sunday or some other special occasion we do, at great sacrifice of personal comfort, bestir ourselves.

It is to this group, of which I blushingly admit I am one, that this letter and those which follow are addressed in the hope that we can sell St. John's Church to you.

Please file this letter as there are several more to come. When the series is completed, I will ask you to read each one through just once more, beginning with the first and continuing to the last without interruption. After that it will be up to you to show whether we have been successful in selling you St. John's Church, the grounds, the building, the traditions, the services, the choirs, and, yes, even the bell.

Sincerely yours,

JOHN GREENO
(hand-signed)

A CHURCH FOR SALE

The Ground, The Buildings, The Traditions

Dear Member,

One hundred years ago, a few churchmen among the early settlers of Buffalo, recognizing the need of a place of worship in what was at that time not much more than a frontier village, got together and organized St. John's Church.

This was no easy task. In those days money was scarce and members were few. One dollar represented a hard day's work—and it took many dollars to buy the land and erect a building that would be suitable as a place where this group of churchmen and their families could gather on Sunday morning and hold services.

Little wonder then that it was a proud and happy day when the first spade full of earth was turned and the project began. Little wonder that it was an even happier and prouder day when the first service was held within its walls.

That was one hundred years ago.

These were men and women of vision and foresight, with no fear of what the future might have in store for them. St. John's Church grew and served its community faithfully and well.

I will not dwell longer on the history of St. John's Church as that history has been written by a far more capable person than I, but looking back down the years we can now see what the "future" held in store for that brave little group. The war between the states, the panic of '93, the plagues and epidemics of the late '90s and the financial crashes of 1907 and 1929, just to name a few.

These problems were met in turn as they arose and St. John's was skillfully guided through these shoals and continued to wield its kindly and beneficent influence on mankind.

Today, we, you and I, are the successors to that same little band of churchmen whose early efforts have given us our opportunity to serve. We are the direct beneficiaries of all that has been done by them. We find ourselves the proud owners of a church building which is a gem of architecture, all built and paid for; but, if that were all we had, we would be poor indeed. Our riches lie in that wealth of experience, tradition, and the example of self-sacrifice which has been handed down to us by those who have gone before. The history of St. John's Church is our inspiration and the future of St. John's Church will be what we make it.

We will have many problems to face during the years of our custodianship. So will those who follow us.

Let us then take a page from the book of our predecessors and look to the future with confidence. Let us be sure that when younger hands take the helm, the good ship, St. John's Church, will be just as sturdy a craft to sail the seas of the uncertainties of tomorrow as it was when we took over.

The only way to be sure of this is to keep our crew pulling together, to avoid dissention in the ranks—to rise above the many little things that annoy us and at all cost avoid letting our group split into factions.

After all, we are the Church. If there is work to be done, we should do it. If there is any credit to be gained by a job well done, we should do it. If there is any blame for the way things are done, we should be blamed.

There are bound to be differences of opinion on the way things are done or why they are done; but, if we keep firmly in our minds the fact that "The Church" is NOT THE BUILDING, NOT THE RECTOR, NOT THE VESTRY, but all of us, each and every one of us, individually and collectively, then we will find a way to adjust our differences of opinion and work together for the common good.

Remember WE ARE THE CHURCH and when we say this or that is wrong with "The Church" what we are really saying is, this or that is wrong with US.

Let's just give this idea a tryout and see if it doesn't give us a little broader perspective and help us to work together to the end that St. John's Church will be able to take a more prominent part in the development of our community.

Sincerely yours,

JOHN GREENO
(hand-signed)

A CHURCH FOR SALE

The Services, The Choir, The Bell

Dear Member,

The services of St. John's Church—am I about to tread heavily on some thin ice?—perhaps, but here goes anyway. Let's kick it around a bit. It will do us good no matter what we think.

Let's start this way: When you read the first line of this letter, did you think of the "Morning Service" held at eleven o'clock on Sunday, or did you think of the term in its broader sense which includes ALL of the MANY services rendered by the Church?

For example, did you think of that all-important service of organizing and maintaining an efficient staff for the religious education of our children, the Church School?

Did you think of the baptism of our babies, the confirmation of our youngsters, the marriage of our young people, and the accurate records that must be kept of all these events?

If you did, fine, for those and many others are the services that we so often overlook.

St. John's Church has always stood high on the lists for its accomplishments both at home and abroad.

Never have the people of St. John's failed to hold up their end in any church activity, and I am sure we can all be justly proud of what has been done in the past.

We want to be equally proud of what we will do in the future, but a church cannot stand still. If we are to be proud of what we do in the future, then, we must plan for the future. If we plan for the future, we must back up our plans with the necessary money to see them through.

A tree stems from roots planted firmly in the ground. The services we hope to render through our parish must stem from our church planted in our community.

If our financial structure is weak, then our plans will collapse; but if we do, as we have always done, look our problems squarely in the face, and back our plans with our money, then St. John's

Church will go forward to greater heights of accomplishments and be in fact the spiritual POWER we all hope and pray for.

Next Sunday, as has been announced, will be LOYALTY SUNDAY. The choir has worked to have a special program of music for this occasion. The warm and friendly chime of St. John's bell which has rung down through the years will bid you WELCOME as you approach the outer doors.

It is on this day that by our presence we demonstrate to our church, to ourselves, and to each other our determination to support St. John's Church and all it stands for.

It is on this day that you will show, by your presence, whether we have been successful in SELLING ST. JOHN'S CHURCH to you, including the grounds, the buildings, the traditions, the services, the choir, and, yes, even the bell.

Sincerely yours,

JOHN GREENO
(hand-signed)

Results of the letters from St. John's

The Reverend Mr. Kirk reports that these three letters were a major factor in obtaining pledges totaling almost 15% higher than the previous year. Equally important was the fact that many brand new givers responded and pledged for the first time.

Chapter 30

Ways to Welcome Worshippers*

When a congregation builds a new church they try to build an inviting one—one that will appeal to the members and attract passers-by. But many congregations are not building new edifices. Nevertheless, the pastor and his congregation want to make their church, whatever its age and architecture, an inviting one so that people who attend will feel welcome and will feel at home in pleasant and dignified surroundings.

To make any church inviting, it must manifest an atmosphere of "welcome." Welcome is one of the warmest and friendliest words in the English language. Cowper once defined it as that feeling which is secured "when the glad soul is made Heaven's Guest." This does not require a lot of money, nor does it mean commencing a major project. Your church can be made an inviting church by thoughtfulness, by paying attention to little things and by putting oneself in another person's position.

There are two aspects of welcoming people to church. The humane aspect, or what people can do; and the physical aspect, or what furnishings and equipment can do. Both are important. Both can work hand

* Most of the material in this chapter appeared in *Your Church* magazine and is reprinted with their permission.

in hand to make one feel like Heaven's Guest. We suggest that the minister and the church leaders take an objective look at their church as they approach it next Sunday morning. Does it say: "This is the Lord's Day"? Or does it look exactly the same as it has on Mondays through Saturdays. On Sunday there should be extra evidence of the warm welcome the church wants to extend to members and visitors.

USING THE CHURCH FLAG: One of the surest ways to create extra evidence of a warm welcome is to fly the church flag over the doorway. It reminds everyone that this is the Lord's Day; that He is waiting inside. It reminds them that His Love, comfort and forgiveness and His inspiration are just inside the door. A church flag always says, "Come in and worship." It should be placed over the doorway where its message is seen by all who pass or enter the church.

USING FLOWERS: Another way to give the church the inviting look on the Lord's Day is to place vases of cut flowers outside on either side of the entrance. Flowers remind everyone that it is God who has given his children the glories of nature. The men's Bible class or the young couples group could assume the responsibility of placing such flowers at the doorway of the church each Sunday. It is also a project that would appeal to garden lovers.

A CHURCH GARDEN: The appearance of a church can be considerably improved if it has a Garden-for-God. The church grounds, in spring, summer and fall should never be barren of blooms. The church members can be nearer to God's heart in a garden on the church grounds. On Sunday's, as members go in and out of the building, they are inspired by God's language of the flowers.

Creation of a fine church garden can be accomplished without taking funds from the regular church budget. A "church garden Sunday" can be organized. On this particular day each family brings a plant, bush or seeds specifically requested by a Garden Committee, and before or after the service the donations can be placed in the garden. The garden plot will have already been dug the day before by a volunteer group of men and women.

THE USES OF LIGHTING: Lighting can be used effectively to make a church more inviting. If a church has a beautiful stained glass window facing the street it can be lit at night. This is a colorful way to warm the hearts of those who pass by. If a proper window is not available for this purpose, then perhaps floodlights can be placed so as to illuminate the steeple or the facade of the church.

THE CHURCH BULLETIN BOARD: The church bulletin board is too often neglected. This piece of equipment can enhance the appearance of the church if it is used properly and kept in good repair. The name of the church and the hours of Sunday service should appear on the board in large enough letters so that someone driving by in an automobile can read it. All essential information should be adequately displayed. In some cases the board may need repainting, and if it does, green is a good color. By all means, the last line on the bulletin board should invite attendance at church services. It can say: "Worship with us this Sunday." Too many congregations fail to visually extend a welcome in this manner.

THE HAND OF FELLOWSHIP: A church can be made more inviting and the feeling of welcome extended if ushers are assigned each Sunday to greet people on the front steps rather than in the vestibule. They shake hands with them and welcome them to the worship service. To be greeted immediately in this fashion is to make one feel instantly at home.

THE VESTIBULE OR NARTHEX: The minister and the church leaders should look objectively at their vestibule or narthex. Does it radiate a welcoming atmosphere, or is it dull and drab in appearance? How long has it been since it was repainted?

A guest book in the narthex is always in order. It is another way of saying: "We're so glad you're with us and we want to know who you are and where you live." Also, the guest book is a good reminder to the minister and the visiting committee to make regular calls on visitors from nearby areas.

Every denomination publishes a number of helpful and inspirational folders and booklets that should be brought to the attention of members and visitors and made available to them. A cordial way of doing this is to display them neatly in an appropriate rack in the narthex. Such a rack can be purchased or made in a home workshop at little cost. Its usefulness will be appreciated by many people.

INTERIOR APPOINTMENTS: As people enter the sanctuary they will notice many small things. The appearance that each gives will add up to the total impression of the physical aspects of the church. The condition and appearance of the carpeting, the prayer hassocks, the pew cushions and the woodwork are all important. Perhaps the former items have not been kept as clean as possible. Maybe the carpets or tile covered floors need to be cleaned. Perhaps the woodwork needs to be waxed or the old paint scraped and the natural grain of the wood beautified by polishing. These are just a few of the things to be considered in helping to create an inviting church interior that, by its appearance, will welcome visitors and members and cause them to want to return again.

The prayer books and hymnals should always be kept in good condition. If they are worn, frayed or contain torn or loose pages, they should be replaced or repaired. Perhaps one of the women's organizations could have a "book repair meeting." It may be that new hymnals are needed. Having old, worn prayer books or hymnals for worshipers is like welcoming a dinner guest in the home with old, worn napkins.

WASHROOMS: Washrooms are very important and necessary. Their appearance can greatly affect the attitude of members or visitors toward the church. They should always be kept clean and painted and have the necessary accessories available at all times. An unclean washroom in a church building is revolting and, more important, unsanitary.

RELIEF FROM HEAT: One way to make a church inviting is to try to provide some relief from the heat in summer months. Hot days can keep people from church if some provision is not made for their comfort. In many instances it is not feasible to install air conditioning units. Yet, some steps can be taken to combat heat oppression. Some congregations have installed fans in the roof or in the windows which exhaust the hot air. Some have used standard floor fans such as those used by retailers to cool their stores. Provision for the opening of more windows in the church can also be considered. Perhaps some carpentry work is needed in order to accomplish this.

People are becoming more and more conscious of air conditioning or cooling. They will begin to take increasing notice of the lack of it in the churches. Perhaps it would be in order to appoint a committee immediately to plan how the church can be made cooler during next summer's hot weather.

USING THE CHURCH BELLS: One of the oldest and most charming ways to welcome people to church and to make the church more inviting is to ring the church bells. The rich tones of the church bells spread a Christian invitation to all within hearing distance. There are many churches which ring their bells every Saturday night from 7:00 to 7:15. This is an old custom in many European churches. In this country, the pealing of the bells at the close of the Jewish Sabbath and on the eve of the Christian Sabbath proclaims to all who hear that we are a God-fearing people, that each week we reaffirm our faith in God, that the best place to reaffirm that faith is at the Sunday worship service, and that all who hear the bells are truly welcome to this service.

PROVISION FOR CHILDREN: The inviting church also makes adequate provision for children—the parishioners of tomorrow. The church should not stop with the usual Sunday school program. It should involve children in other activities that build proper relationships and help assure continued growth and Christian influence. Provision should be made for small children so that parents can attend church services. An outdoor recreation area with good equipment can make the church more inviting to small ones and parents as well. Many churches have adequate grounds for this purpose. They should recognize God's love of little children and provide facilities for making this ground useful and inviting.

St. Joseph of Arimathea in Elmsford, New York, has a heart-warming way of announcing the birth of babies born to parishioners. They are publicly welcomed into the congregation in the following manner.

Before the beginning of his sermon, the Rev. Walter McNeely announces: "During the doxology the church bell will be rung to spread the good news that another child has been born into our church family. He (or she) is (name) the son (or daughter) of Mr. and Mrs. (name) and grandchild of Mr. and Mrs. (name)."

Many times the bell is actually tolled by the proud father or the super-proud grandfather.

After the doxology, the Reverend McNeely says the following prayer:

"O Lord Christ who didst lay thy quiet hands on the shining heads of little children, Take this child, ——, also to thy heart. Give —— thy gentleness. Give —— thy strength. Fill —— with love for thee and for —— brethren here on earth. Help us to send —— out among —— fellows with a strong and healthy body, with a clean fearless mind, with a generous heart, untiring in thy service.
Use ——, we pray Thee, Lord Christ."

Then a copy of this prayer is typed on a card showing a picture of the church and sent to the parents.

The Rev. McNeely does not know the author of this prayer. Neither can he find the author of the following prayer.

"Grant, O God, that because we have met together here, life may grow greater for some who have contempt for it, simpler for some who are confused by it, happier for some who are tasting the bitterness of it, safer for some who are feeling the peril of it, more friendly for some who are feeling the loneliness of it, serener for some who are throbbing with the flavor of it, holier for some to whom life has lost all dignity, beauty and meaning. Through Jesus Christ our Lord."

If some reader can identify either authors, please write the Rev. McNeely.

After church services it is important for the older members of the congregation to approach the new ones and the visitors, introduce themselves, and say how pleased they were to have them present. To keep the church inviting, these after-service greetings should not be over-zealous approaches to try to get them to join the church or one of its organizations, or to buy a ticket to a church social function, or to bake a cake for the cake sale. It must be remembered that the visitors came to worship and thus should be greeted on a spiritual rather than organizational level. A good way to make the after-service greetings effective is to serve light refreshments such as tea, coffee, or soup-on-the-rocks in the parish house after worship services. Here, new members and visitors can be pleasantly engaged in informal and interesting conversation and can be properly introduced to other members of the church.

CONCLUSION: There are a number of other ways in which the local church can be made more inviting to both members and visitors. It may be in order to form a special committee of interested individuals to determine ways and means of physically improving the appearance of the church without undergoing a major remodeling project and to discuss methods by which present members can make new members and visitors more welcome in their midst.

The House of God, regardless of its age, architecture or site, should be as noble and as dignified as the congregation can make it. It must be inviting. It must manifest a spirit of welcome. It must be neat, clean and trim. Of all the buildings in the community, the church building should be the one which stands first in its invitation and its welcome to the public.

250
P72m
C.1.